KNITTING VAN GOGH

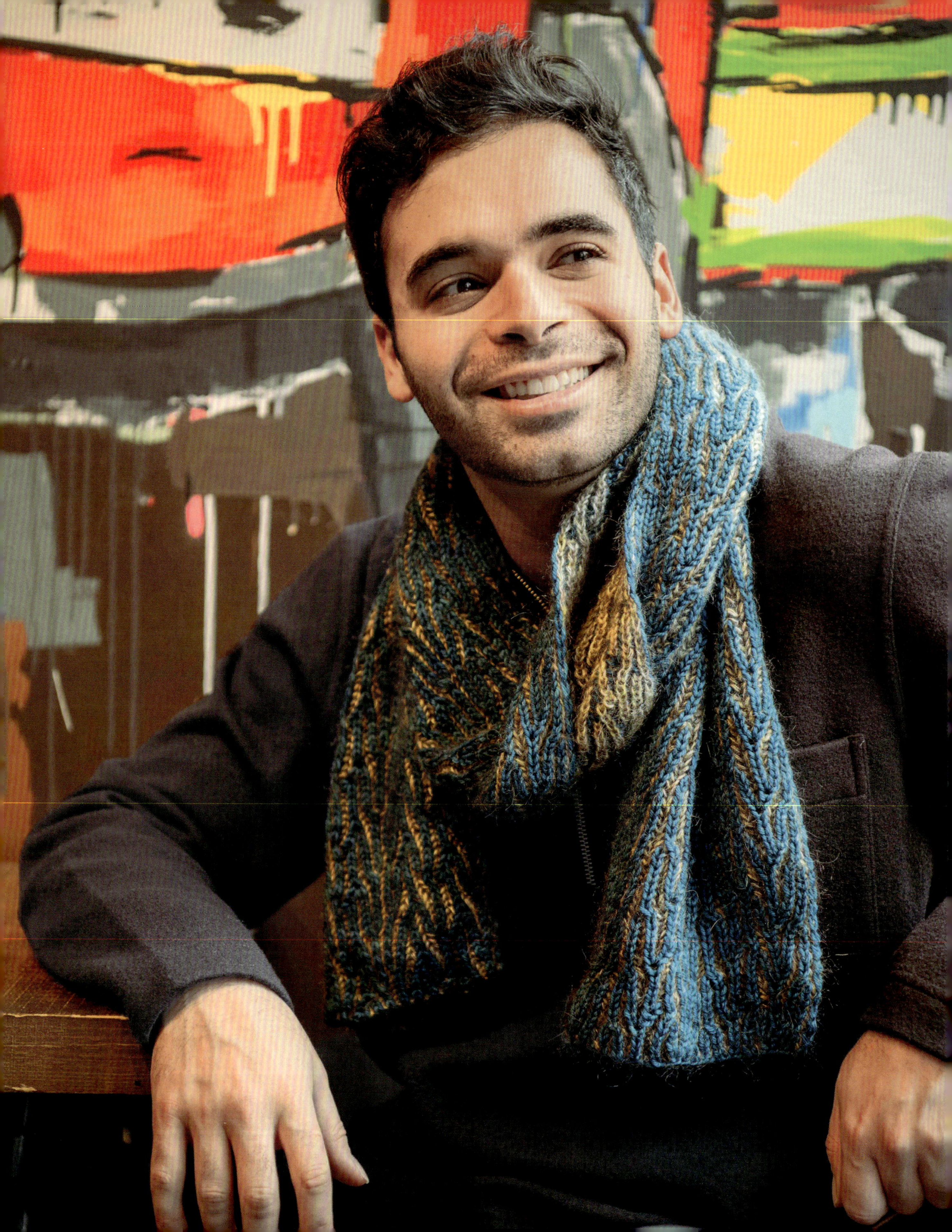

KNITTING VAN GOGH

KNIT YOUR OWN MASTERPIECE INSPIRED BY THE WORK OF VINCENT VAN GOGH

KRISTA ANN

weldonowen

CONTENTS

INTRODUCTION

When I was a child, my elementary school had an art enrichment program. An art expert would bring a painting to class and we would discuss the life of the artist, their body of work, and then (my favorite part) we would create our own masterpiece influenced by that week's artist. I remember van Gogh's *Starry Night* being one of the works of art we discussed. I enjoyed swirling paint around on a piece of paper to mimic the swirls of his skies and using thick paint to try and mimic his bold brushstrokes.

When I was in college, I took a children's art class. We spent an entire month discussing van Gogh's self-portraits. We learned about his life and dove deep into his moods and how they reflected how he chose to portray himself on canvas. At the end of the month, I had to create my own self-portrait that reflected my current mood. Sadly, my paint and canvas skills are fairly terrible and so my mood appeared to be messy and lopsided!

In the spring of 2022, my husband and I vacationed in Amsterdam and we spent a day touring the Van Gogh Museum. Winding through the rooms filled with his original paintings, drawings, and journal pages was awe-inspiring. My nose was inches away from where his brush touched canvas and for the first time in my life, I could actually see the depth of his brushstrokes and the fine details of the colors.

Without really knowing it, van Gogh has been a part of my artistic upbringing for my entire life. I feel sadness that his talents were not embraced and celebrated during his own lifetime. I feel joy at what he left behind for the world to appreciate and enjoy for hundreds of years to come. And when I was asked to write this book, I felt anxiety to create something worthy of his name.

As a fiber artist, I knew translating oil on canvas into stitches with yarn was not going to be an easy transition. Rather than trying to copy his intricate details and reproduce his flowers or fields of wheat, I wanted to design pieces that give tribute to his brilliant use of colors. My goal was to create fabrics that invoked the motion and texture of his brushstrokes.

This book is filled with patterns that knitters like you will not only enjoy making, but you will also finish with wearable garments that summon your own artistic love for color and texture. With each piece I designed, I never wanted to try and replicate van Gogh's paintings, but rather find colors and fabric textures that are inspired by his work.

It was a great honor to write this book, and it allowed me a reason to dive back into van Gogh's masterpieces and look for more inspiration from one of the world's truly most influential artists.

I hope you enjoy knitting these designs. Don't be afraid to find textures and colors that inspire you in ways you never thought possible!

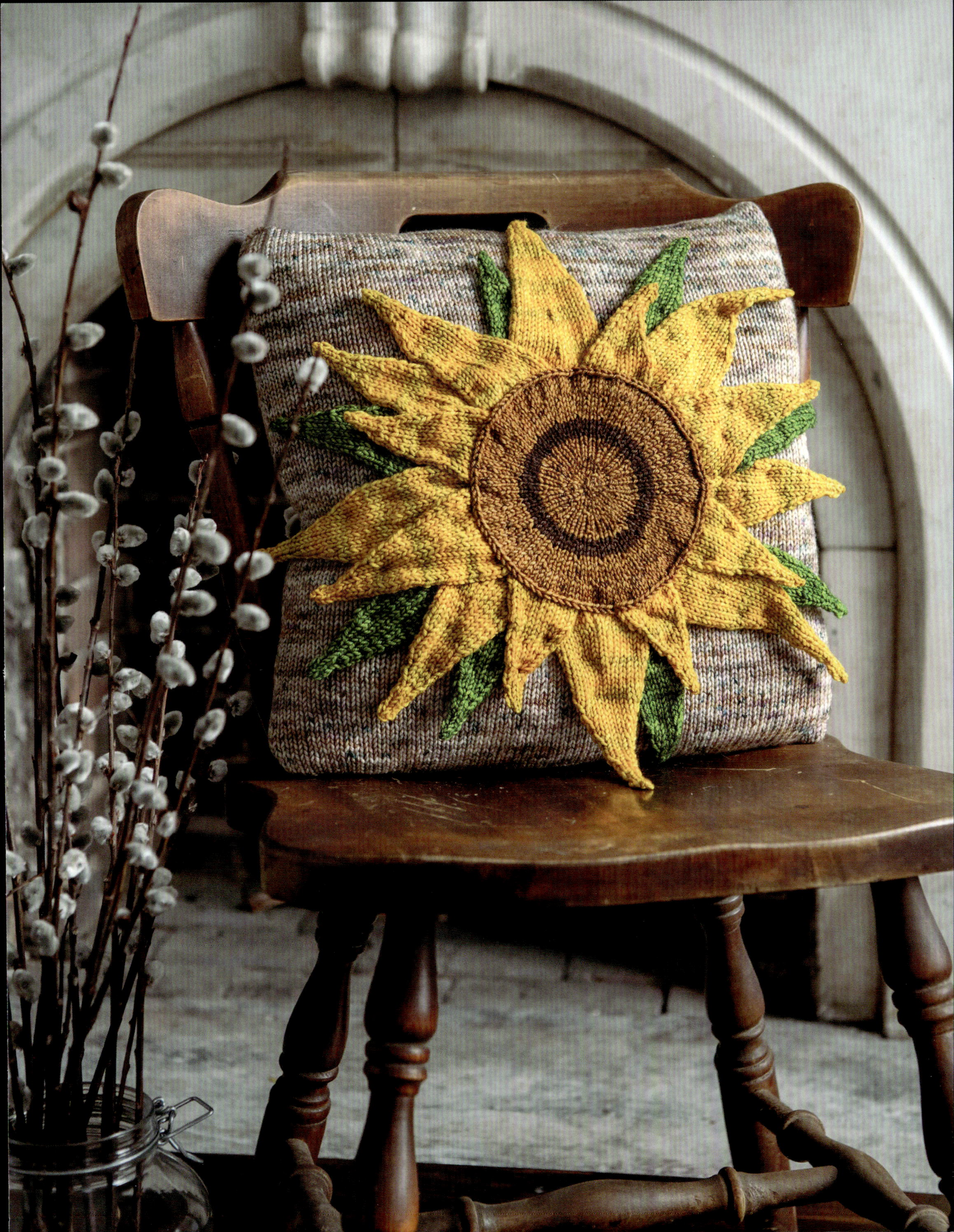

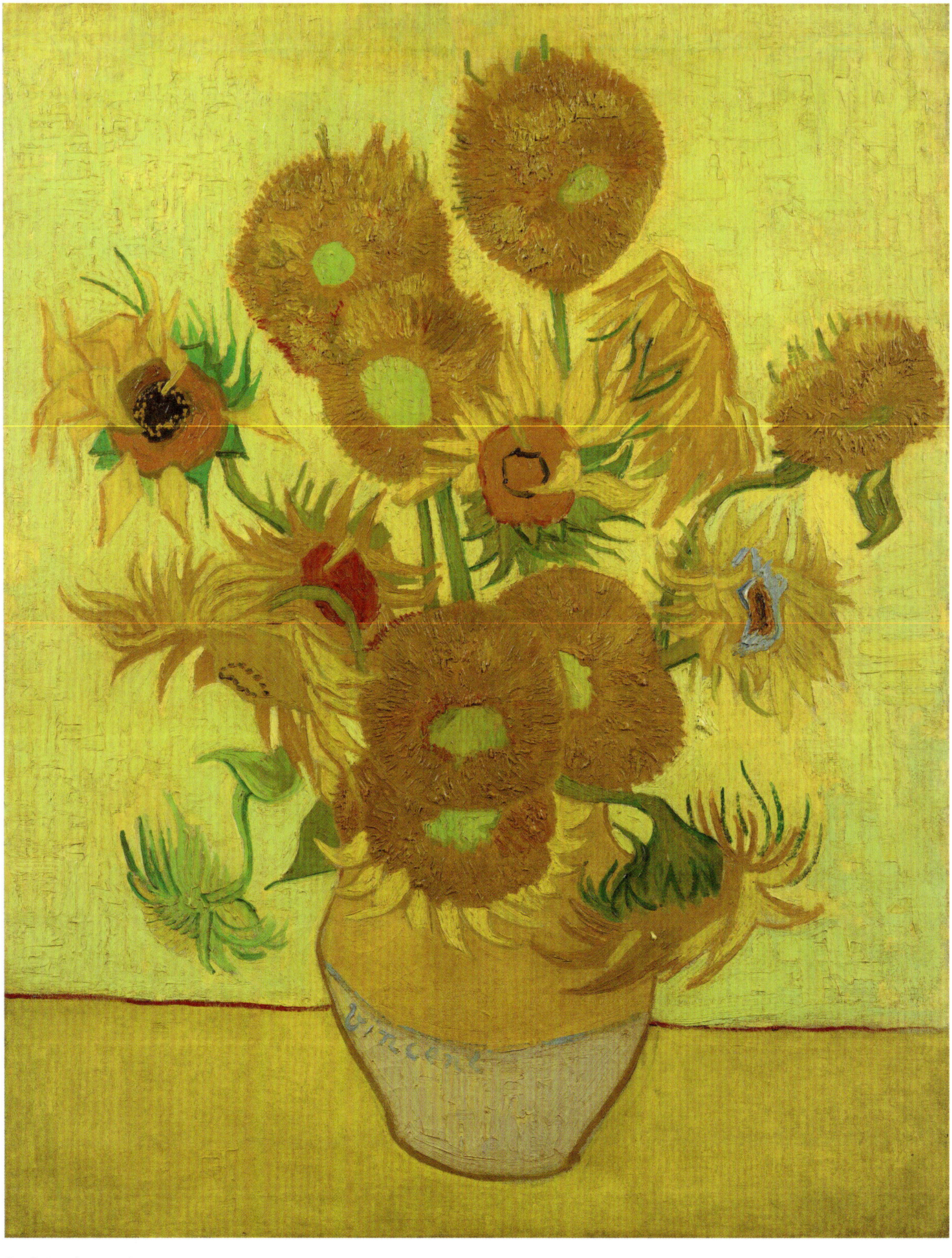

Sunflowers (p. 91, 115)

"HOW MUCH THERE IS
IN ART THAT IS BEAUTIFUL,
IF ONLY ONE CAN REMEMBER
WHAT ONE HAS SEEN,
ONE IS NEVER EMPTY
OR TRULY LONELY,
AND NEVER ALONE."

—Vincent van Gogh to his brother Theo,
November 13-16, 1878

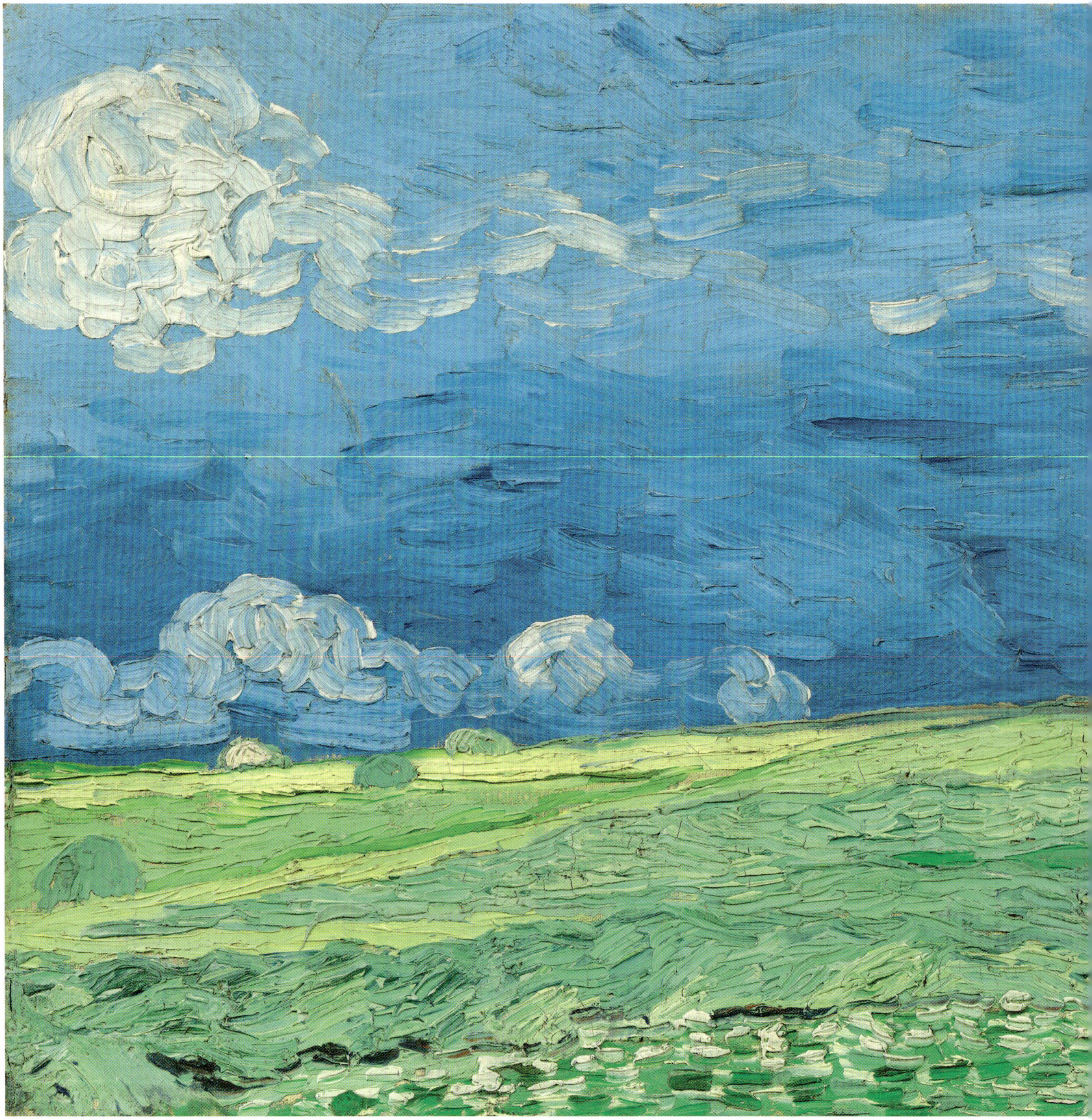

Wheatfield under Thunderclouds (p. 49)

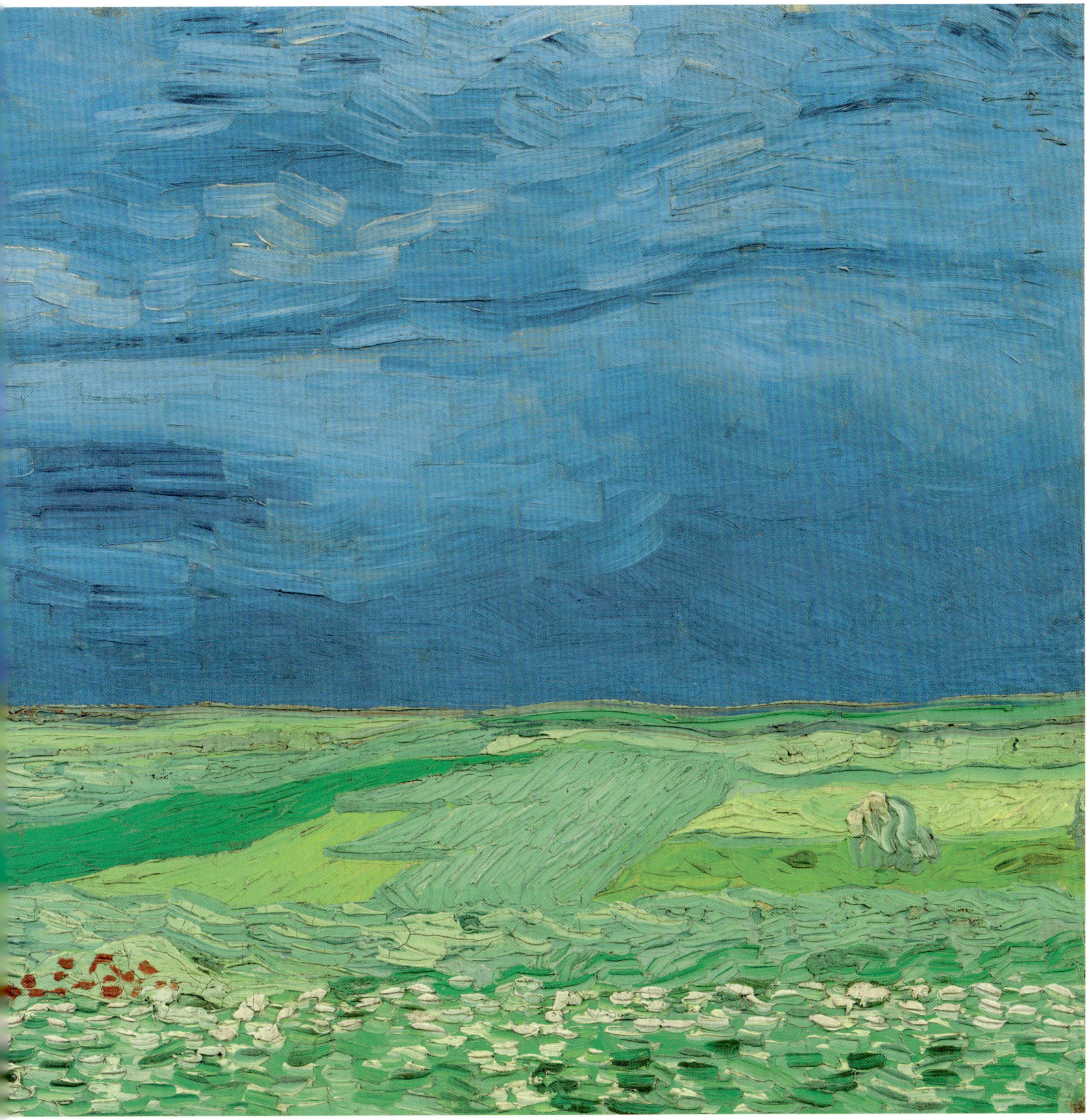

ARTISTIC APPAREL

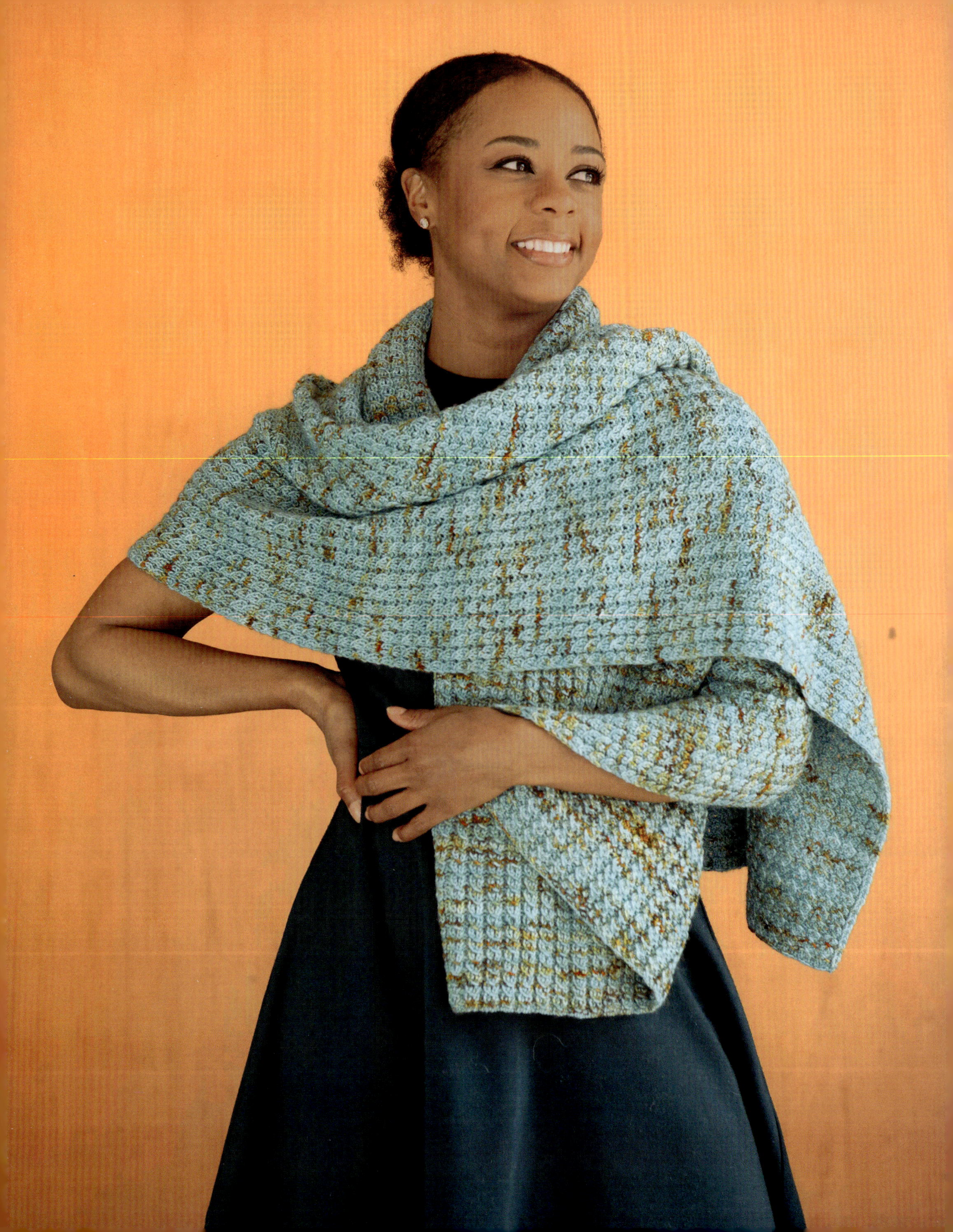

PEACH TREE WRAP

Inspired by *The Pink Peach Tree*

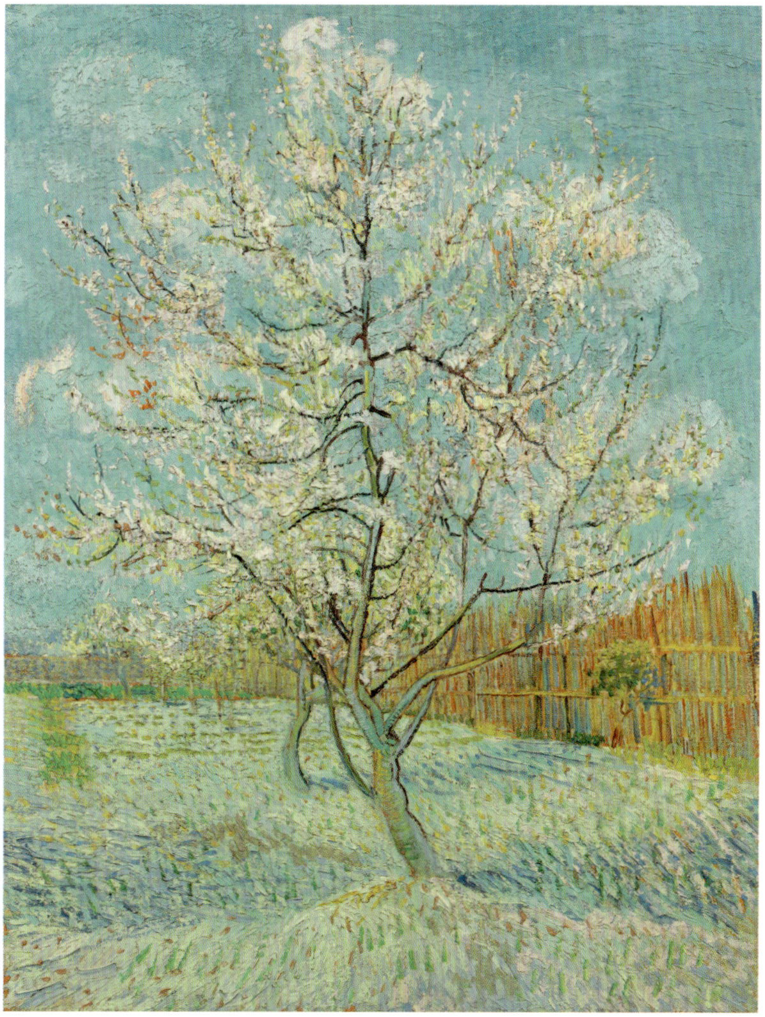

Van Gogh's use of texture and movement in this painting is extraordinary, and what I wanted to convey in this delicate wrap. I used a yarn that had the same color to mimic the spots of brown grass and the swaying movement we see in the painting; the light blue yarn pulls in the image of the sky against the pink peach tree and the shading along the blades of grass. The blue sky and portrayal of wind blowing put me in the mind of a late winter or early spring day, the perfect time to wrap up in something soft and cozy.

For more information on van Gogh's *The Pink Peach Tree*, see p. 138.

SIZES
One size

FINISHED MEASUREMENTS
27 in. / 68.5 cm wide and 72 in. / 183 cm long

YARN
La Bien Aimée "Cashmerino"
75% Merino Wool, 15% Cashmere, 10% Nylon; Fingering (100 g / 474 yd. / 433 m)

Sanho – 5 skeins

NEEDLES
- US size 2 / 2.75 mm, 24 in. / 60 cm long circular knitting needles

Or size needed to obtain gauge

NOTIONS
- Scissors
- Tapestry needle for weaving in ends

GAUGE
34 stitches and 40 rows = 4 in. / 10 cm over pattern stitch after blocking
29 stitches and 40 rows = 4 in. / 10 cm in stockinette stitch

NOTES
- This shawl is worked flat, widthwise across the shawl. There is no WS or RS, so this pattern is completely reversible.
- Slip all stitches purlwise with yarn held to the back.
- If you want to make your shawl wider or narrower, this pattern is a multiple of 6 + 2 stitches.
- As written, this pattern uses up almost all of your yarn. If you would like to make your scarf longer or wider, you will need more yarn.

KNITTING INSTRUCTIONS
Cast on 230 sts.

Row 1: Sl1, *K3, P3* to last st, P1.
Row 2: Sl1, *sl1, K2, pass sl st over 2 sts, P3* to last st, p1—192 sts.
Row 3: Sl1, *sl1, K2, pass sl st over 2 sts, P1, YO, P1* to last st, P1.
Row 4: Sl1, *K3, P1, YO, P1* to last st, P1—230 sts.

Rep Rows 1–4 until piece measures 72 in. / 183 cm or desired length. End after working Row 1.

Bind off as follows: Sl1, K1, psso, *K2tog, pass 1st over second st on RH needle, P1, pass 1st over second st on RH needle, P2tog, pass 1st over second st on RH needle, K1, pass 1st over second st on RH needle* to end.

Break yarn and pull tail through remaining loop; pull tight to secure.

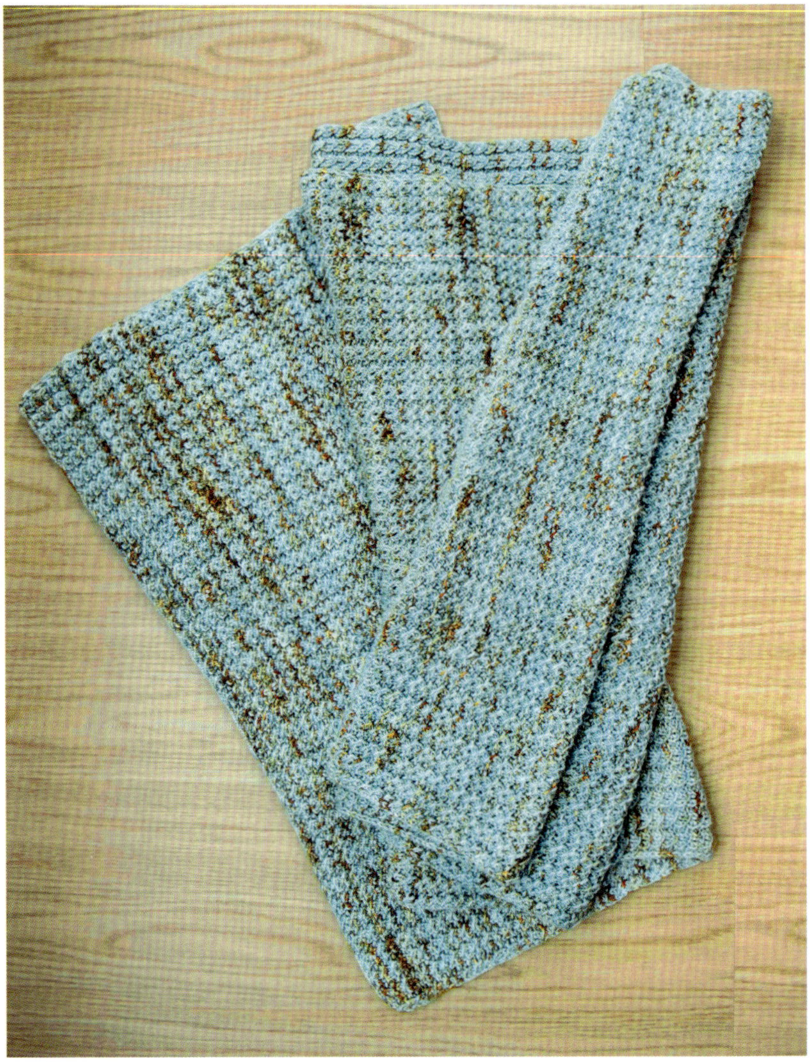

FINISHING
Weave in all tails (see p. 133).

Lightly wet block shawl to measurements (see p. 136).

"SOMETIMES I LONG SO MUCH TO DO LANDSCAPE, JUST AS ONE WOULD FOR A LONG WALK TO REFRESH ONESELF, AND IN ALL OF NATURE, IN TREES FOR INSTANCE, I SEE EXPRESSION AND A SOUL, AS IT WERE. A ROW OF POLLARD WILLOWS SOMETIMES RESEMBLES A PROCESSION OF ORPHAN MEN."

—Vincent van Gogh to his brother Theo,

December 10, 1882

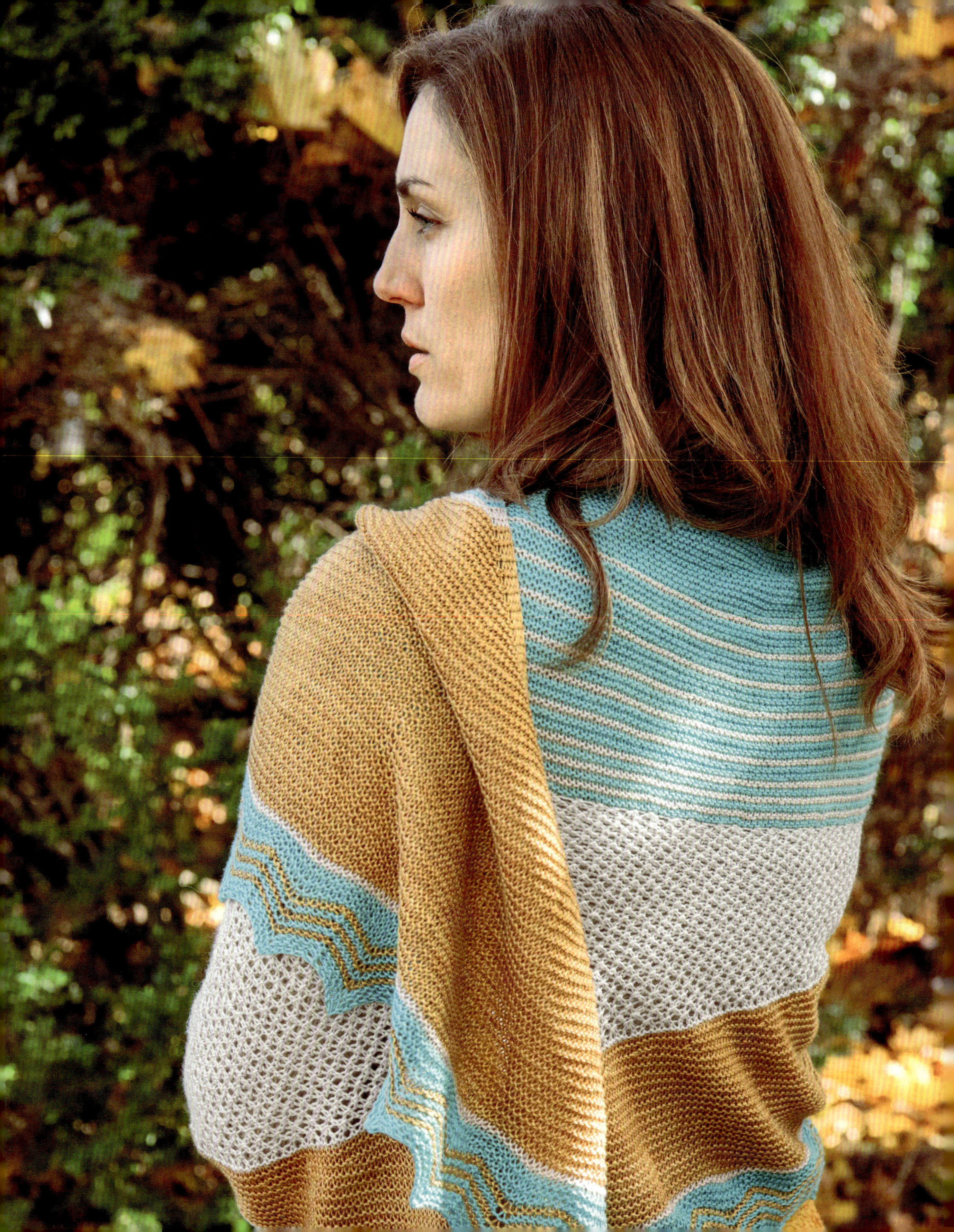

ALMOND BLOSSOM SHAWL

Inspired by *Almond Blossom*

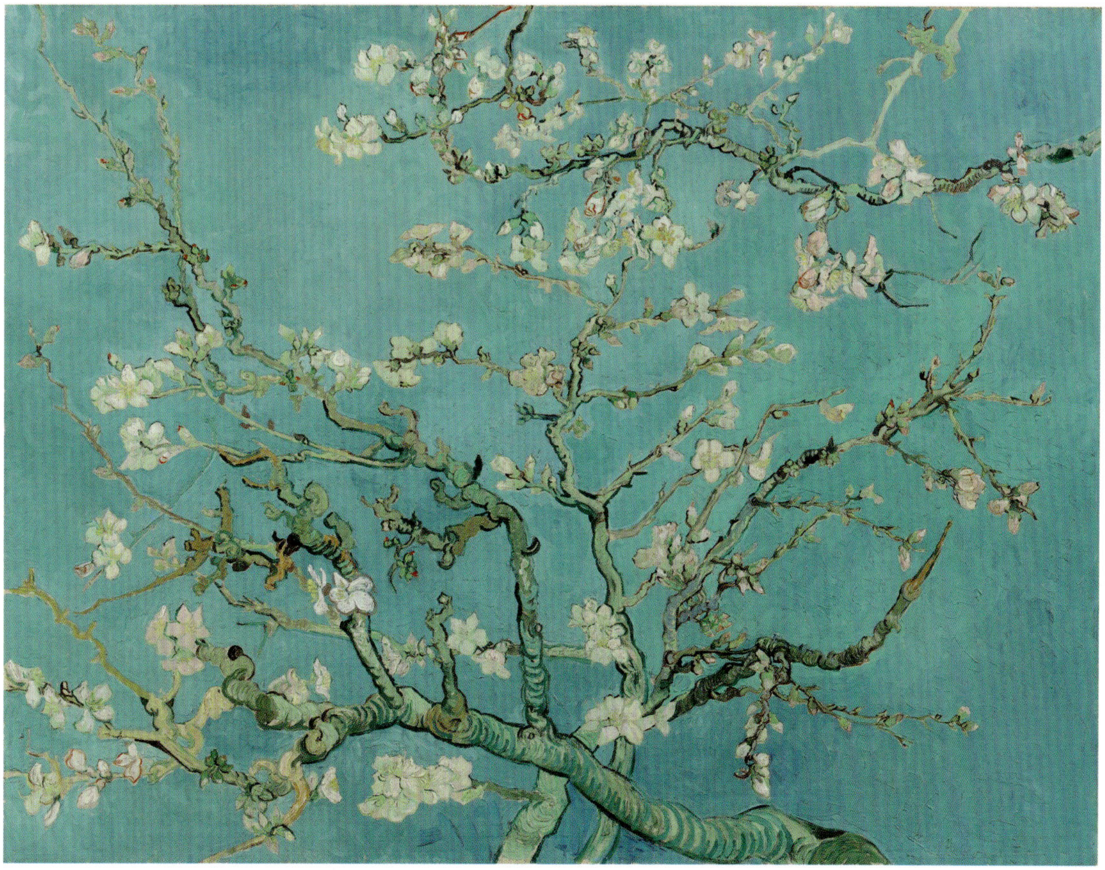

Large branches against a vibrant blue sky, like the ones featured here in *Almond Blossom*, were one of van Gogh's favorite subjects. He painted almond blossoms often, but he created this particular painting as a gift for his newborn nephew, and it nods to the innocence and softness of nature. I designed this shawl using silk because it knits up into a wonderfully delicate and light fabric that offers a breezy weightlessness as it drapes over the shoulders. The curves of the fabric mimic the light and airy petals moving with the wind. I pulled in the captivating teals and gold colors we see in the sky and on the branches, along with the soft white representing the silky petals of the spring blooms.

For more information on van Gogh's *Almond Blossoms*, see p. 138.

SIZES
One size

FINISHED MEASUREMENTS
Approximately 58 in. / 147 cm in wingspan and 22 in. / 56 cm at center depth

YARN
Hand Maiden "Sea Silk" 70% Silk, 30% Seacell; Fingering (100 g / 437 yd. / 400 m)

- **C1**: Piscine–1 skein
- **C2**: Bone–1 skein
- **C3**: Gold–1 skein

NEEDLES
- US size 2 / 2.75 mm, 32 in. / 60 cm long circular knitting needles

Or size needed to obtain gauge

NOTIONS
- Scissors
- Tapestry needle for weaving in ends
- Blocking mats
- Blocking pins
- Spray bottle of water

GAUGE
27 stitches and 40 rows = 4 in. / 10 cm in garter stitch after blocking

NOTES
In sections where 2 colors are used, do not cut yarns unless instructed. Carry the unused yarn up the edge to save on yardage and ends to weave in.

KNITTING INSTRUCTIONS

SECTION 1
Using C1, CO 3 sts.

Knit 11 rows. Don't turn at the end of 11th row. Rotate piece 90 degrees clockwise and pick up 5 sts along long side. Rotate 90 degrees clockwise again and pick up 3 sts along CO edge—11 sts.

Setup Row (WS): K3, YO, K1, kf&b, K1, kf&b, K1, YO, K3—15 sts.

Row 1 (RS): K3, drop YO, K1, kf&b twice, K to last 7 sts, kf&b twice, K1, drop YO, K3—2 sts inc.
Row 2 (WS): K3, YO, K1, kf&b, K to last 5 sts, kf&b, K1, YO, K3—4 sts inc.

Rep Rows 1–2 until you have 183 sts. End after working Row 2.

SECTION 2
Join C2.

Row 1 (RS, C2): K3, drop YO, K1, kf&b twice, K to last 7 sts, kf&b twice, K1, drop YO, K3—2 sts inc.
Row 2 (WS, C2): K3, YO, K1, kf&b, K to last 5 sts, kf&b, K1, YO, K3—4 sts inc.

Rows 3, 5, & 7 (C1): K3, drop YO, K1, kf&b twice, K to last 7 sts, kf&b twice, K1, drop YO, K3—2 sts inc.
Rows 4, 6, & 8 (C1): K3, YO, K1, kf&b, K to last 5 sts, kf&b, K1, YO, K3—4 sts inc.

Rep Rows 1–8 two *more* times—255 sts.

Work Rows 1–6 a total of 3 times—309 sts.

Work Rows 1–4 a total of 3 times—345 sts.

Work Rows 1–2 one *more* time—351 sts.

Cut C1.

SECTION 3
This section uses C2 only.

Short Row 1 (RS): K3, drop YO, K1, kf&b twice, K1, bring 3rd st on LH up and over first two sts and off the needle, K1, YO, K1, turn—1 st inc.
Short Row 2 (WS): P to last 5 sts, kf&b, K1, YO, K3—2 sts inc.

Short Row 3: K3, drop YO, K1, kf&b twice, *bring 3rd st on LH up and over first two sts and off the needle, K1, YO, K1* to one st before turn from previous RS row, *bring 3rd st on LH up and over first two sts and off the needle, K1, YO, K1* three *more* times, turn—1 st inc.
Short Row 4: P to last 5 sts, kf&b, K1, YO, K3—2 sts inc.
Short Row 5: K3, drop YO, K1, kf&b twice, K1, *bring 3rd st on LH up and over first two sts and off the needle, K1, YO, K1* to two sts before turn from previous RS row, *bring 3rd st on LH up and over first two sts and off the needle, K1, YO, K1* three *more* times, turn—1 st inc.

Short Row 6: P to last 5 sts, kf&b, K1, YO, K3—2 sts inc.

Rep Short Rows 3–6 twenty *more* times—480 sts.

Next Row: K3, drop YO, K1, kf&b twice, *bring 3rd st on LH up and over first two sts and off the needle, K1, YO, K1* to last 8 sts, K1, kf&b twice, K1, drop YO, K3—482 sts.
Next Row: K3, YO, K1, kf&b, K to last 5 sts, kf&b, K1, YO, K3—486 sts.

Don't cut C2; carry it up the edge of Section 4 to use again in Section 5.

SECTION 4

Join C3.

Row 1 (RS): K3, drop YO, K1, kf&b twice, K to last 7 sts, kf&b twice, K1, drop YO, K3—488 sts.
Row 2 (WS): K3, YO, K1, kf&b, K to last 5 sts, kf&b, K1, YO, K3—492 sts.
Row 3: K3, drop YO, K1, kf&b twice, K to last 7 sts, kf&b twice, K1, drop YO, K3—494 sts.
Short Rows 4–5: K3, YO, K1, kf&b, K7, w&t, K to last 7 sts, kf&b twice, K1, drop YO, K3—497 sts.

Short Rows 6–7: K3, YO, K1, kf&b, K to previous w&t, K the wrapped st with its wrap, K7, w&t, K to last 7 sts, kf&b twice, K1, drop YO, K3—3 sts inc.

Rep Short Rows 6–7 forty-one *more* times—623 sts.

Next Row (WS): K3, YO, K1, kf&b, K to last 5 sts picking up the w&t when you get to it, kf&b, K1, YO, K3—627 sts.

Work Rows 1–2 once more—633 sts.

SECTION 5

Row 1 (RS, C2): K3, drop YO, K1, kf&b twice, K to last 7 sts, kf&b twice, K1, drop YO, K3—2 sts inc.
Row 2 (WS, C2): K3, YO, K1, kf&b, K to last 5 sts, kf&b, K1, YO, K3—4 sts inc.

Cut C2; join C1.

Work Rows 1–2 in C1 three *more* times—657 sts.

Row 9 (C3): K3, drop YO, K1, kf&b twice, K to last 7 sts, kf&b twice, K1, drop YO, K3—659 sts.
Row 10 (C3): K4, kf&b, K to last 4 sts, kf&b, K3—661 sts.

You are now done increasing. You will have 661 sts for the remainder of the piece.

Row 11 (C1): *K1, M1L, K4, sl2K1p2sso, K4, M1R* to last st, K1.
Row 12 (C1): Knit.
Row 13 (C3): *K1, M1L, K4, sl2K1p2sso, K4, M1R* to last st, K1.
Row 14 (C3): Knit.

Rep Rows 11–12 one *more* time.

Cut C3.

With C1, work Rows 11–12 two *more* times. Work Row 11 one *more* time.

Bind off loosely.

FINISHING

When you are ready to block your shawl, do not soak it in water. Block the shawl dry according to the measurements. The edges of the shawl curl up and the peaks along the bottom should be stretched using blocking pins. Once your shawl is the shape you want it to be, use spray bottle to spritz the entire piece with water until the yarn is saturated, but not soaking wet. Let it dry for at least 24 hours (see p. 136 for more on blocking).

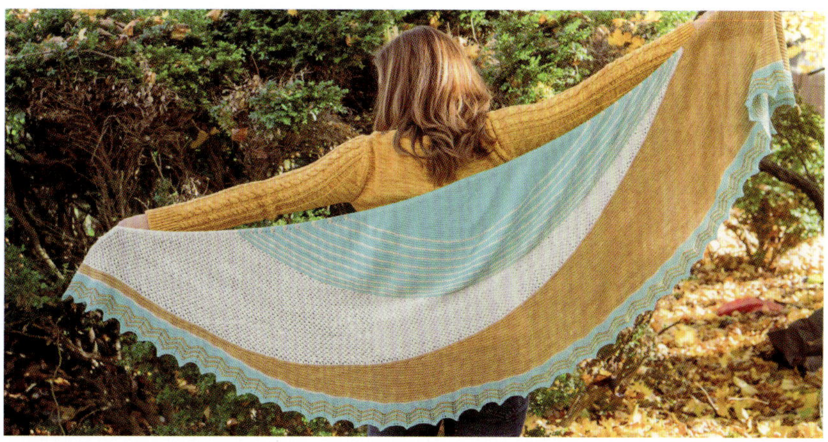

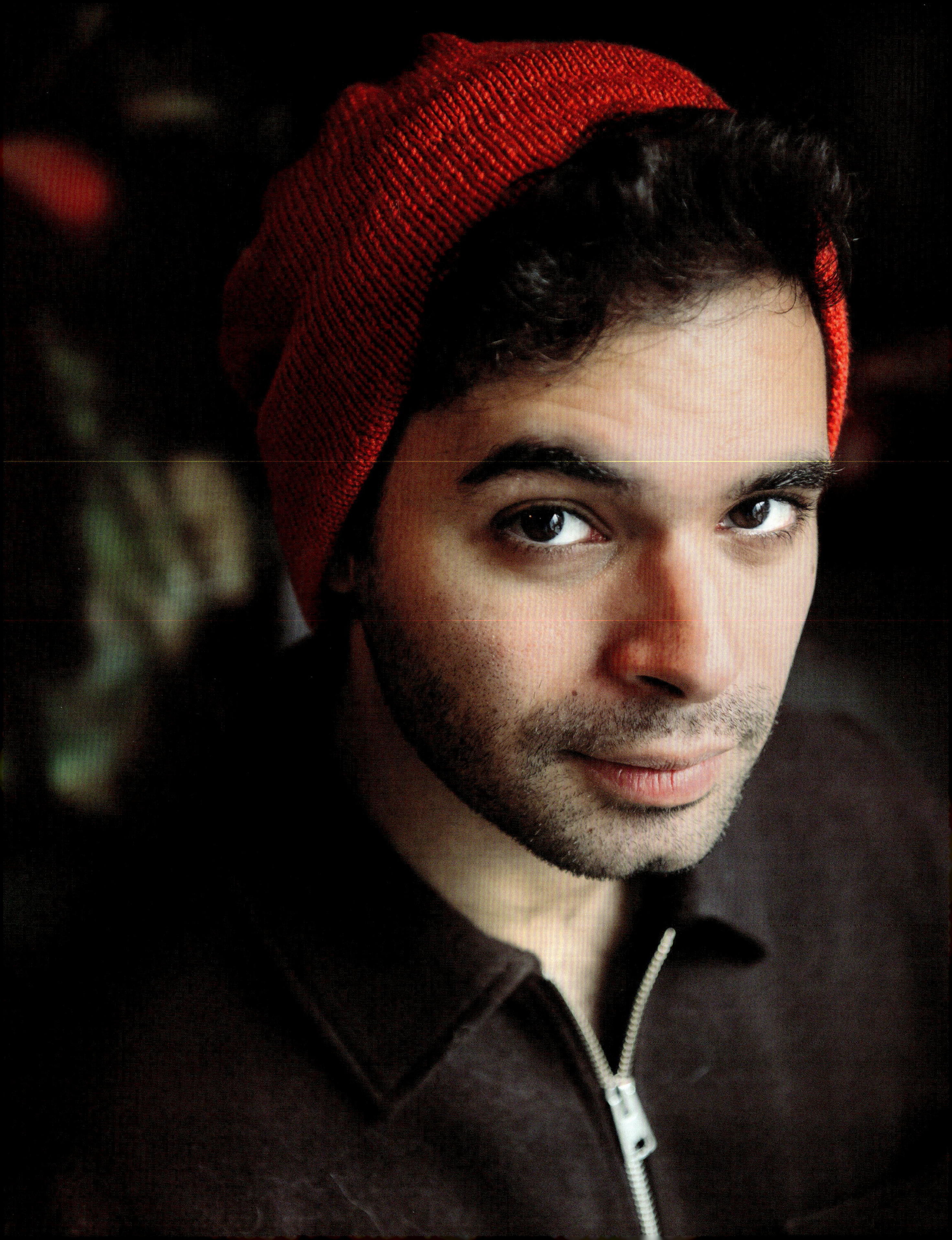

SLOUCH HAT

Inspired by *Head of a Woman*

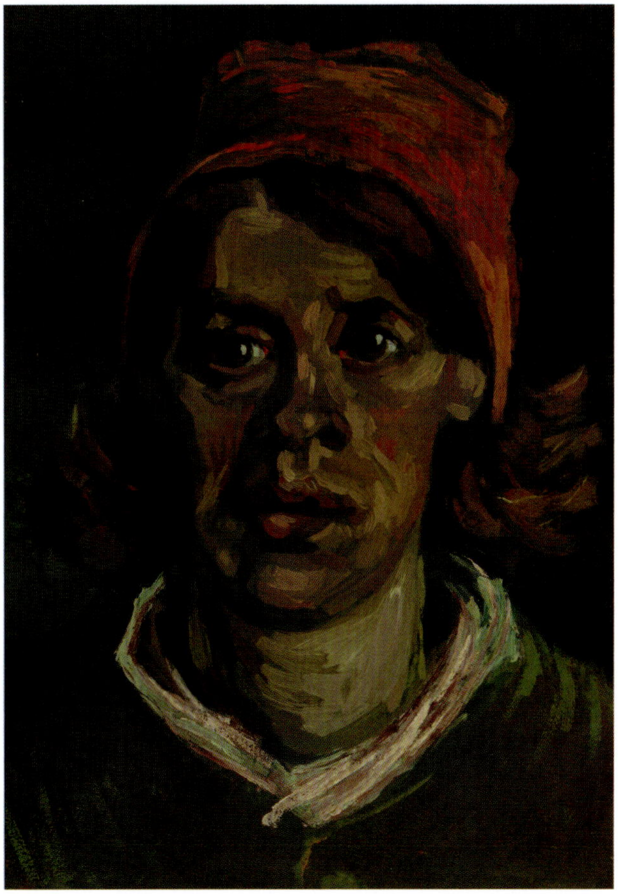

At one point in his career, van Gogh painted the heads of more than forty farmworkers. He hoped that focusing on the features and strokes of the human face would help him become better at painting figures. Van Gogh enjoyed choosing laborers as the focus of his paintings; he viewed them as a special kind of people. This simple red hat, with its slouchy fit, mimics the woman's hat, of course, as well as her expression and demeanor. This pattern has a double thickness that is perfect for peak warmth and comfort in colder seasons. The vibrant red is a unique element to this rather dark-toned painting, and this hat could be the same on a gloomy winter day.

For more information on van Gogh's *Head of a Woman*, see p. 138.

SIZES

One size fits an average female adult sized head

FINISHED MEASUREMENTS

10.5 in. / 27 cm wide, 17 in. / 43 cm tall, and 21 in. / 53 cm circumference unstretched and unfolded

YARN

Cascade Yarns "Heritage Silk" 85% Superwash Merino, 15% Silk; Fingering (100 g / 437 yd. / 400 m)

#5642 Blood Orange – 1 skein

NEEDLES

- US size 2 / 2.75 mm, 16 in. / 40 cm long circular knitting needles
- US size 2 / 2.75 mm, double pointed needles (DPNs)

Or size needed to obtain gauge

NOTIONS

- Scissors
- Stitch marker
- Tapestry needle for weaving in ends

GAUGE

30 stitches and 42 rows = 4 in. / 10 cm in stockinette stitch

NOTES

This hat is worked in the round from the top down. Change from DPNs to circular needle and back to DPNs when needed. Hat is designed to be a baggy fit. If you want a snugger fit, work fewer increase rounds.

KNITTING INSTRUCTIONS

Using DPNs, CO 8 sts.

Join to work in the round; place sm to note bor.

INCREASE SECTION

Rnd 1 and all Odd Rnds: Knit.
Rnd 2: *K1, M1L* around—16 sts.
Rnd 4: *K2, M1L* around—24 sts.
Rnd 6: *K3, M1L* around—32 sts.
Rnd 8: *K4, M1L* around—40 sts.
Rnd 10: *K5, M1L* around—48 sts.
Rnd 12: *K6, M1L* around—56 sts.
Rnd 14: *K7, M1L* around—64 sts.
Rnd 16: *K8, M1L* around—72 sts.
Rnd 18: *K9, M1L* around—80 sts.
Rnd 20: *K10, M1L* around—88 sts.
Rnd 22: *K11, M1L* around—96 sts.
Rnd 24: *K12, M1L* around—104 sts.
Rnd 26: *K13, M1L* around—112 sts.
Rnd 28: *K14, M1L* around—120 sts.
Rnd 30: *K15, M1L* around—128 sts.
Rnd 32: *K16, M1L* around—136 sts.
Rnd 34: *K17, M1L* around—144 sts.
Rnd 36: *K18, M1L* around—152 sts.
Rnd 38: *K19, M1L* around—160 sts.

CENTER BODY

Work in st. st for 5 in. / 12.5 cm.
Next Rnd: *K8, K2tog* around—144 sts.
Knit for 1 in. / 2.5 cm.
Next Rnd: *K16, K2tog* around—136 sts.
Knit for 2.5 in. / 6.5 cm.
Next Rnd: *K17, M1L* around—144 sts.
Knit for 1 in. / 2.5 cm.
Next Rnd: *K9, M1L* around—160 sts.
Work in st. st for 3 in. / 7.5 cm.

DECREASE SECTION

Rnd 1: *K8, K2tog* around—144 sts.
Rnd 2 and every Even Rnd: Knit.
Rnd 3: *K7, K2tog* around—128 sts.
Rnd 5: *K6, K2tog* around—112 sts.
Rnd 7: *K5, K2tog* around—96 sts.
Rnd 9: *K4, K2tog* around—80 sts.
Rnd 11: *K3, K2tog* around—64 sts.
Rnd 13: *K2, K2tog* around—48 sts.

Turn hat inside out and weave in all of your ends (see p. 133). Turn right side out to finish hat.

Rnd 15: *K1, K2tog* around—32 sts.
Rnd 16: *K2tog* around—16 sts.
2tog* around—16 sts.

FINISHING

Cut yarn leaving a tail to weave in. Using a tapestry needle, weave tail through remaining live stitches and cinch tight (see p. 133).

Fold the piece in on itself to create a double layered hat.

If necessary, block lightly (see p. 136 for more on blocking).

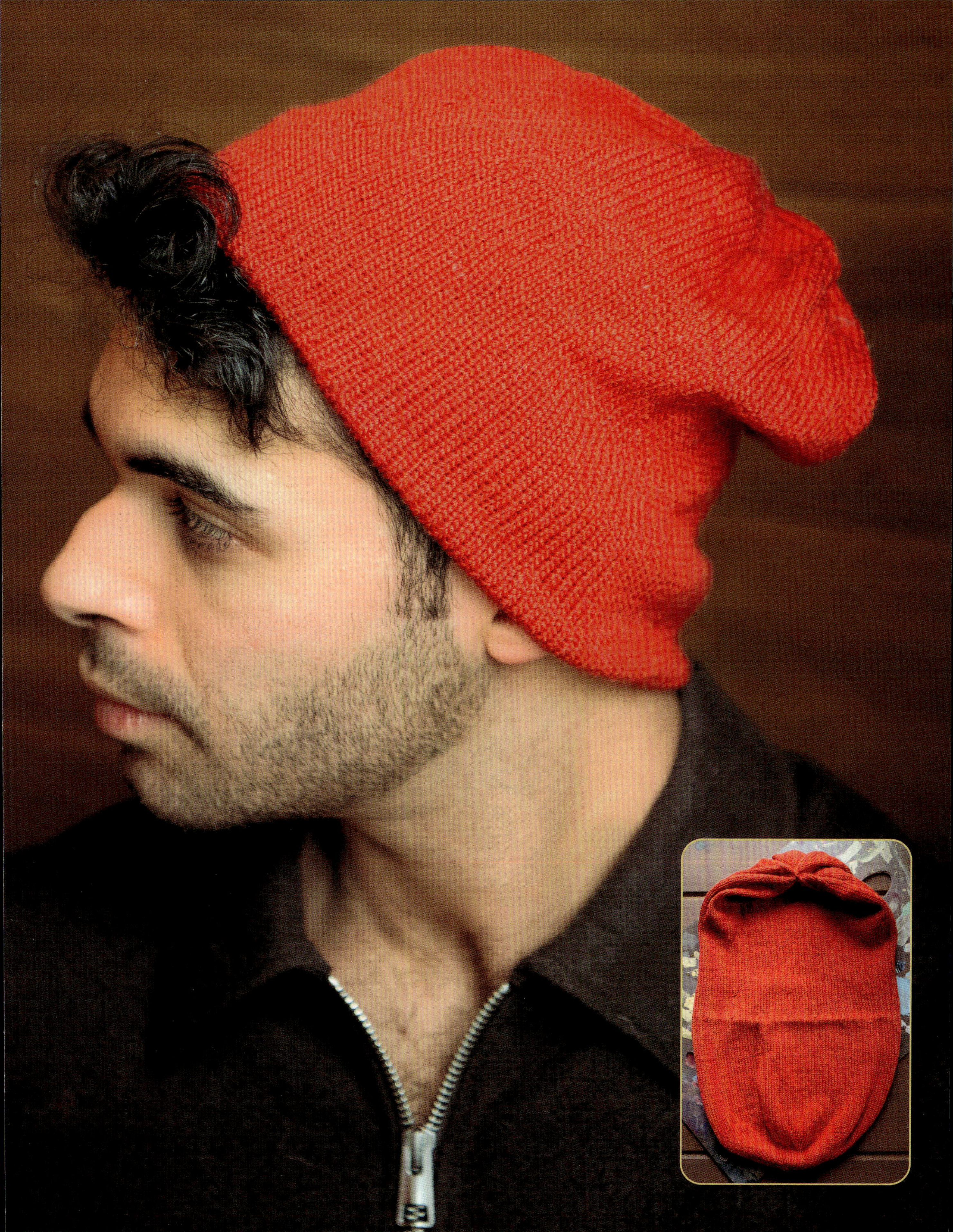

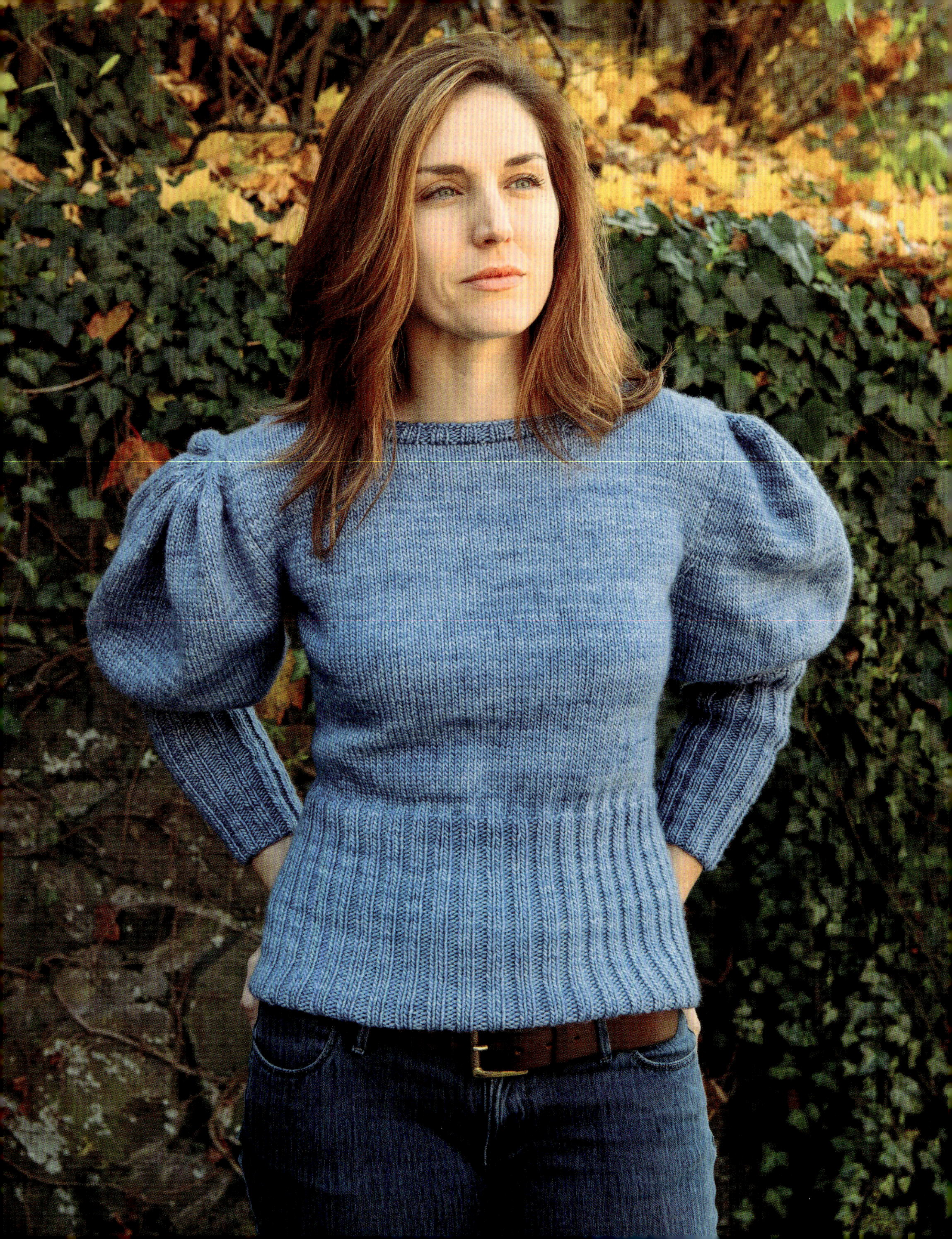

SKILL LEVEL 3

PEASANT SWEATER

Inspired by *Peasant Woman Binding Sheaves* (after Millet)

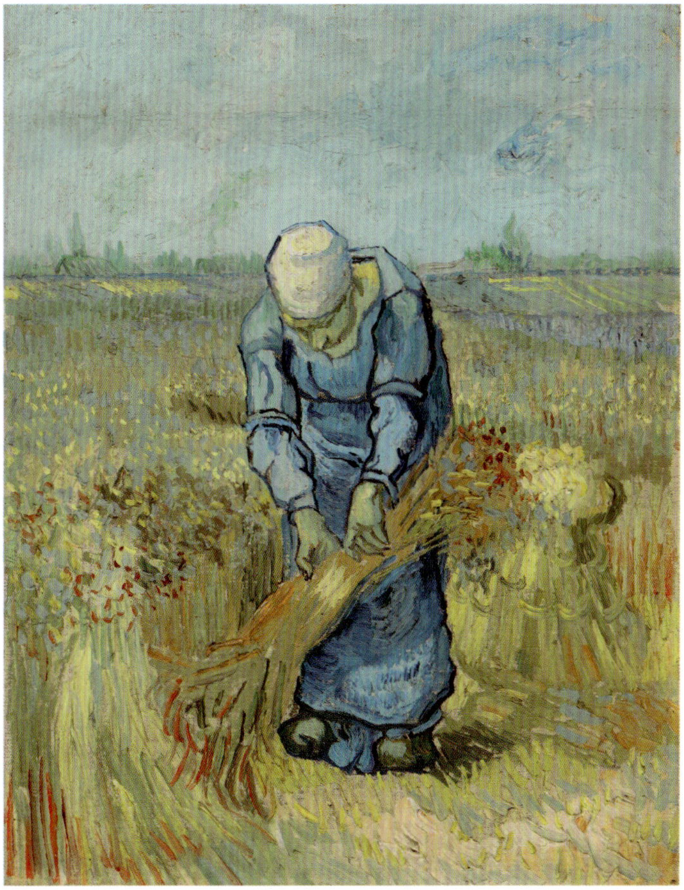

Van Gogh found comfort in painting like many of us find comfort in knitting. During his stay at the psychiatric hospital of Saint-Rémy-de-Provence, van Gogh spent time recreating prints, like this peasant woman, by Jean-François Millet. He studied the work of Millet during this time to give his mind a break, while still practicing his craft. The puffy sleeves and blue color of this sweater mimic the woman's dress in the painting. The heathered appearance also draws in the strokes of the crops she's tending to, the different shades of blue due to the portrayal of the sun hitting her, and the textured sky above her.

For more information on van Gogh's *Peasant Woman Binding Sheaves* (after Millet), see p. 138.

SIZES

XS (S, M, L, XL) [2XL, 3XL, 4XL, 5XL]

FINISHED MEASUREMENTS

34 (36, 38, 40, 42) [46, 48, 50, 52] in. / 86.5 (91.5, 96.5, 101.5, 106.5) [117, 122, 127, 132] cm circumference at underarm. Model is wearing size Medium. Sweater is designed to be worn with 2 in. / 5 cm of positive ease.

YARN

Malabrigo "Worsted"100% Merino Wool; Worsted (100 g / 210 yd. / 192 m)

#608 Bijou Blue – 6 (7, 7, 8, 8) [9, 10, 10, 11] skeins

NEEDLES

- US size 8 / 5 mm, 16" / 40 cm long circular needle for the collar, 24-40" in. / 60-100 cm long circular needles for body ribbing and set of DPNs for the cuffs
- US size 9 / 5.5 mm, 24-40 in. / 60-100 cm long circular needles for the body and set of DPNs for the sleeves

Or size needed to obtain gauge

NOTIONS

- Scissors
- Stitch markers
- Tapestry needle for weaving in ends
- Scrap yarn

GAUGE

19 stitches and 30 rows = 4 in. / 10 cm over stockinette stitch in the round using larger needles, taken after blocking

NOTES

Sweater is worked starting from the bottom up and separates for the sleeve openings. The front and the back are then worked separately. Sleeves are worked in the round up to the armhole opening. Sleeves are eased into the armhole opening at the end.

KNITTING INSTRUCTIONS

BODY

Using smaller and longer needles, CO 160 (172, 180, 192, 200) [216, 228, 236, 248] sts.

Join to work in the round being careful not to twist. Place sm to note bor.

K2, P2 until piece measures 8 in. / 20.5 cm from cast on edge.

Change to larger and longer circular needles.

Work in st. st until the body measures 16 in. / 41 cm from cast on edge.

UNDERARM BIND OFF

Next Rnd: K 76 (82, 86, 92, 96) [104, 110, 114, 120] sts (these are your Front sts), BO 8, K to 4 sts before end of rnd (these are your Back sts), BO 8 sts removing sm when you get to it.

You now have 72 (78, 82, 88, 92) [100, 106, 110, 116] sts for both Back and Front. Place Back sts onto scrap yarn. You will now be working back and forth on Front sts.

FRONT ARMHOLE SHAPING

Row 1 (RS): K2, SSK, K to last 4 sts, K2tog, k2—2 sts dec.

Row 2 (WS): Purl.

Rep Rows 1–2 two *more* times—66 (72, 76, 82, 86) [94, 100, 104, 110] sts rem.

Continue in st. st until piece measures 5 (5.5, 5.5, 6, 6.5) [7, 7.5, 7.5, 8] in. / 12.5 (14, 14, 15, 16.5) [18, 19, 19, 20.5] cm from underarm bind off. End after working a WS row.

Separation Row (RS): K 21 (24, 25, 28, 29) [33, 35, 37, 39] sts (these are your Left Front sts), BO center 24 (24, 26, 26, 28) [28, 30, 30, 32] sts, K to end.

Place Left Front sts onto scrap yarn. You will now be working the Right Front only.

Next Row (WS): Purl.

RIGHT FRONT

Row 1 (RS): K2, SSK, K to end—1 st dec.

Row 2 (WS): Purl.

Rep Rows 1–2 four *more* times—16 (19, 20, 23, 24) [28, 30, 32, 34] sts rem.

Continue in st. st until piece measures 7.5 (8, 8, 8.5, 9) [9.5, 10, 10, 10.5] in. / 19 (20.5, 20.5, 21.5, 23) [24, 25.5, 25.5, 26.5] cm from underarm bind off. End after working a WS row.

Cut yarn leaving a tail and place remaining 16 (19, 20, 23, 24) [28, 30, 32, 34] sts onto scrap yarn.

LEFT FRONT

Place Left Front sts onto larger needle. Join yarn with WS facing.

Row 1 (WS): Purl.
Row 2 (RS): K to last 4 sts K2tog, K2—1 st dec.

Rep Rows 1–2 four *more* times—16 (19, 20, 23, 24) [28, 30, 32, 34] sts rem.

Continue in st. st until piece measures 7.5 (8, 8, 8.5, 9) [9.5, 10, 10, 10.5] in. / 19 (20.5, 20.5, 21.5, 23) [24, 25.5, 25.5, 26.5] cm from underarm bind off. End after working a WS row.

Cut yarn leaving a tail and place remaining 16 (19, 20, 23, 24) [28, 30, 32, 34] sts onto scrap yarn.

BACK

Place Back sts onto larger needle. Join yarn with RS facing.

Row 1 (RS): K2, SSK, K to last 4 sts, K2tog, k2—2 sts dec.
Row 2 (WS): Purl.

Rep Rows 1–2 two *more* times—66 (72, 76, 82, 86) [94, 100, 104, 110] sts rem.

Continue in st. st until piece measures 6 (6.5, 6.5, 7, 7.5) [8, 8.5, 8.5, 9] in. / 15 (16.5, 16.5, 18, 19) [20.5, 21.5, 21.5, 23] cm from underarm bind off. End after working a WS.

Separation Row (RS): K 18 (21, 22, 25, 26) [30, 32, 34, 36] sts (these are your right back sts), BO center 30 (30, 32, 32, 34) [34, 36, 36, 38] sts, K to end.
Place Right Back sts onto scrap yarn. You will now be working the Left Back only.
Next Row: Purl.

LEFT BACK

Row 1 (RS): K2, SSK, K to end—1 st dec.
Row 2 (WS): Purl.

Rep Rows 1–2 one *more* time—16 (19, 20, 23, 24) [28, 30, 32, 34] sts rem.

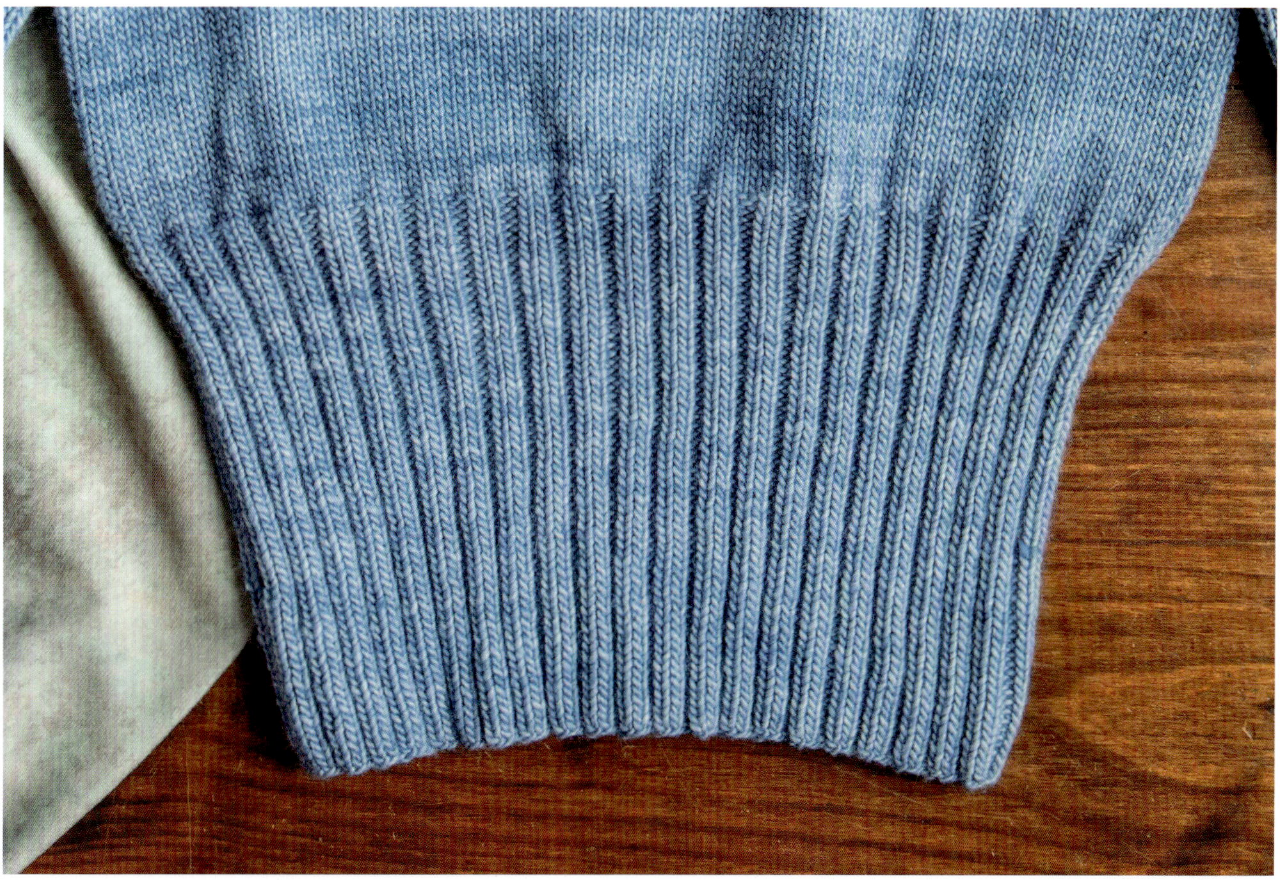

(Pattern continues on next page)

Continue in st. st until piece measures 7.5 (8, 8, 8.5, 9) [9.5, 10, 10, 10.5] in / 19 (20.5, 20.5, 21.5, 23) [24, 25.5, 25.5, 26.5] cm from underarm bind off. End after working a WS row. Do not break yarn.

Place Left Front sts onto second larger needle. With RS facing each other, work three-needle bind off (see p. 132).

RIGHT BACK

Place Right Back sts onto larger needle. Join yarn with WS facing.

Row 1 (WS): Purl.
Row 2 (RS): K to last 4 sts K2tog, K2—1 st dec.

Rep Rows 1–2 one *more* time—16 (19, 20, 23, 24) [28, 30, 32, 34] sts rem.

Continue in st. st until piece measures 7.5 (8, 8, 8.5, 9) [9.5, 10, 10, 10.5] in / 19 (20.5, 20.5, 21.5, 23) [24, 25.5, 25.5, 26.5] cm from underarm bind off. End after working a WS row. Do not break yarn.

Place Right Front sts onto second larger needle. With RS facing each other, work three-needle bind off (see p. 132).

SLEEVES (MAKE 2)

Using smaller DPNs, CO 36 (40, 44, 44, 48) [52, 52, 56, 60] sts.
Join to work in the round being careful not to twist. Place sm to note bor.

Rnds 1–6: K1, P2, *K2, P2* to last st, K1.
Rnd 7: K1, M1L, *P2, K2* to last 3 sts, P2, M1R, K1—2 sts inc.
Rnds 8–14: *K2, P2* to last 2 sts, K2.
Rnd 15: K1, M1L, K1, *P2, K2* to last 4 sts, P2, K1, M1R, K1—2 sts inc.
Rnds 16–22: P1, *K2, P2* to last 3 sts, K2, P1.
Rnd 23: P1, M1LP, *K2, P2* to last 3 sts, K2, M1RP, P1—2 sts inc.
Rnds 24–30: *P2, K2* to last 2 sts, P2.
Rnd 31: P1, M1PL, P1, *K2, P2* to last 4 sts, K2, P1, M1RP, P1—2 sts inc.
Rnds 32–38: K1, *P2, K2* to last 3 sts, P2, K1.

Rep Rnds 7–38 one *more* time—52 (56, 60, 60, 64) [68, 68, 72, 76] sts.

Change to larger DPNs.

Rnd 1: K1, M1L, K to last st, M1R, K1—2 sts inc.
Rnds 2–8: Knit.

Rep Rnds 1–8 two *more* times—58 (62, 66, 66, 70) [74, 74, 78, 82] sts.

Setup Rnd: K 26 (28, 30, 30, 32) [34, 34, 36, 38], *place sm, K2* 3 times, place sm, K to end—4 sm placed.

Rnd 1: *K to sm, slm, M1R* twice, *K to sm, M1L, slm* twice, K to end—4 sts inc.
Rnds 2–4: Knit.

Rep Rnds 1–4 four *more* times—78 (82, 86, 86, 90) [94, 94, 98, 102] sts.

Rnd 21: *K to sm, slm, M1R* twice, K5, place sm, M1R, K2, M1L, place sm, *K to sm, M1L, slm* twice, K to end—6 sts inc.

Rnds 22–24: Knit.

Rnd 25: *K to sm, slm, M1R* three times *K to sm, M1L, slm* three times, K to end—6 sts inc.

Rep Rnds 22–25 two *more* times—102 (106, 110, 110, 114) [118, 118, 122, 126] sts.

Rnd 34: K to end removing all sm except bor sm.

Work in st. st until sleeve measures 20 in. / 51 cm from cast on edge. The sleeve should extend just past your wrist bone, but it should be worn at the wrist bone. This helps give puff to the upper part of the sleeve.

Next Rnd: K to last 4 sts, BO 8 sts removing bor sm when you get to it—94 (98, 102, 102, 106) [110, 110, 114, 118] sts rem.

You will now be working back and forth in rows.

Row 1 (RS): K2, SSK, K to last 4 sts, K2tog, K2—2 sts dec.
Row 2 (all WS rows): Purl.

Rep Rows 1–2 two *more* times—88 (92, 96, 96, 100) [104, 104, 108, 112] sts.

Continue in st. st until the sleeve measures 6 (6.5, 6.5, 7, 7.5) [8, 8.5, 8.5, 9] in. / 15 (16.5, 16.5, 18, 19) [20, 22, 22, 23] cm from underarm bind off. End after working a WS row.

SHORT ROWS

Short Rows 1–2: K to last 4 sts, w&t, P to last 4 sts, w&t.
Short Rows 3–4: K to last 8 sts, w&t, P to last 8 sts, w&t.
Short Rows 5–6: K to last 12 sts, w&t, P to last 12 sts, w&t.
Short Rows 7–8: K to last 16 sts, w&t, P to last 16 sts, w&t.

Short Row 9 (RS): K to end picking up and knitting all w&t when you come to them.

Row 10 (WS): P to end picking up and knitting all w&t when you come to them.

SLEEVE CAP

Row 1 (RS): K 44 (46, 48, 48, 50) [52, 52, 54, 56], place sm, K to end.
Row 2 (WS): Purl.
Row 3: K2, *SSK* to sm, slm, *K2tog* to last 2 sts, K2—46 (48, 50, 50, 52) [54, 54, 56, 58] sts.
Row 4: Purl.
Row 5: K 3 (2, 3, 3, 2) [3, 3, 2, 3] *SSK* to sm, slm, *K2tog* to last 3 (2, 3, 3, 2) [3, 3, 2, 3] sts, K to end—26 (26, 28, 28, 28) [30, 30, 30, 32] sts.
Row 6: Purl.
Row 7: K 3 (3, 2, 2, 2) [3, 3, 3, 2], *SSK* to sm, slm, *K2tog* to last 3 (3, 2, 2, 2) [3, 3, 3, 2] sts, K to end—16 (16, 16, 16, 16) [18, 18, 18, 18] sts.
Row 8: Purl.
Row 9: K 2 (2, 2, 2, 2) [3, 3, 3, 3], *SSK* to sm, slm, *K2tog* to last 2 (2, 2, 2, 2) [3, 3, 3, 3] sts, K to end—10 (10, 10, 10, 10) [12, 12, 12, 12] sts.
Row 10: Purl and remove sm when you get to it.

With RS facing, bind off knitwise.

Ease the sleeves into the body of the sweater and use mattress stitch (see p. 136) to attach sleeves to body.

COLLAR

Using smaller 16 in. / 40 cm circular needles, pick up around the neckline edge. Pick up 1 st for every stitch along the Back and Front bind off and 3 sts for every 4 rows along the vertical edges. The number of stitches you pick up is not important as long as it is a multiple of 4.

K2, P2 around neck edge for 1 in. / 5 cm.

FINISHING

Work sewn bind off (see p. 132).

Weave in tails (see p. 133).

Lightly spray block (see p. 136).

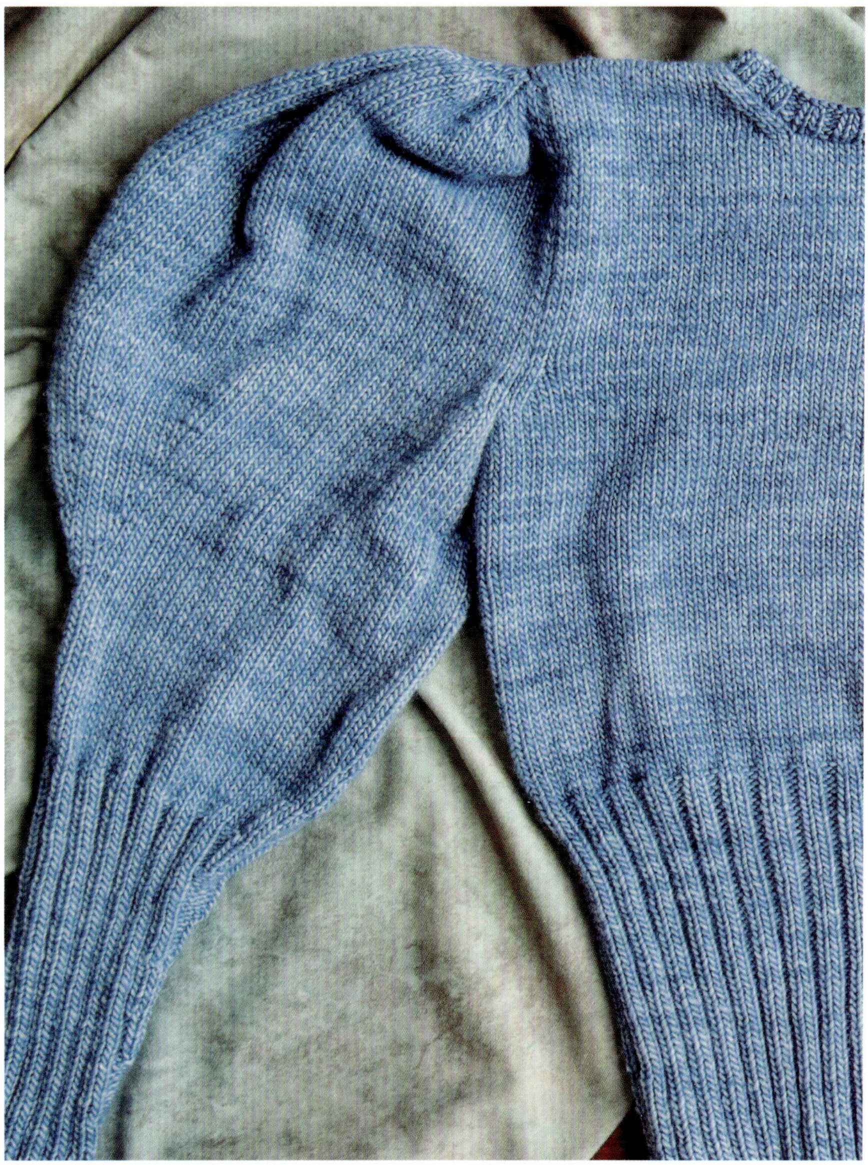

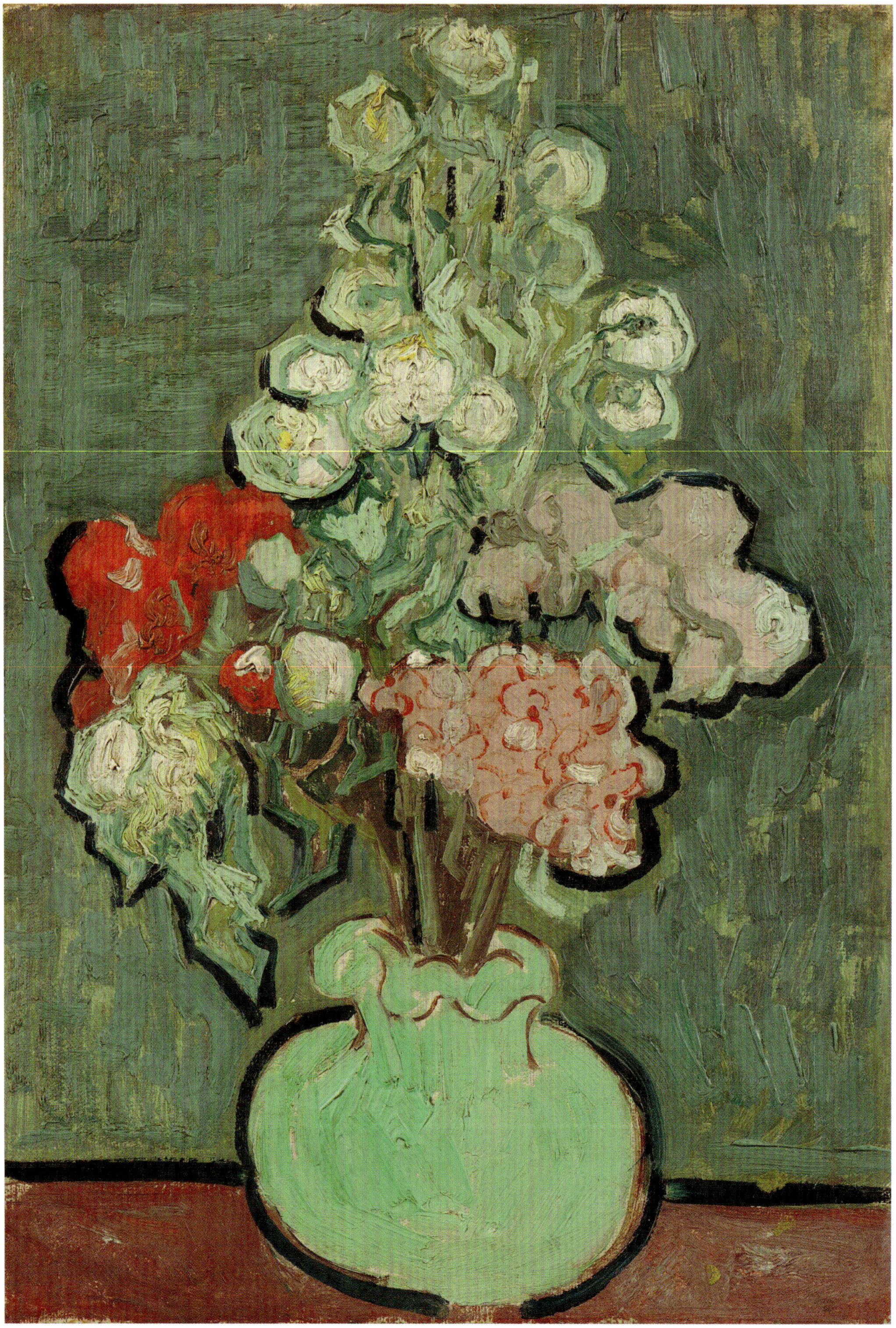

Vase of Flowers (p. 73)

"SUCCESS IS SOMETIMES THE OUTCOME OF A WHOLE STRING OF FAILURES."

—Vincent van Gogh to his brother Theo,
October 1, 1882

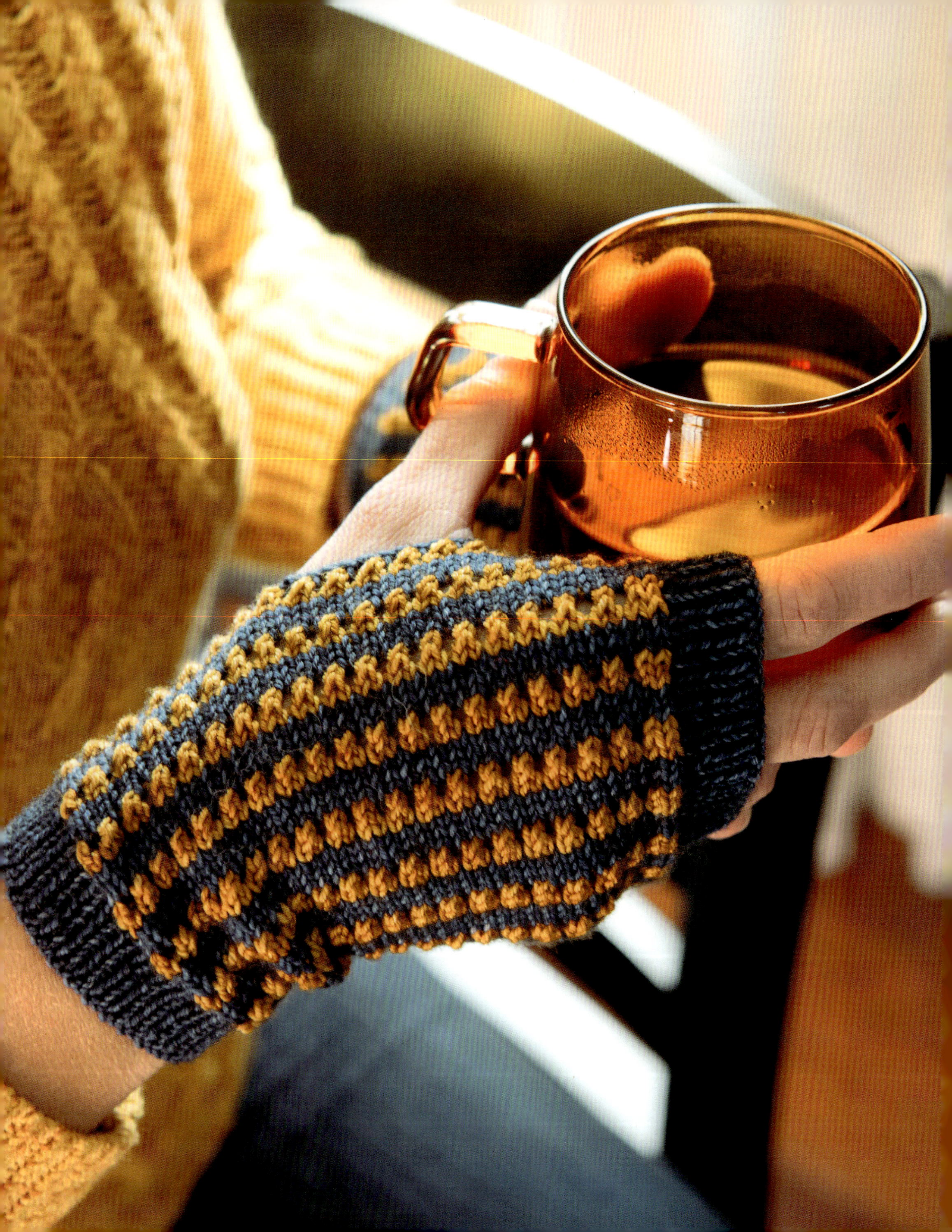

SKILL LEVEL **2**

FINGERLESS GLOVES

Inspired by *Irises*

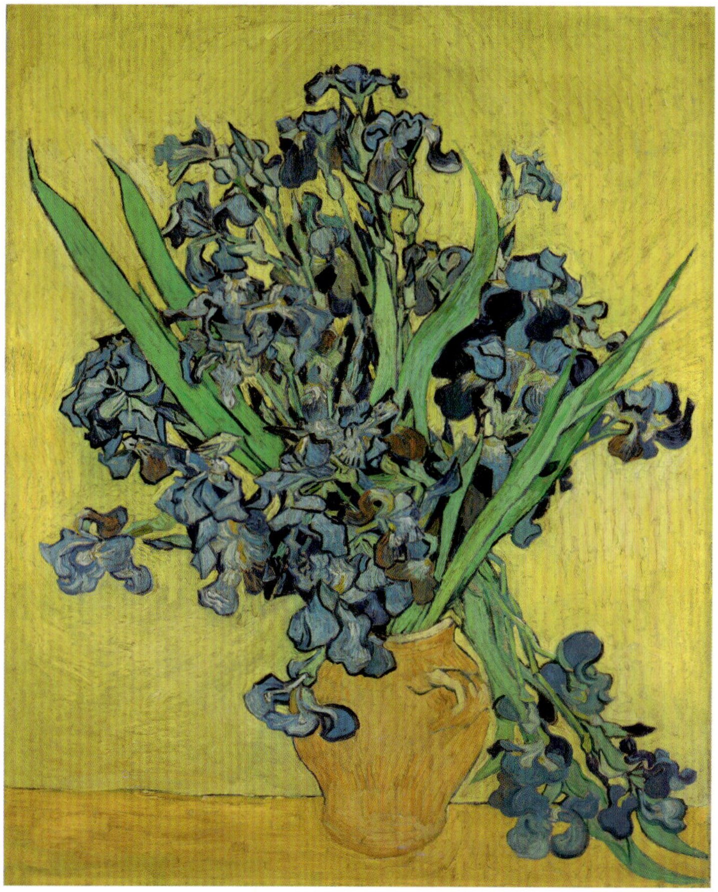

A simple vase with beautiful, vibrant flowers is one of van Gogh's signature subjects. With this painting, he set out to achieve a clear color contrast, which is a goal I maintained when creating this pattern. The irises in this painting were originally purple, but as the pigment faded over time, they turned blue. The strong yellow and blue colors alternating in these fingerless gloves make for a stunning pattern. I also thought of a painter's hands for this pattern. I wanted to design a pair of fingerless gloves that would allow a painter to wear them and keep warm without hindering their fingers from creating their next great masterpiece.

For more information on van Gogh's *Irises*, see p. 138.

SIZES

One size

FINISHED MEASUREMENTS

6.5 in. / 16.5 cm tall (including ribbed edges) and 7 in. / 18 cm circumference

YARN

Malabrigo "Ultimate Sock" 75% Superwash Merino Wool, 25% Nylon; Fingering (100 g / 420 yd. / 385 m)

MC: #150 Azul Profundo – 1 skein

CC: #013 Oro – 1 skein

NEEDLES

- US size 0 / 2.0 mm, set of double pointed needles
- (2) US size 1 / 2.25 mm, 16 in. / 40 cm circular knitting needles

Or size needed to obtain gauge

NOTIONS

- Scissors
- Stitch marker
- Tapestry needle for weaving in ends
- Scrap yarn (for provisional cast on)
- Crochet hook (for provisional cast on)

GAUGE

30 stitches and 48 rows = 4 in. / 10 cm in stockinette stitch worked flat on larger needles

NOTES

- These fingerless gloves are knit flat worked from side to side. Make two the same.
- If you want longer or shorter gloves, the stitch pattern is a multiple of 2 stitches.
- To make your gloves larger in circumference, continue in pattern to desired pre-seamed length, being sure to end after working Row 10.

KNITTING INSTRUCTIONS

Using larger needles and CC, provisionally CO 40 sts using the crochet chain provisional cast on method (see p. 131). Do not join to work in the round.

Row 1 (MC, WS): Purl.
Row 2 (CC, RS): Knit.
Row 3 (CC, WS): P2, *P2tog, YO* to last 2 sts, P2.
Row 4 (CC, RS): K to end of row, do not turn, slide sts to other end of the needle.
Row 5 (MC, RS): Knit.
Row 6 (MC, WS): Purl.
Row 7 (MC, RS): Knit.
Row 8 (CC, WS): Purl.
Row 9 (CC, RS): K2, *YO, K2tog* to last 2 sts, K2.
Row 10: (CC, WS): P to end of row, do not turn, slide sts to other end of the needle.
Row 11 (MC, WS): Purl.
Row 12 (MC, RS): Knit.

Rep Rows 1–12 five *more* times.

Work Rows 1–10 one *more* time.

Next Row: P14, BO 12 sts purlwise, P to end.

Cut CC yarn leaving a tail to weave in. Cut MC yarn leaving a 24 in. / 61 cm tail.

Pull out provisional cast on and put all 40 live sts onto second larger needle.

Hold the two needles parallel with the RS facing out. The cast on sts should be on the needle furthest from you; this will be the Back needle. The live sts remaining from the top of the glove will be on the needle closest to you; this will be the Front needle.

Using 24 in. / 61 cm MC tail, graft the first 14 sts of the Front and Back needles together using Kitchener stitch (see p. 130).

Pass over bind off the next 12 sts on the Back needle (see p. 131). Move the remaining sts to the left-hand Back needle purlwise. 14 sts now remain on each of the Front and Back needles.

Graft the remaining sts from the Front and Back needles together using Kitchener stitch.

TOP EDGE

Using smaller needles and MC, pick up and knit 3 sts for every 4 rows around top edge of glove. While an exact number of sts is not required, be sure you have an even number of sts. The original design has 64 sts at each ribbed edge. Place sm to note bor.

K1, P1 for 10 rnds.

Bind off in pattern.

BOTTOM EDGE

Work the bottom edge cuff of the band the same as the Top Edge.

FINISHING

Weave in tails (see p. 133).

Do not block fingerless gloves so that the texture of the pattern does not disappear.

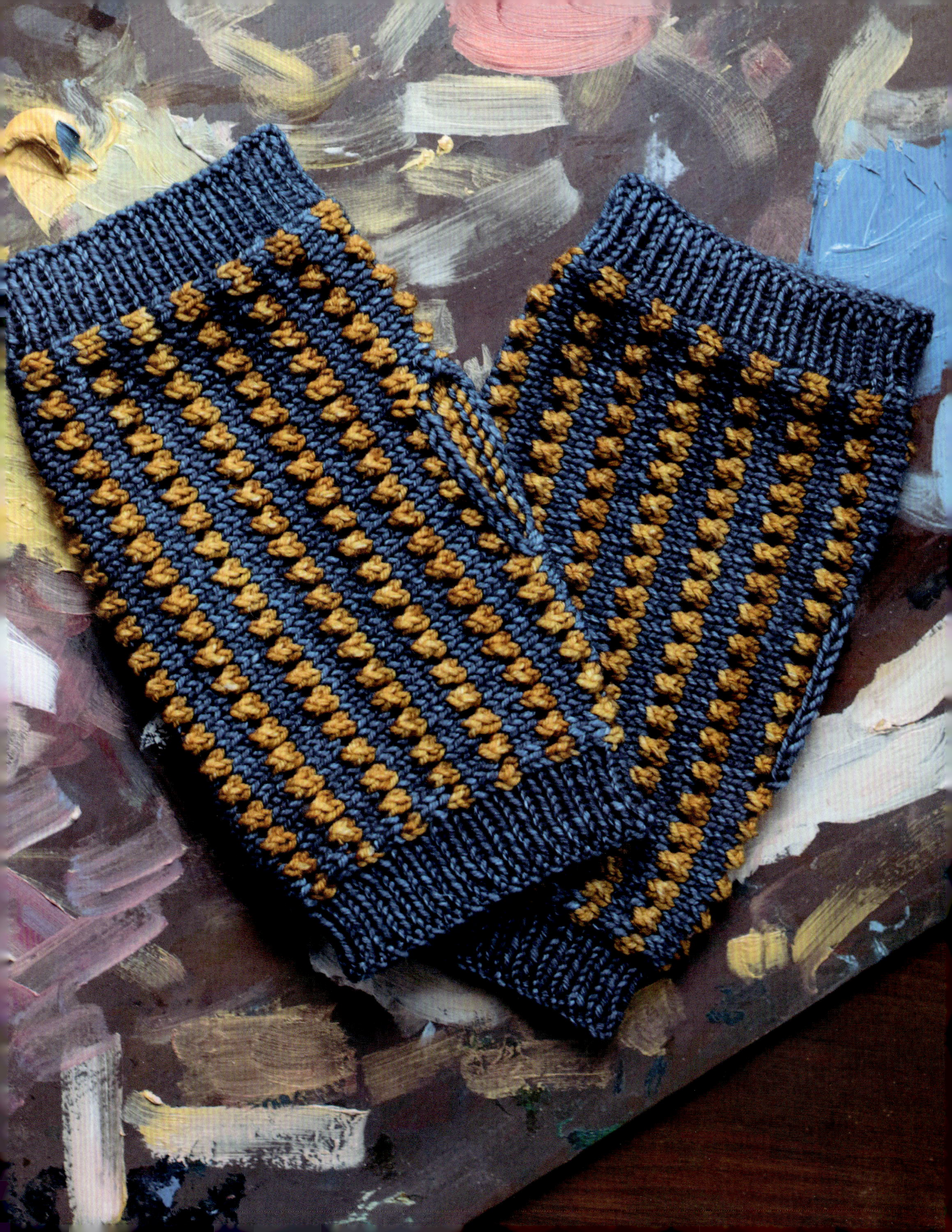

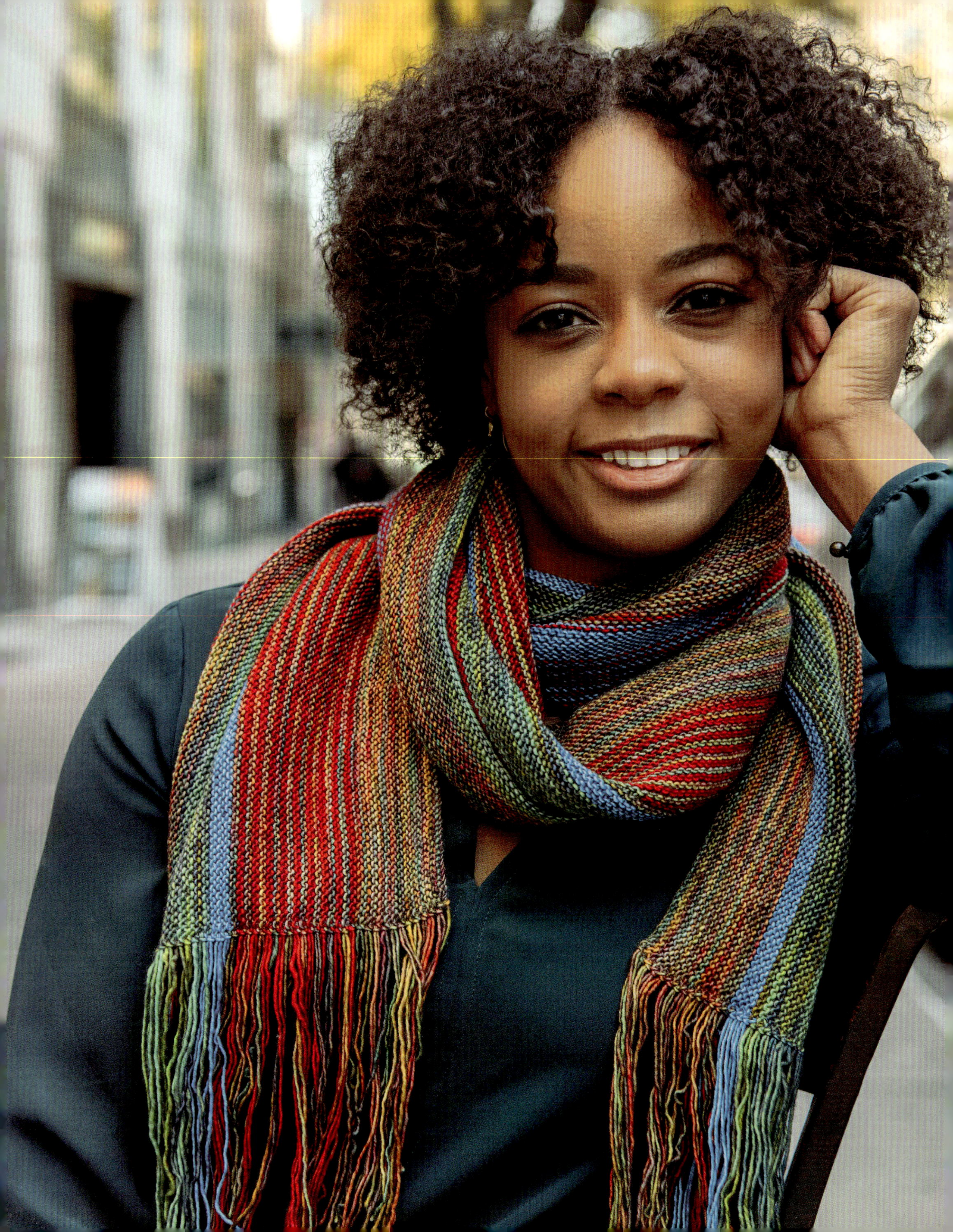

BAMBOO SCARF

Inspired by *Courtesan* (after Eisen)

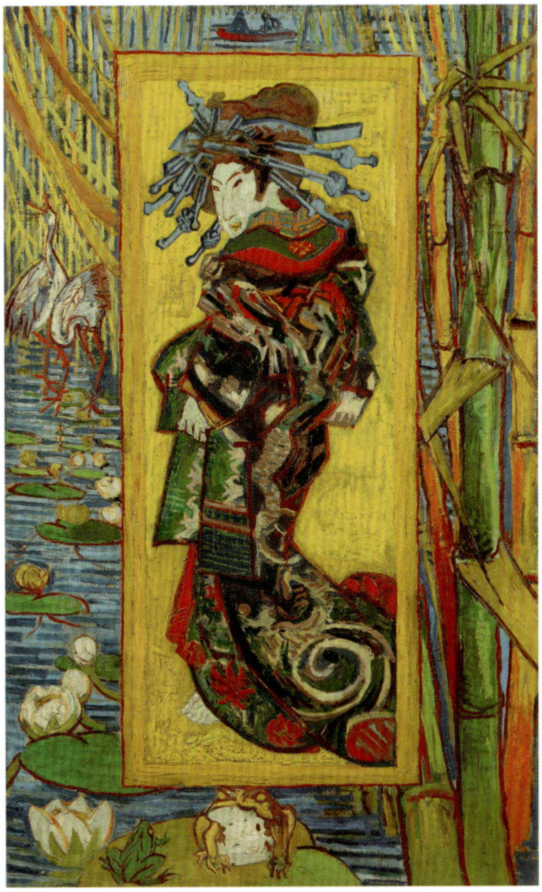

There is plenty to absorb in this painting, with the courtesan's colorful garment and her surroundings of water lilies, bamboo stems, cranes, and frogs. However, the colorful bamboo stalks were my immediate inspiration for this vertical knit scarf. The vertical knit pattern is the perfect way to translate the long and straight lines of the bamboo onto a fashionable accessory. Van Gogh modeled this painting after a woodcut by Japanese artist Kesai Eisen, who is credited in the title. He made use of bold reds, yellows, greens, blues, and oranges that came together beautifully, both in the painting and in this cozy scarf.

For more information on van Gogh's *Courtesan* (after Eisen), see p. 138.

SIZE
Finished scarf measures 8.5 in. / 22 cm wide and 70 in. / 178 cm long (without fringe) or 82 in / 208 cm long (with fringe)

YARN
Malabrigo "Mechita" 100% Superwash Merino Wool; Fingering (100 g / 420 yd. / 384 m)

- **C1:** #886 Diana – 1 skein
- **C2:** #033 Cereza – 1 skein
- **C3:** #806 Impressionist Sky – 1 skein
- **C4:** #880 Hojas – 1 skein

NEEDLES
- US size 3 / 3.25 mm, 32 or 40 in. / 80 or 100 cm long circular knitting needles

Or size needed to obtain gauge

NOTIONS
- Scissors
- Crochet hook for attaching fringe
- Tapestry needle for weaving in ends

GAUGE
28 stitches and 56 rows = 4 in. / 10 cm in garter stitch

NOTES
- Scarf is worked lengthwise. Fringe is added at the end.
- In Section One, odd-numbered rows are WS rows. In Sections Two and Three, odd-numbered rows are RS rows.
- Carry unused yarns up the edge of the scarf to save on yardage and ends to weave in; only cut colors when instructed.

KNITTING INSTRUCTIONS

Using long tail cast on (see p. 130) and C1, CO 500 sts.

SECTION ONE

Starting with a WS row, work Rows 1—25 using C1 as follows:
Sl1, K to last st, P1.

Join C2. Begin short rows.

Short Rows 26–27 (C2): Sl1, K249, w&t (see p. 134), K to last st, P1.
Short Rows 28–29 (C1): Sl1, K to 5 sts before last turn, w&t, K to last st, P1.
Short Rows 30–31 (C2): Sl1, K to 5 sts before last turn, w&t, K to last st, P1.

Rep Short Rows 28–31 seven *more* times. You will have a total of 9 C2 stripes.

Cut C2.

Row 60 (C1): Sl1, K to last st picking up the w&t sts when you get to them, P1.
Row 61 (C1): Sl1, K to last st, P1.

Cut C1. Join C3.

Rows 62–67 (C3): Sl1, K to last st, P1.

Cut C3.

SECTION TWO

Join C4.

Rows 1–18 (C4): Sl1, K to last st, P1.
Row 19 (RS): Sl1, K to last st, P1.

Begin short rows. Pick up the w&t sts when you get to them.

Short Rows 20–21: Sl1, K274, w&t, K to last st, P1.
Short Rows 22–23: Sl1, K279, w&t, K to last st, P1.
Short Rows 24–25: Sl1, K284, w&t, K to last st, P1.
Short Rows 26–27: Sl1, K289, w&t, K to last st, P1.
Short Rows 28–29: Sl1, K294, w&t, K to last st, P1.
Row 30 (WS): Sl1, K to last st, P1.

Cut C4. Join C2 and C3.

Rows 31–40 (C2): Sl1, K to last st, P1.

Rows 41–42 (C3): Sl1, K to last st, P1.
Rows 43–44 (C2): Sl1, K to last st, P1.

Rep Rows 41–44 four *more* times. You will have a total of 5 C3 stripes.

Row 61 (C3): Sl1, K to last st, P1.

Begin short rows. Pick up the w&t sts when you get to them. (This part only uses C3. Keep C2 joined.)

Short Rows 62–63: Sl1, K249, w&t, K to last st, P1.
Short Rows 64–65: Sl1, K254, w&t, K to last st, P1.
Short Rows 66–67: Sl1, K259, w&t, K to last st, P1.

Short Rows 68–69: Sl1, K264, w&t, K to last st, P1.
Short Rows 70–71: Sl1, K269, w&t, K to last st, P1.

Row 72 (WS): Sl1, K to last st, P1.

Cut C3.

Rows 73–74 (C2): Sl1, K to last st, P1.

Cut C2.

SECTION THREE

Join C1.

Rows 1–7 (C1): Sl1, K to last st, P1.

Begin short rows. Pick up the w&t sts when you get to them.

Short Rows 8–9: Sl1, K299, w&t, K to last st, P1.
Short Rows 10–11: Sl1, K304, w&t, K to last st, P1.
Short Rows 12–13: Sl1, K309, w&t, K to last st, P1.
Short Rows 14–15: Sl1, K314, w&t, K to last st, P1.
Short Rows 16–17: Sl1, K319, w&t, K to last st, P1.
Short Rows 18–19: Sl1, K324, w&t, K to last st, P1.
Short Rows 20–21: Sl1, K329, w&t, K to last st, P1.

Rows 22–24: Sl1, K to last st, P1.

Cut C1. Join C4.

Rows 25–30 (C4): Sl1, K to last st, P1.

Loosely bind off all sts knitwise using C4.

FINISHING

Weave in tails (see p. 133).

Add fringe as follows: Cut each piece of fringe to be about 13 in. / 33 cm in length. Each piece of fringe that is applied to the scarf should match the adjoining edge stitch color of the scarf. For example, if the piece of fringe is being added to a C3 slipped edge stitch, then the fringe piece should also be in C3.
Apply 1 length of fringe to each slipped edge stitch along both short edges of the scarf.
Once all of your fringe is added, lightly trim the edges so the pieces are roughly the same length: 6 in. / 15 cm (see p. 134 for more on adding fringe).

If necessary, lightly block your scarf (see p. 136).

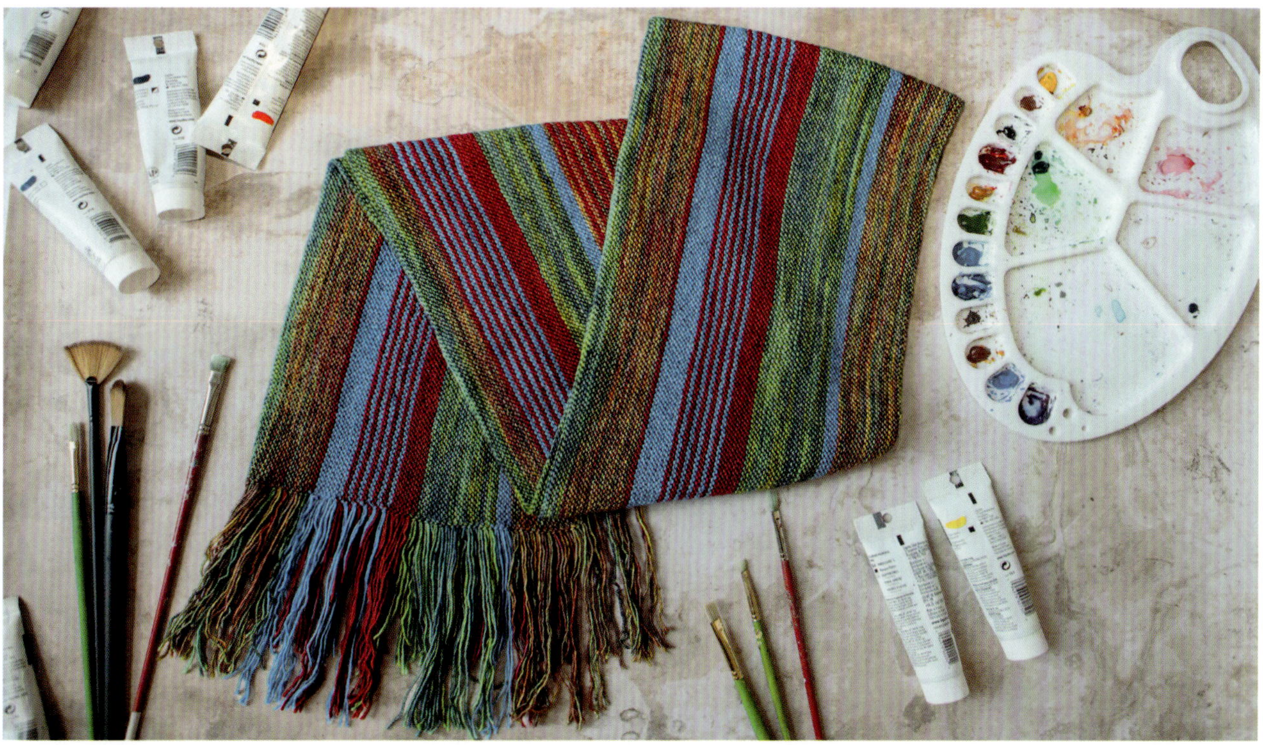

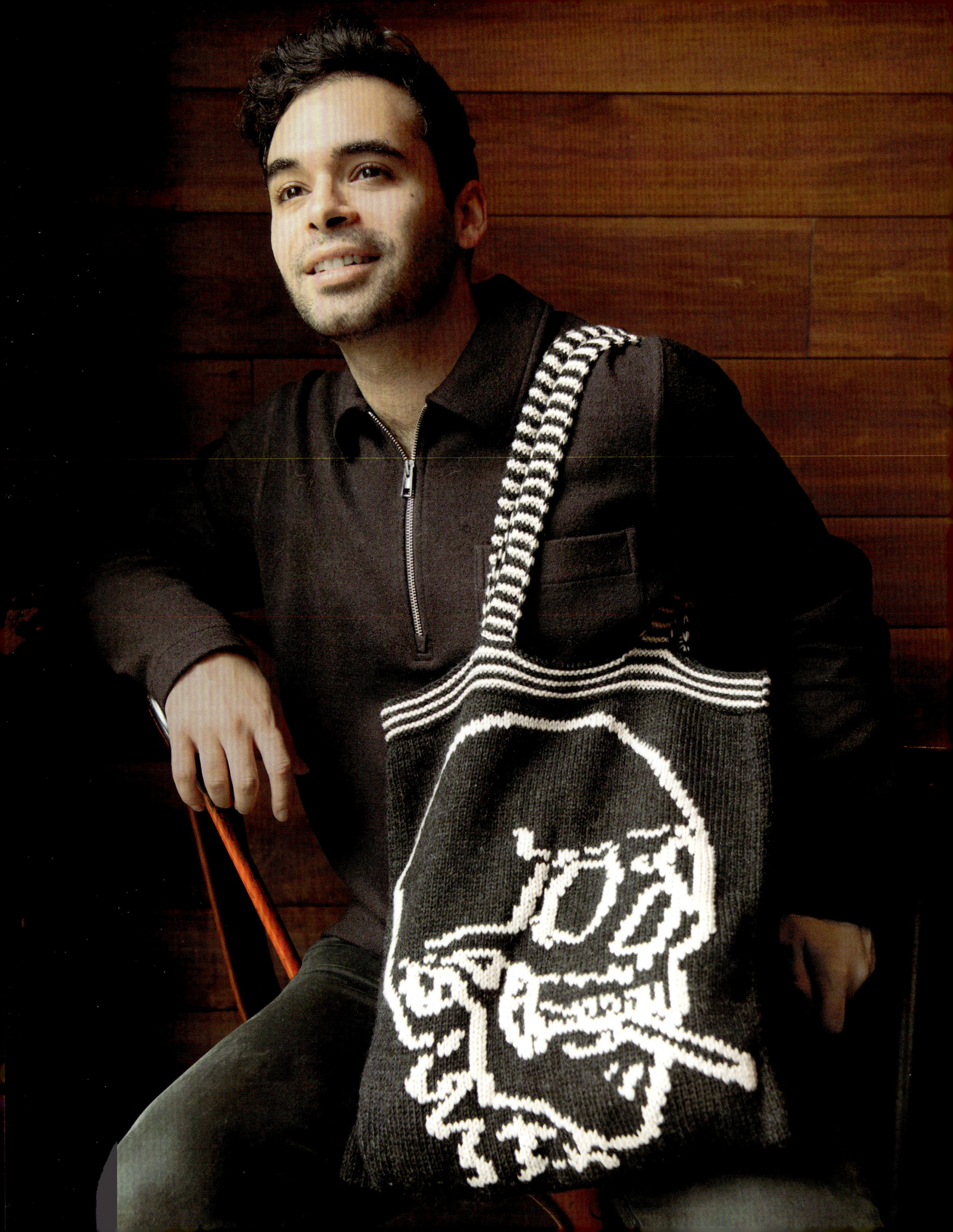

SMOKING SKELETON TOTE

Inspired by *Head of a Skeleton with Burning Cigarette*

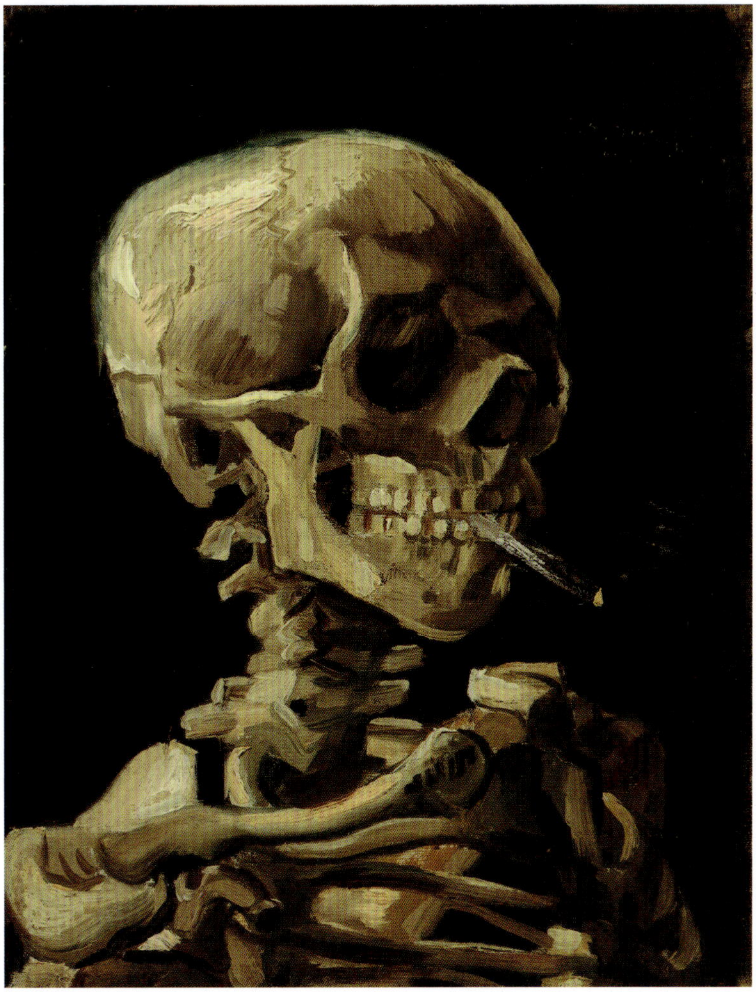

Van Gogh painted this skeleton with a cigarette as a joke, finding humor in the idea of enjoying a fleeting mundane element of life after death. The inspiration for this fashionable tote is glaringly clear. I mimicked the shape of van Gogh's image directly onto the tote and chose a stark, black yarn background to match the background of the painting. The beauty of this graphic is that it's a duplicate stitch, meaning it can be placed on this bag or a sweater, blanket, pillow, or anything you'd like. Get creative and have fun with it!

For more information on van Gogh's *Head of a Skeleton with Burning Cigarette*, see p. 138.

SIZES

One size

FINISHED MEASUREMENTS

14.5 in. / 37 cm wide, 15 in. / 38 cm tall (not including the handles)

YARN

Cascade "220 Superwash"
100% Superwash Wool; DK / Light Worsted (100 g / 220 yd. / 200 m)

■ MC: #1913 Jet – 2 balls

□ CC: #228 Frosted Almond – 1 ball

NEEDLES

- US size 5 / 3.75 mm, 16 in. / 40 cm long circular knitting needles
- (2) US size 6 / 4.0 mm, 16 in. / 40 cm long circular knitting needles

Or size needed to obtain gauge

NOTIONS

- Scissors
- Scrap yarn
- Stitch marker
- Tapestry needle for weaving in ends
- Blunt tapestry needle for duplicate stitching
- Crochet hook for provisional cast on.

GAUGE

22 stitches and 30 rows = 4 in. / 10 cm in stockinette stitch on larger needles

NOTES

- This bag is worked flat from the bottom up.
- The chart for the graphic is the same number of stitches wide and tall as your bag. Duplicate stitch your graphic onto the front piece before seaming your pieces together.
- The handles are applied after the bag is seamed.

KNITTING INSTRUCTIONS

FRONT

Using larger needles and MC, provisionally CO 80 sts using the crochet chain provisional cast on method (see p. 129). Do not join to work in the round.

Starting with a Purl row, work in st. st for 104 rows (end after working a Knit row).

With purl side facing, bind off loosely purlwise. Cut yarn leaving a tail to weave in later.

Duplicate stitch graphic (see p. 46) onto RS (knit side) of Front of bag using CC (see p. 135 for more on duplicate stitch).

BACK

When working the Back of your bag, leave a tail about 10 ft. / 3 m long to be used later when seaming up the bottom of your bag.

Using larger needles and MC, provisionally CO 80 sts using the crochet chain provisional cast on method. Do not join to work in the round.

Starting with a Purl row, work in st. st for 104 rows (end after working a Knit row).

With purl side facing, bind off loosely purlwise. Cut yarn leaving a tail to weave in later.

SEAMING BAG

Pull out provisional cast on from Front piece and place sts onto first larger needle. Pull out provisional cast on from Back piece and place sts onto second larger needle.

Holding the two needles parallel, with the RS together (WS facing out), graft the two edges together using the three-needle bind off (see p. 132) and the long tail from the Back of the bag.

With the WS together (RS facing out), using mattress stitch (see p. 136), seam up the two sides of your bag from bottom to top.

TOP BORDER

Begin at the right side seam with Front of bag facing you. Using smaller needles and MC, pick up and knit 77 sts across the top Front edge to the left side seam (see p. 133). Then pick up and knit 77 sts across the top Back edge to the right side seam. Place sm to note bor—154 sts.

Rnd 1 (MC): Purl.
Rnd 2 (CC): Knit.
Rnd 3 (CC): Purl.
Rnd 4 (MC): Knit.

Rep Rnds 1–4 two *more* times.

Cut CC.

Rnd 13: BO 20 sts purlwise, P7 (8 sts on RH needle—this is

Group A), BO 21 sts purlwise, P7 (this is Group B), BO 40 sts purlwise, P7 (this is Group C), BO 21 sts purlwise, P7 (this is Group D), BO purlwise to end of rnd. You should have four sets of 8 sts on your needle.

Cut MC.

STRAPS

Put sts in Groups B, C, and D onto scrap yarn. Keep 8 sts in Group A on working needle. With the Front of the bag facing, rejoin CC.

Row 1 (CC, RS): Sl1, K6, P1.
Row 2 (CC, WS): Sl1, K6, P1.
Row 3 (MC, RS): Sl1, K6, P1.
Row 4 (MC, WS): Sl1, K6, P1.

Rep Rows 1–4 until your strap measures 16 in. / 41 cm. End after working Row 3. Make a note of the total number of rows worked so the remaining strap is worked to the same length. Leave the live sts on the working needle.

Place 8 Group B sts onto a second needle and hold parallel with the live stitches at the end of the strap from Group A. Make sure your right sides are facing each other. Using MC, graft the two sets of live sts together using the three-needle bind off (see p. 132).

Place 8 Group C sts onto smaller needle. With the Back of the bag facing you, join CC.

Beginning with Row 1, work as for the first strap, making sure the straps are the exact same length.

Repeat the strap grafting with the live stitches from Group D.

FINISHING

Weave in all your tails carefully (see p. 133).

Block your bag. Place a couple of books on top to be sure the stitches of your graphic lay nice and flat (see p. 136).

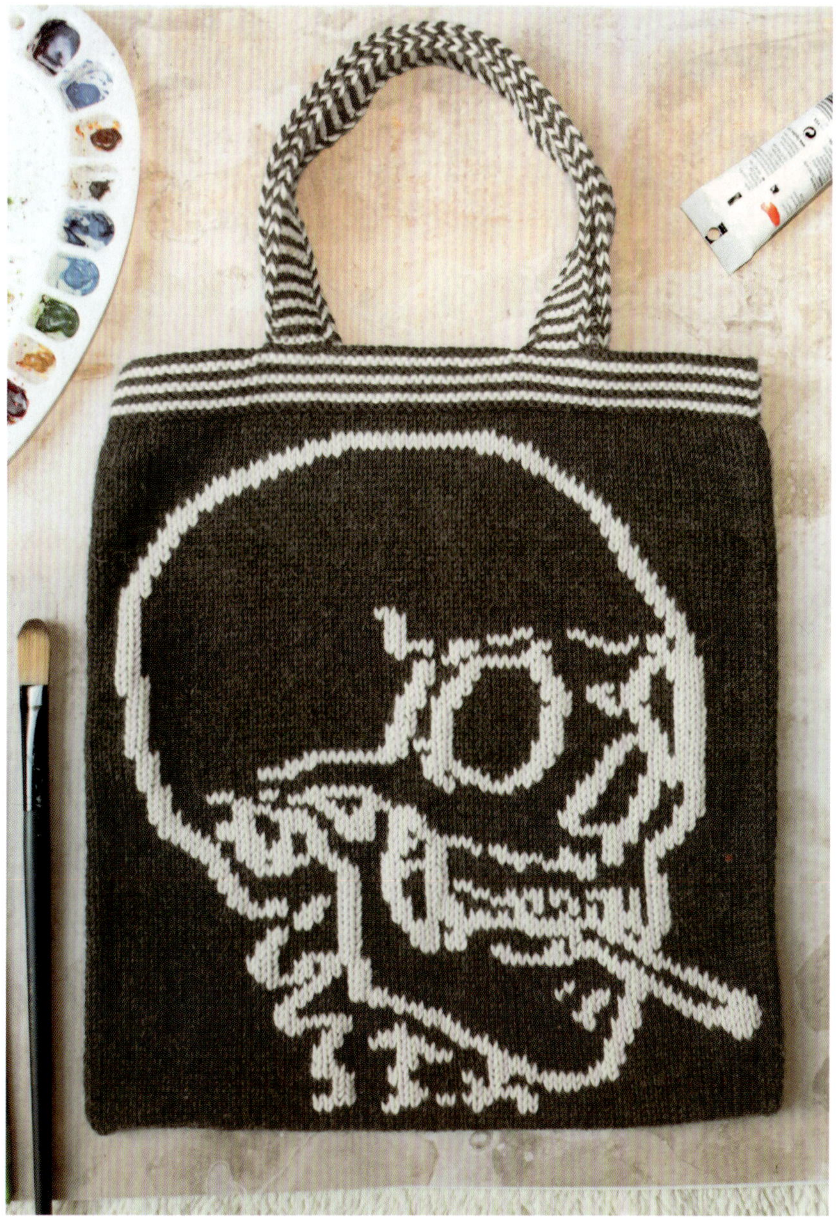

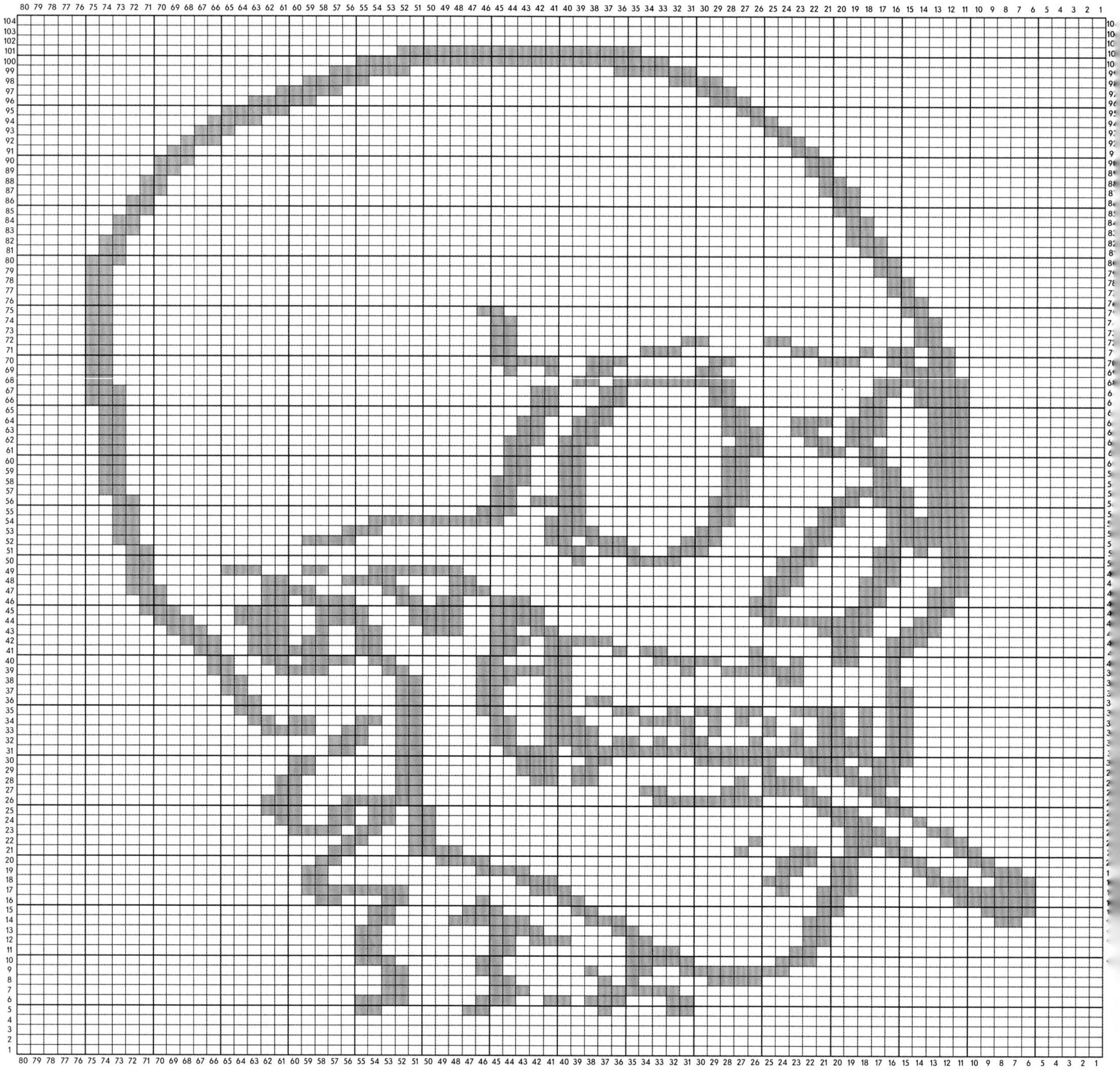

"IF SOMETHING IN YOU YOURSELF SAYS 'YOU AREN'T A PAINTER'—IT'S THEN THAT YOU SHOULD PAINT, OLD CHAP, AND THAT VOICE WILL BE SILENCED TOO."

—Vincent van Gogh to his brother Theo,
October 28, 1883

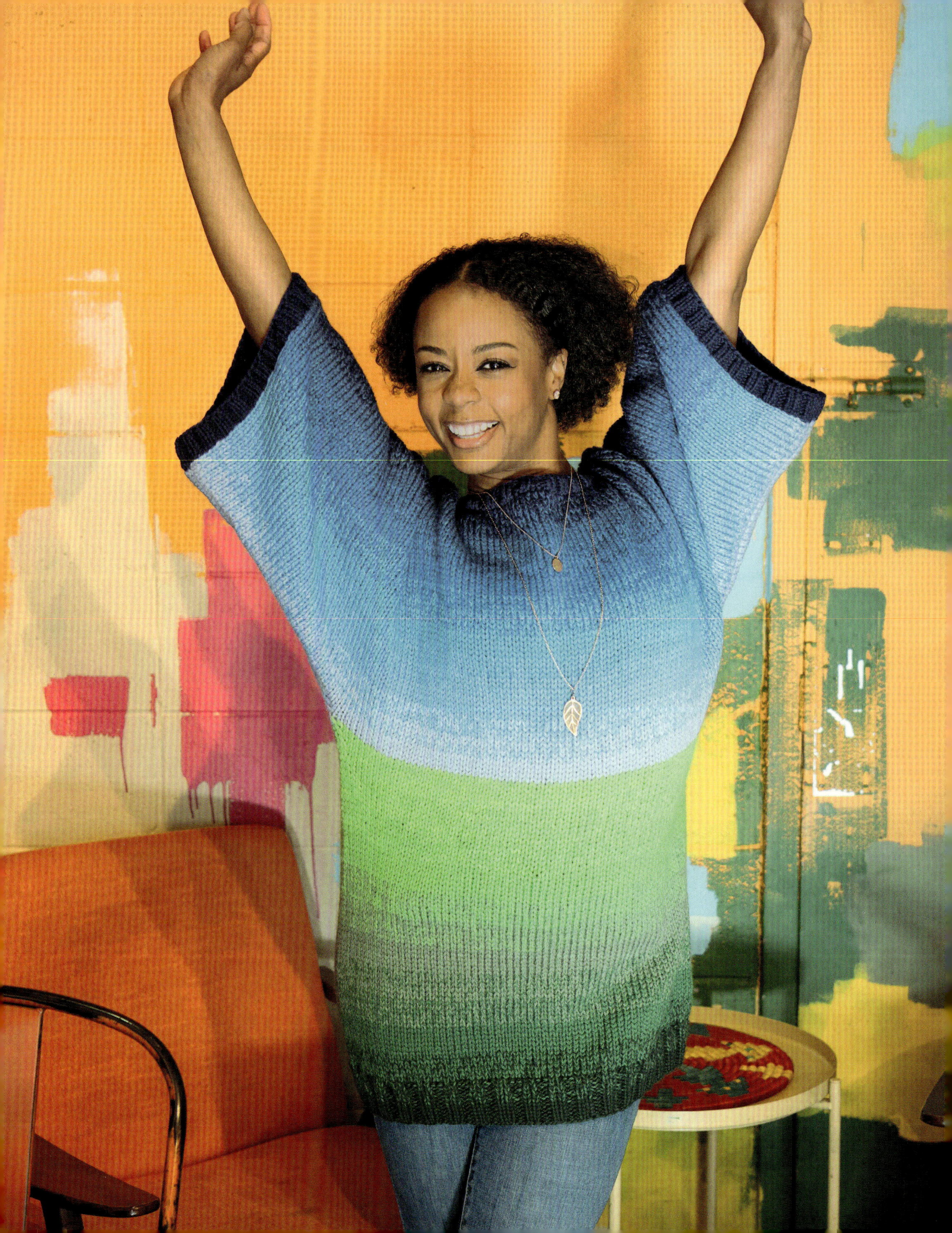

STORMY OMBRÉ TUNIC

Inspired by *Wheatfield under Thunderclouds*

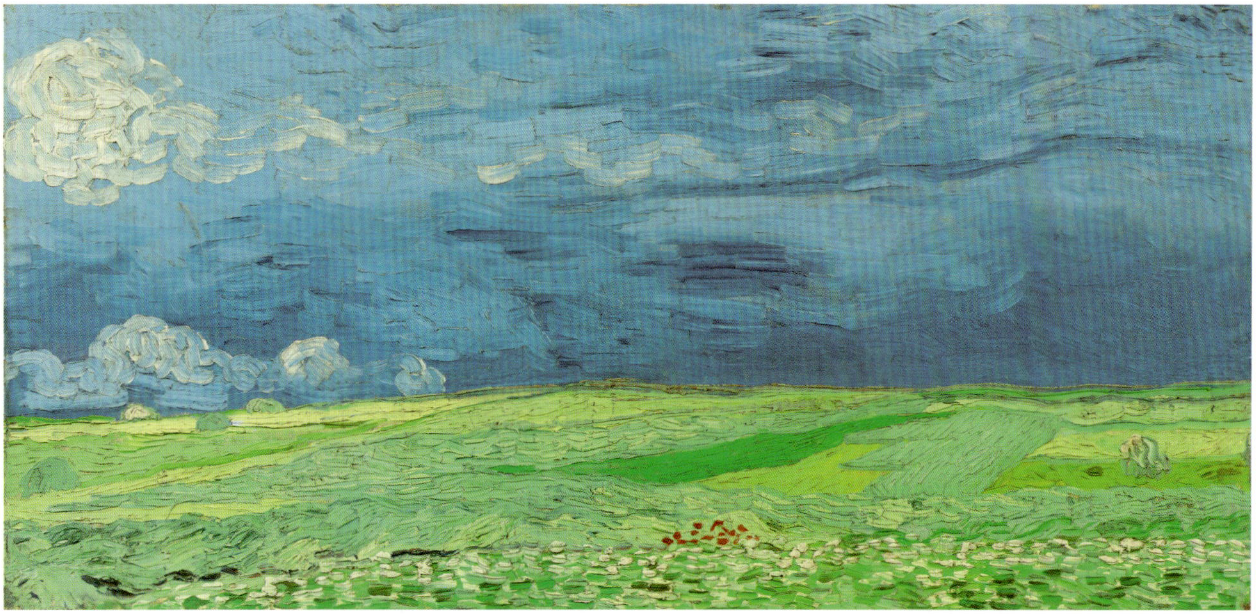

Van Gogh experienced overwhelming emotions when painting nature, and tried to express a sense of loneliness and sadness in the landscapes he painted near the end of his life, including this one. I think the essence that he captured also summons something freeing, positive, and beautiful. I chose the ombré technique with light and deep blues and greens to symbolize the sky and land meeting on the horizon. The wide sleeves, and free-flowing fit, give a sense of the wide-open field we see in the painting, with plenty of space to move around comfortably and without feeling confined.

For more information on van Gogh's *Wheatfield under Thunderclouds*, see p. 139.

SIZES

XS (S, M, L, XL) [2XL, 3XL, 4XL, 5XL]

FINISHED MEASUREMENTS

37.5 (40, 42.25, 44.5, 47) [49, 51.5, 53.75, 56] in. / 96 (101.5, 107.5, 113, 119.5) [124.5, 131, 136.5, 142] cm circumference at underarms

- Model is wearing size Large.
- Sweater is designed to be worn with 4–6 in. / 10–15 cm of positive ease.

YARN

Knit Picks "Palette"
100% Peruvian Highland Wool; Fingering (50g / 231 yd. / 211 m)

- C1: Color 2098 Ivy – 1 (1, 1, 1, 1) [2, 2, 2, 2] balls
- C2: Color 1982 Grass – 1 (1, 1, 1, 1) [2, 2, 2, 2] balls
- C3: Color 2196 Spearmint – 1 (1, 1, 1, 1) [2, 2, 2, 2] balls
- C4: Color 6315 Peapod – 1 (1, 1, 1, 1) [2, 2, 2, 2] balls
- C5: Color C967 Limeade Heather – 1 (1, 1, 1, 1) [2, 2, 2, 2] balls
- C6: Color 1983 Bluebell – 1 (1, 1, 1, 1) [2, 2, 2, 2] balls
- C7: Color 6873 Pool – 1 (1, 1, 1, 1) [2, 2, 2, 2] balls
- C8: Color 1981 Whirlpool – 1 (1, 1, 1, 1) [2, 2, 2, 2] balls
- C9: Color 6874 Blue – 1 (1, 1, 1, 1) [2, 2, 2, 2] balls
- C10: Color 2425 Delta – 1 (1, 1, 1, 1) [2, 2, 2, 2] balls
- C11: Color 1019 Jay – 1 (1, 1, 1, 1) [2, 2, 3] balls

NEEDLES

- US size 9 / 5.5 mm, 16 in. / 40 cm and 32 to 40 in. / 80 to 100 cm long circular knitting needles
- US size 10 / 6.0 mm, 16 in. / 40 cm and 32 to 40 in. / 80 to 100 cm long circular knitting needles

Or size needed to obtain gauge

NOTIONS

- Scissors
- Stitch markers
- Tapestry needle for weaving in ends
- Scrap yarn for placing stitches on hold
- Yarn for seaming underside of sleeves

GAUGE

14 stitches and 20 rows = 4 in. / 10 cm in stockinette stitch holding three strands together using larger needles

NOTES

- You will be working entire piece with three strands of yarn held together throughout. If you only have one ball of yarn, divide it into three equal balls as follows: Weigh the ball of yarn without the ball band label. Divide that number by three and wind up three equal sized balls of yarn. For example, if your ball of yarn weighs 50 grams, you should have three balls of yarn that each weigh (roughly) 16.5 grams.
- This sweater is worked from the bottom up. The body is worked in the round to the underarms. The yoke is divided and worked flat to create the front and back of the sweater and the sleeves simultaneously.

COLOR CHANGING INSTRUCTIONS

You will always be working with three strands of yarn held together. When the body is worked in the round (the bottom half of the sweater), work six rounds of each color before changing color. After six rounds have been worked, cut one color leaving a tail and join the next color. In the top half of the sweater (the blue section, after the yoke has been divided and you are working flat), work four rows in each color before changing color.

For example, start the piece by casting on with three strands of C1 (C1/C1/C1). After working six rounds, cut one strand of C1 and join one strand of C2 (C1/C1/C2). After working six rounds, cut one strand of C1 and join another strand of C2 (C1/C2/C2). After working six rounds, cut last strand of C1 and join another strand of C2 (C2/C2/C2). After working six rounds, cut one strand of C2 and join one strand of C3 (C2/C2/C3), etc.

This is the method you will use throughout the entire tunic.

Continue this method of changing colors even when you begin working back and forth on the yoke and sleeves section.

KNITTING INSTRUCTIONS

Using smaller 32 or 40 in. / 80 or 100 cm circular needles and C1, CO 120 (128, 136, 144, 152) [160, 168, 176, 184] sts

Join to work in the round being careful not to twist. Place sm to note bor.

K2, P2 for 12 rounds.

Change to larger 32 or 40 in. / 80 or 100 cm circular needles.

Work in st. st (knitting every round), changing colors as indicated in the Color Changing Instructions, for 60 rnds. Piece should measure approx. 14 in. / 35.5 cm from cast on edge. You should be ready to work with three strands of C5.

YOKE SETUP

Rnd 1: K 60 (64, 68, 72, 76) [80, 84, 88, 92] sts, pm, K to end.

Rnd 2 (Inc Rnd): *K1, M1R, K to 1 st before sm, M1L, K1, slm* twice—4 sts inc.
Rnd 3: Knit.

Rep Rnds 2–3 one *more* time.
Work Rnd 2 one *more* time—132 (140, 148, 156, 164) [172, 180, 188, 196] sts.

You will now be setting up the piece to work the Front and Back separately. Cut all three strands of C5 leaving tails to weave in later. No further blending will occur with C5.

DIVIDE FOR YOKE

Setup Row 1 (RS): Using three strands of C6, K to sm, remove sm, place next 66 (70, 74, 78, 82) [86, 90, 94, 98] sts onto scrap yarn. These are the Back sts and can hang out on the scrap yarn for now. Remove bor sm. Using backwards loop cast on (see p. 130), CO 38 sts.

Setup Row 2 (WS): Purl across all sts. CO 38 sts using the backward loop cast on—142 (146, 150, 154, 158) [162, 166, 170, 174] sts.

Work two *more* rows in st. st using three strands of C6.

Work in st. st (knitting every RS row and purling ever WS row), changing colors every 4 rows, for 60 rows. The sleeve should measure approx. 12 in. / 30.5 cm from backwards loop cast on. You should be ready to work with three strands of C11. End after working a WS row.

Remainder of Front Yoke is worked using three strands of C11.

DIVIDE FOR FRONT NECKLINE

Row 1 (RS): K52 (54, 56, 58, 60) [62, 64, 66, 68]; place these sts onto scrap yarn or leave on the working needle. These are the Front Left sts and will remain unworked temporarily. BO center 38 sts, K to end.

FRONT RIGHT SHOULDER AND SLEEVE

Row 2 (WS): Purl.
Row 3 (Dec Row): K2, SSK, K to end—1 st dec.
Row 4: Purl.

Cut three strands of C11 leaving tails to weave in later. Place remaining 51 (53, 55, 57, 59) [61, 63, 65, 67] sts onto scrap yarn.

FRONT LEFT SHOULDER AND SLEEVE

Place the Front Left sts onto larger 32 in. / 80 cm circular needles.

With WS facing you, join three strands of C11 at neck edge.

Row 2 (WS): Purl.
Row 3 (Dec Row): K to last 4 sts, K2tog, K2 – 1 st dec.
Row 4: Purl.

Cut three strands of C11 leaving tails to weave in later. Place remaining 51 (53, 55, 57, 59) [61, 63, 65, 67] sts onto scrap yarn.

BACK

Place 66 (70, 74, 78, 82) [86, 90, 94, 98] live Back sts from scrap yarn onto larger 32 in. / 80 cm circular needles.

With RS facing, join three strands of C6.

Setup Row 1 (RS): Knit across all sts. Using backwards loop cast on, CO 38 sts.
Setup Row 2 (WS): Purl across all sts. Cast on 38 sts using the backwards loop cast on. 142 (146, 150, 154, 158) [162, 166, 170, 174] sts.

Work two *more* rows in st. st using three strands of C6.

Work in st. st (knitting every RS row and purling ever WS row), changing colors every 4 rows, for 60 rows (this length will match the Front). You should be ready to work with three strands of C11. End after working a WS row.

Remainder of Back Yoke is worked using three strands of C11.

(Pattern continues on next page)

DIVIDE FOR BACK NECKLINE

Row 1 (RS): K52 (54, 56, 58, 60) [62, 64, 66, 68]; place these sts onto scrap yarn or leave on the working needle. These are the Back Right sts and will remain unworked temporarily. BO center 38 sts, K to end.

BACK LEFT SHOULDER AND SLEEVE

Row 2 (WS): Purl.
Row 3 (Dec Row): K2, SSK, K to end—1 st dec.
Row 4: Purl.

Place 51 (53, 55, 57, 59) [61, 63, 65, 67] live Front Left shoulder and sleeve sts from scrap yarn onto larger 16 in. / 40 cm circular needles.

Turn piece inside out so the RS are facing each other. Using three strands of C11, work three-needle bind off (see p. 132) along all left shoulder and sleeve stitches. Turn piece right side out.

BACK RIGHT SHOULDER AND SLEEVE

Place the Back Right sts onto larger 32 in. / 80 cm circular needles.

With WS facing you, join three strands of C11 at neck edge.

Row 2 (WS): Purl.
Row 3 (Dec Row): K to last 4 sts, K2tog, K2—1 st dec.
Row 4: Purl.

Place 51 (53, 55, 57, 59) [61, 63, 65, 67] live Front Right shoulder and sleeve sts from scrap yarn onto larger 16 in. / 40 cm circular needles.

Turn piece inside out so the RS are facing each other. Using three strands of C11, work three-needle bind off along all right shoulder and sleeve stitches. Turn piece right side out.

SLEEVE RIBBING

(Both sleeves should be worked the same and have the same number of picked up stitches.)

Using yarn for seaming and mattress stitch (see p. 136), seam up the undersides of both sleeves.

Using smaller 16 in. / 40 cm circular needles and three strands of C11, starting at the seam at the underside of the sleeve, pick up and knit a multiple of 4 sts around hem of sleeve. (Should be approximately 96 sts.)

K2, P2 for 6 rnds.

Work sewn bind off (see p. 132).

NECK

Using smaller 16 in. / 40 cm circular needles and three strands of C11, starting at one shoulder seam, pick up and knit a multiple of 4 sts around neck opening. (Should be approximately 92 sts.)

K2, P2 for 4 rnds.

FINISHING

Work sewn bind off (see p. 130).

Weave in tails (see p. 133).

Lay the piece flat and lightly block (see p. 136).

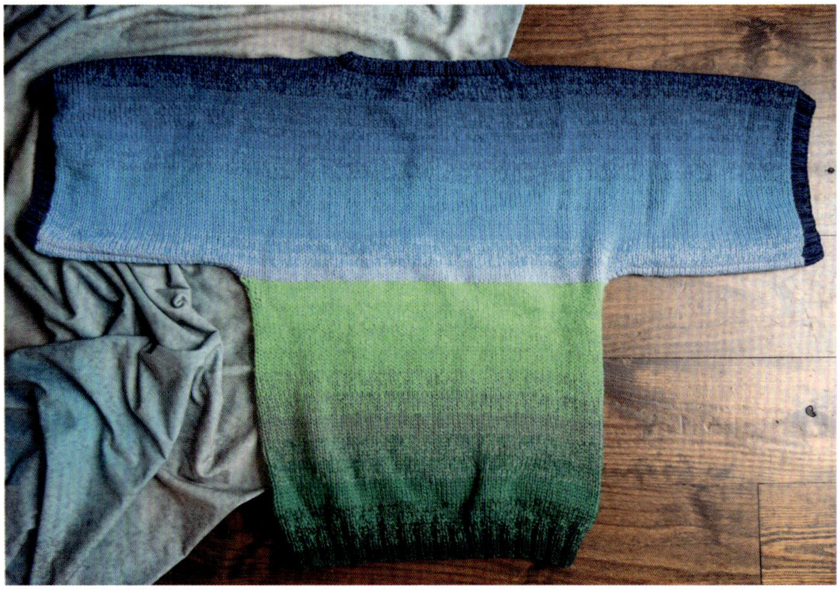

"COLOUR EXPRESSES
SOMETHING IN ITSELF.
ONE CAN'T DO WITHOUT IT;
ONE MUST MAKE USE OF IT.
WHAT LOOKS BEAUTIFUL, REALLY
BEAUTIFUL—IS ALSO RIGHT."

—Vincent van Gogh to his brother Theo,
October 28, 1885

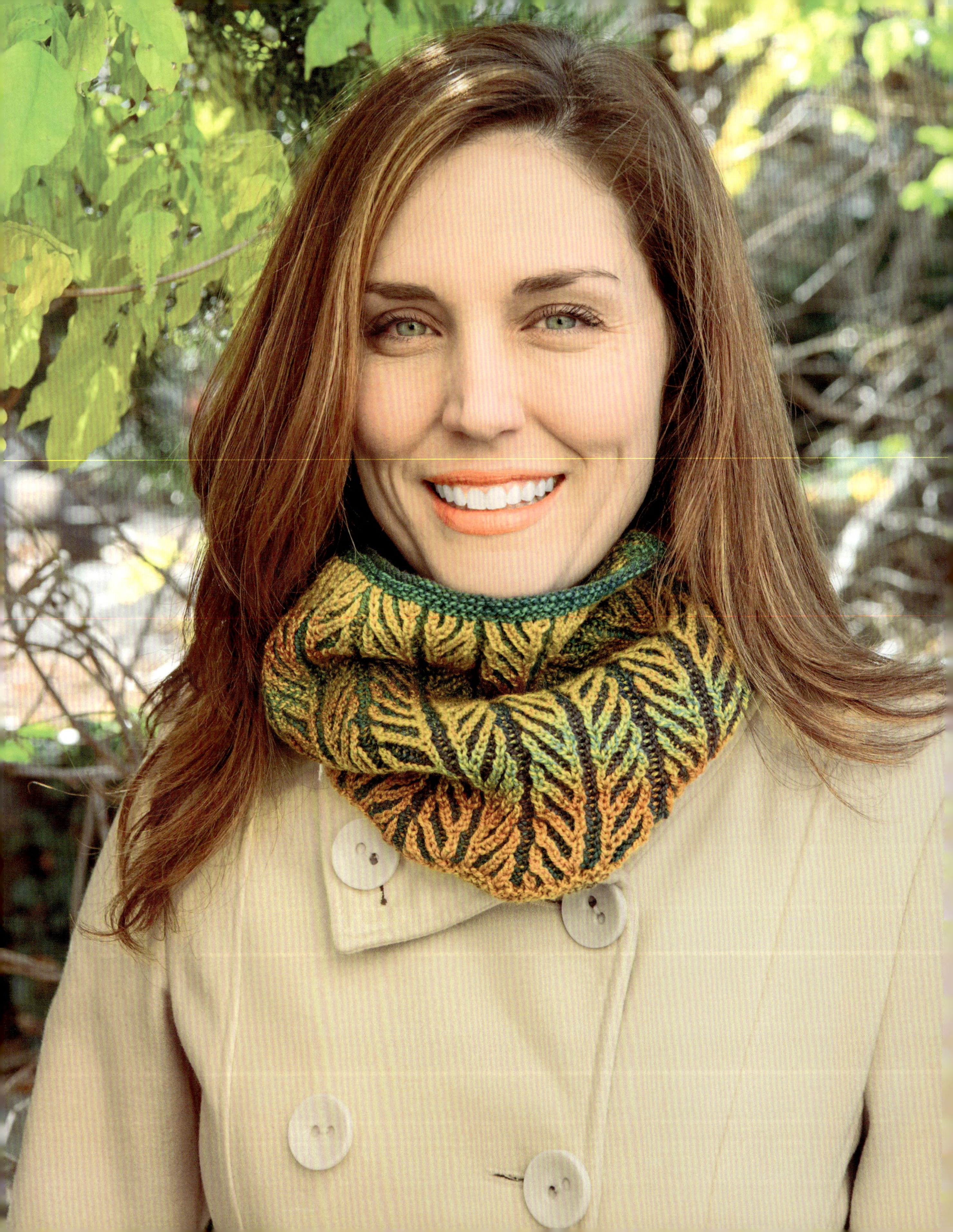

WHEATFIELD BRIOCHE COWL

Inspired by *Wheatfield*

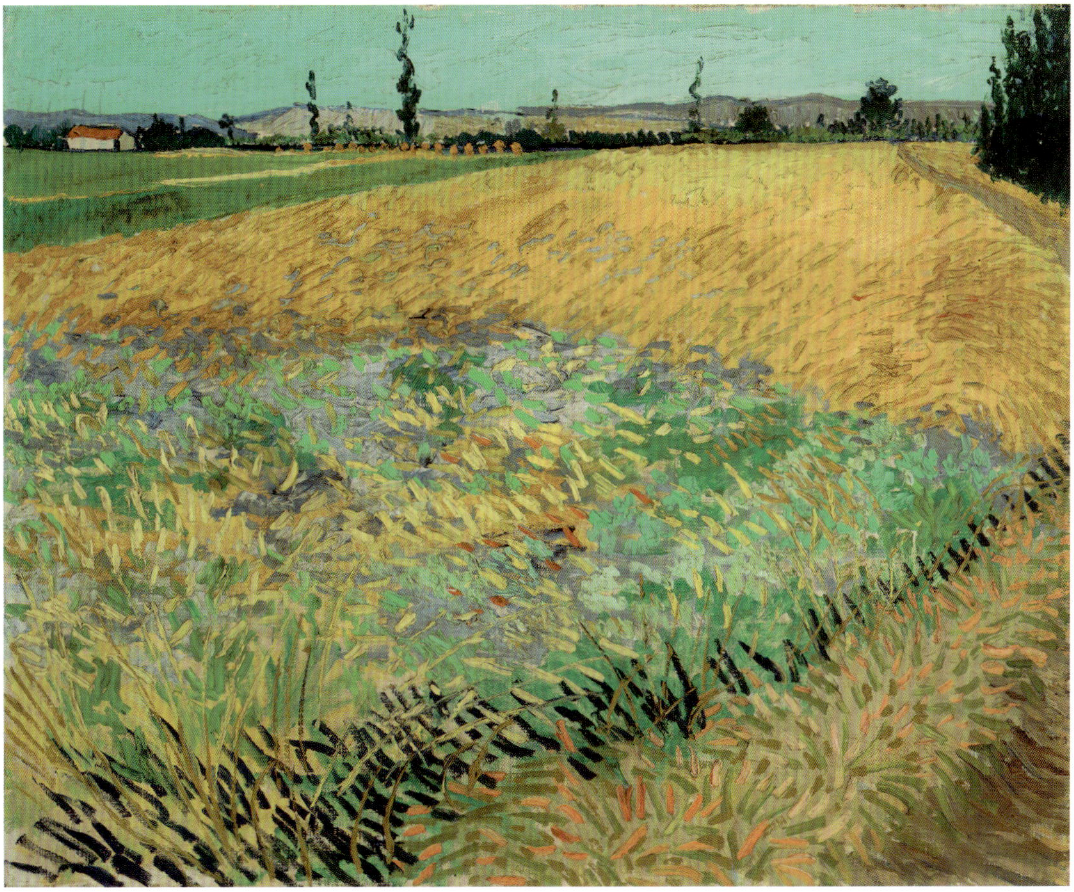

This painting of the wheatfields in Arles is another example of van Gogh's interest in landscapes and movement in nature. The horizon of this painting is high, so the wheatfield takes up most of the canvas and was a clear focus for me in designing this pattern. This vibrant cowl mimics the blowing wheatfields using a ribbed brioche texture pattern. I chose a yarn that creates subtle oranges, yellows, and greens to represent the color and shading van Gogh utilized in portraying the flowers and other plants in the foreground of the wheatfield. The solid green lining along the top of the cowl represents the distant but visible passage of grass and trees.

For more information on van Gogh's *Wheatfield*, see p. 139.

SIZE

Finished cowl measures 11.5 in. / 29 cm wide, 9.5 in. / 24 cm tall, and 23 in. / 58 cm circumference lying flat

YARN

Spincycle Yarns "Dyed in the Wool" 100% American Wool Superwashed; Sport (200 yd. / 183 m)

- C1: Salty Dog – 1 skein
- C2: Afternoon Delight – 1 skein

NEEDLES

- US size 1 / 2.5 mm, 16 in. / 40 cm long circular knitting needles
- US size 3 / 3.25 mm, 16 in. / 40 cm long circular knitting needles

Or size needed to obtain gauge

NOTIONS

- Scissors
- Stitch marker
- Tapestry needle for weaving in ends

GAUGE

29 stitches and 60 rows = 4 in. / 10 cm in garter stitch using larger needles

NOTES

- If you want to make your cowl larger or smaller, the pattern repeat is a multiple of 14 stitches. If you make your cowl larger or taller than the original design, you will need more yarn.
- Cowl is knit using up almost all of your yarn. Pull out your gauge swatch so that you can use that yarn.

KNITTING INSTRUCTIONS

Using C1 and larger needles, CO 168 sts.

Join to work in the rnd being careful not to twist. Place sm to note bor.

Rnd 1: Purl.
Rnd 2: Knit.

Rep Rnds 1-2 one *more* time.

Work Rnd 1 one *more* time.

Change to smaller needles.

Setup Rnd A (C1): *K1, sl1YO* to end.

Setup Rnd B (C2): *Sl1YO, brp1* to end.

Rnd 1A (C1): (BrkRdec, *sl1YO, brk1* two times, sl1YO, brkYObrk, *sl1YO, brk1* two times, sl1YO) around.

Rnd 1B (C2): (*Sl1YO, brp1* three times, sl1YO, P1, *sl1YO, brp1* three times) around.

Rnd 2A (C1): *Brk1, sl1YO* around.

Rnd 2B (C2): *Sl1YO, brp1* around.

Rnd 3A (C1): (*Brk1, sl1YO* two times, brkYObrk, *sl1YO, brk1* two times, sl1YO, brkLdec, sl1YO) around.

Rnd 3B (C2): (*Sl1YO, brp1* two times, sl1YO, P1, *sl1YO, brp1* 4 times) around.

Rnd 4A (C1): *Brk1, sl1YO* around.

Rnd 4B (C2): *Sl1YO, brp1* around.

Rep Rnds 1–4 until you have used almost all of your C1 yarn, or the cowl is desired height. End after completing Rnd 2 or Rnd 4.

Cut C1 leaving a tail to weave in later. Finish cowl using C2.

Next Rnd: *rkB1, K1* around.

Switch to larger needles.

Next Rnd: Purl.
Next Rnd: Knit.

Rep last two rnds one *more* time.

Last Rnd: Purl.

FINISHING

Work sewn bind off (see p. 132).
Weave in tails (see p. 133).
Spray block lightly (see p. 136).

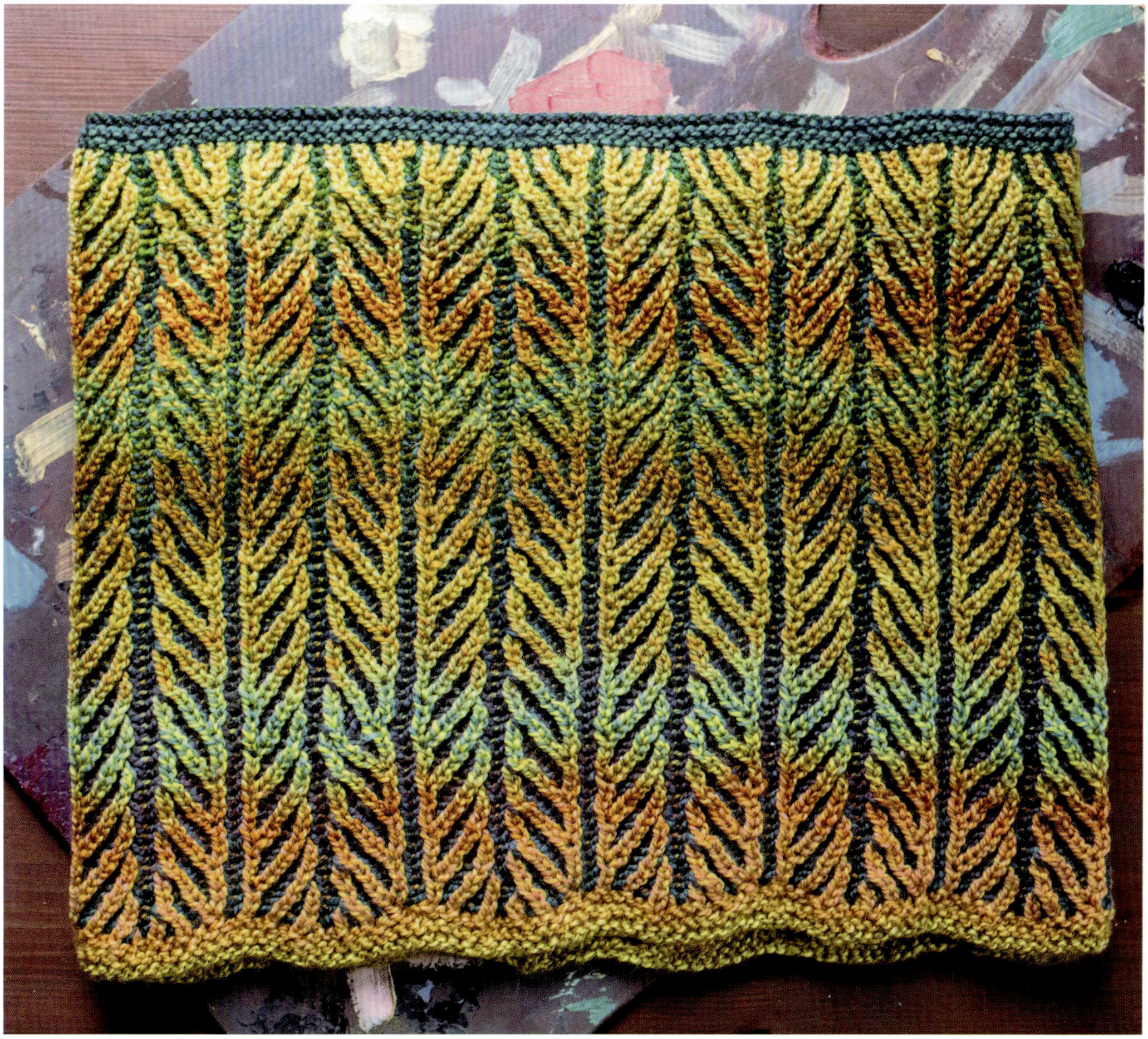

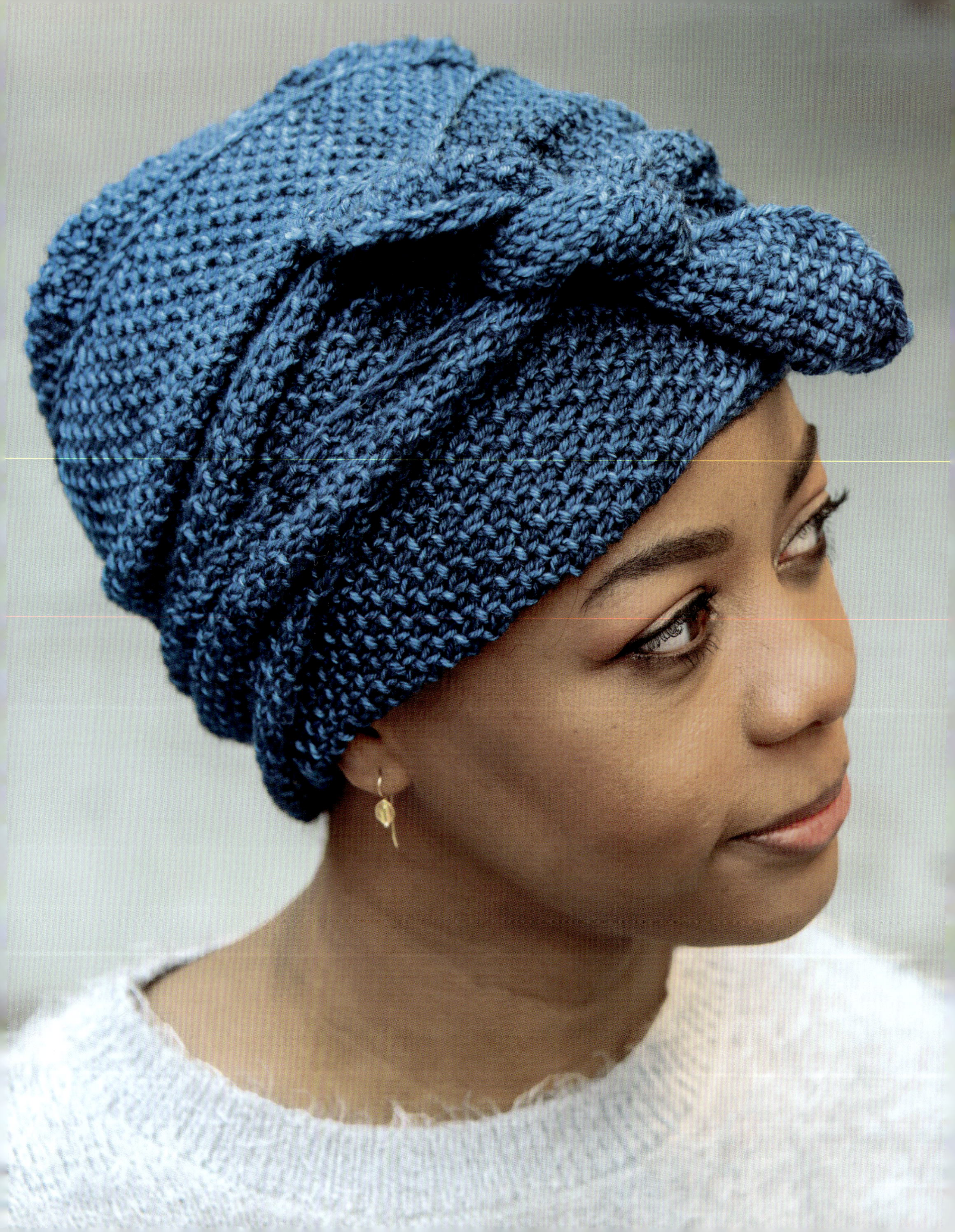

SKILL LEVEL 3

ARLES HEAD WRAP

Inspired by *An Old Woman of Arles*

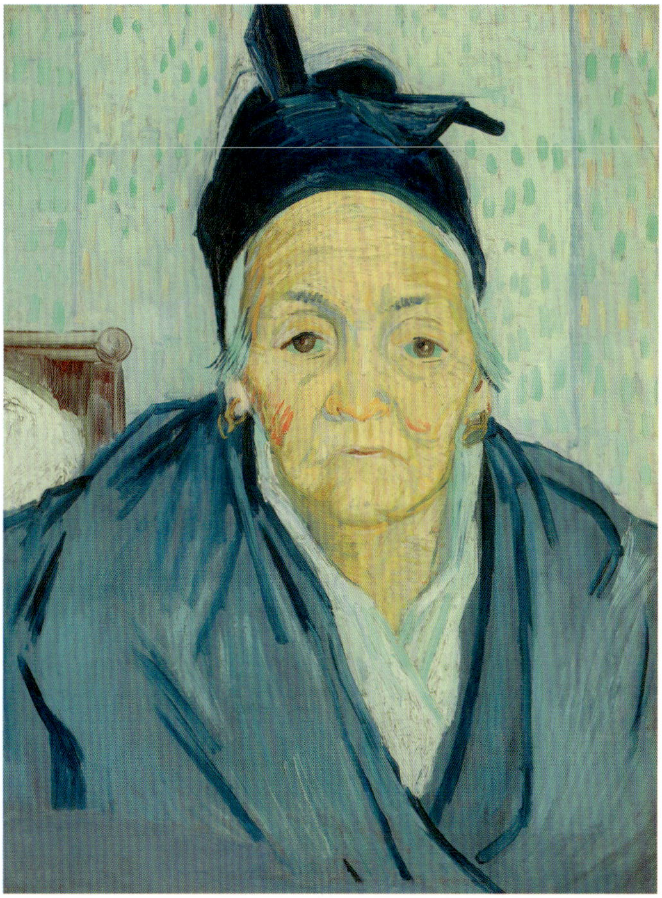

The woman in this painting was a widow van Gogh met at a hotel in Arles. Van Gogh found interest in those in mourning, in poverty, and those who seemed to be in a similar mental battle or hardship as his own. The head wrap the woman bears was a typical element of a widow's mourning attire. I wondered what material it was made of. Though I may never know for sure, this knitted version of the head wrap is loose-fitting and lax, mimicking the fit of the old woman's head wrap in the painting and making for comfortable wear. The blue color also pulls from the woman's head wrap along with the shawl or wrap we see her draped in.

For more information on van Gogh's *An Old Woman of Arles*, see p. 138.

SIZES

One size fits an average adult sized head.

FINISHED MEASUREMENTS

7.5 in. / 19 cm tall (not including wrap) and 17.75 in. / 45 cm circumference unstretched

YARN

Malabrigo "Rios" 100% Merino Wool; Worsted (100 g / 210 yd. / 192 m)

#150 Azul Profundo – 2 skeins

NEEDLES

- US size 9 / 5.5 mm, 16 in. / 40 cm long circular knitting needles
- US size 2 / 2.75 mm double pointed needles (DPNs)

Or size needed to obtain gauge

NOTIONS

- Locking stitch markers
- Scissors
- Stitch markers
- Tapestry needle for weaving in ends

GAUGE

20 stitches and 32 rows = 4 in. / 10 cm over seed stitch

NOTES

- Always slip stitch purlwise with yarn in back, unless otherwise noted.
- Hat is made by first knitting the long strip from side to side. The brim of the hat is then picked up in the middle of the strip and worked in the round up toward the crown decreasing.
- To help differentiate RS from WS, clip a locking marker to the RS of the work.

KNITTING INSTRUCTIONS

Using circular needles, CO 4 sts.

Setup Row 1 (WS): Wyif sl1, K1, P2.
Setup Row 2 (RS): Sl1, (K1, P1) into next st, K1, P1—5 sts.
Setup Row 3: Sl1, (P1, K1) into next st, P1, K1, P1—6 sts.
Setup Row 4: Sl1, (P1, K1) into next st, P1, K1, P2—7 sts.
Setup Row 5: Sl1, (K1, P1) into next st, *K1, P1* twice, P1—8 sts.

Row 1 (RS): Sl1, (K1, P1) into next st, *K1, P1* to end—9 sts.
Row 2 (WS): Sl1, (P1, K1) into next st, *P1, K1* to last st, P1—10 sts.
Row 3: Sl1, (P1, K1) into next st, *P1, K1* to last 2 sts, P2—11 sts.
Row 4: Sl1, (K1, P1) into next st, *K1, P1* to last st, P1—12 sts.

Row 5: Sl1, *P1, K1* to last st, P1.
Row 6: Sl1, *K1, P1* to last st, P1.

Rep Rows 5–6 five *more* times.

Row 17 (RS): Sl1, (K1, P1) into next st, *K1, P1* to end—13 sts.
Row 18 (WS): Sl1, (P1, K1) into next st, *P1, K1* to last st, P1—14 sts.

Row 19: Sl1, *K1, P1* to last st, P1.
Row 20: Sl1, *P1, K1* to last st, P1.

Rep Rows 19–20 ten *more* times.

Work Rows 3–18 one *more* time—18 sts.

Row 57 (RS): Sl1, (P1, K1) into next st, *P1, K1* to last 2 sts, P2—19 sts.
Row 58 (WS): Sl1, (K1, P1) into next st, *K1, P1* to last st, P1—20 sts.
Row 59: Sl1, *P1, K1* to last st, P1.
Row 60: Sl1, *K1, P1* to last st, P1.

Row 61: Sl1, (K1, P1) into next st, *K1, P1* to end—21 sts.
Row 62: Sl1, (P1, K1) into next st, *P1, K1* to last st, P1—22 sts.
Row 63: Sl1, *K1, P1* to last st, P1.
Row 64: Sl1, *P1, K1* to last st, P1.
Row 65: Sl1, (P1, K1) into next st, *P1, K1* to last 2 sts, P2—23 sts.
Row 66: Sl1, (K1, P1) into next st, *K1, P1* to last st, P1—24 sts.
Row 67: Sl1, *P1, K1* to last st, P1.
Row 68: Sl1, *K1, P1* to last st, P1.
Row 69: Sl1, (K1, P1) into next st, *K1, P1* to end—25 sts.
Row 70: Sl1, (P1, K1) into next st, *P1, K1* to last st, P1—26 sts.

Row 71: Sl1, *K1, P1* to last st st, P1.
Row 72: Sl1, *P1, K1* to last st, P1.

Rep Rows 71–72 until piece measures 52 in. / 132 cm from CO. End after working Row 72.

DECREASE SECTION

Row 1 (RS): Sl1, P2tog, *K1, P1* to last st, P1—25 sts.
Row 2 (WS): Sl1, K2tog, *P1, K1* to last 2 sts, P2—24 sts.
Row 3: Sl1, *P1, K1* to last st, P1.
Row 4: Sl1, *K1, P1* to last st, P1.
Row 5: Sl1, K2tog, *P1, K1* to last st, P1—23 sts.
Row 6: Sl1, P2tog, *K1, P1* to end—22 sts.
Row 7: Sl1, *K1, P1* to last st, P1.
Row 8: Sl1, *P1, K1* to last st, P1.
Row 9: Sl1, P2tog, *K1, P1* to last st, P1—21 sts.
Row 10: Sl1, K2tog, *P1, K1* to last 2 sts, P2—20 sts.

Row 11: Sl1, *P1, K1* to last st, P1.
Row 12: Sl1, *K1, P1* to last st, P1.
Row 13: Sl1, K2tog, *P1, K1* to last st, P1—19 sts.
Row 14: Sl1, P2tog, *K1, P1* to end—18 sts.
Row 15: Sl1, P2tog, *K1, P1* to last st, P1—17 sts.
Row 16: Sl1, K2tog, *P1, K1* to last 2 sts, P2—16 sts.

Row 17: Sl1, *P1, K1* to last st, P1.
Row 18: Sl1, *K1, P1* to last st, P1.

Rep Rows 17–18 five *more* times.

Row 29: Sl1, K2tog, *P1, K1* to last st, P1—15 sts.
Row 30: Sl1, P2tog, *K1, P1* to end—14 sts.

Work Rows 7–8 eleven *more* times.

Row 53: Sl1, P2tog, *K1, P1* to last st, P1—13 sts.
Row 54: Sl1, K2tog, *P1, K1* to last 2 sts, P2—12 sts.

Work Rows 17–18 six *more* times.

Row 67: Sl1, K2tog, *P1, K1* to last st, P1—11 sts.
Row 68: Sl1, P2tog, *K1, P1* to end—10 sts.
Row 69: Sl1, P2tog, *K1, P1* to last st, P1—9 sts.
Row 70: Sl1, K2tog, *P1, K1* to last 2 sts, P2—8 sts.
Row 71: Sl1, K2tog, *P1, K1* twice, P1—7 sts.
Row 72: Sl1, P2tog, *K1, P1* twice—6 sts.
Row 73: Sl1, P2tog, K1, P2—5 sts.
Row 74: Sl1, K2tog, P2—4 sts.
Row 75: Sl1, P1, K1, P1.
Bind off knitwise.

Fold piece in half so RS are facing each other and place a locking sm on the center edge slipped stitch. (It doesn't matter which edge you place sm on.)

Count 26 slipped edge stitches to each side of the center sm and place a locking sm on the edge slipped stitch. Remove center sm. You should have 51 edge slipped sts BETWEEN the two sm.

Starting with the sm on the right, pick up and knit 1 st into each edge slipped stitch up to and including the sm on the left. You should have 53 sts on your needle. Remove all locking sm.

Using knitted CO (see p. 131), CO 10 *more* sts.

Place bor sm. Join to work in the round—63 sts

Setup Rnd: *K1, (P1, K1) in next st, P1, (K1, P1) in next st* 13 times, *K1, P1* to last st, K1—89 sts.

Rnd 1: *P1, K1* to last st, P1.
Rnd 2: *K1, P1* to last st, K1.

Rep Rows 1–2 twenty *more* times.

Rnd 43: (*P1, K1* 11 times, pm) 3 times, *P1, K1* 11 times, P1.

CROWN DECREASING

Rnd 1: (K3tog, *P1, K1* 8 times, P3tog, slm) 3 times, K3tog, *P1, K1* 8 times, P3tog, K1—73 sts.
Rnd 2: *P1, K1* to last st, P1.
Rnd 3: *K1, P1* to last st, K1.
Rnd 4: *P1, K1* to last st, P1.
Rnd 5: (K3tog, *P1, K1* 6 times, P3tog, slm) 3 times, K3tog, *P1, K1* 6 times, P3tog, K1—57 sts.
Rnd 6: *P1, K1* to last st, P1.
Rnd 7: *K1, P1* to last st, K1.
Rnd 8: *P1, K1* to last st, P1.
Rnd 9: (K3tog, *P1, K1* 4 times, P3tog, slm) 3 times, K3tog, *P1, K1* 4 times, P3tog, K1—41 sts.
Rnd 10: *P1, K1* to last st, P1.
Rnd 11: *K1, P1* to last st, K1.
Rnd 12: *P1, K1* to last st, P1.

Rnd 13: (K3tog, *P1, K1* 2 times, P3tog, remove sm) 3 times, K3tog, *P1, K1* 2 times, P3tog, K1—25 sts.
Rnd 14: *P1, K1* to last st, P1.
Rnd 15: *K1, P1* to last st, K1.
Rnd 16: *P2tog, K2tog* to last 5 sts, P2tog, K3tog—12 sts.

Cut yarn leaving a 10 in. / 25.5 cm tail. Using a tapestry needle, weave tail through remaining live stitches and cinch tight. Weave in your ends (see p. 133).

FINISHING

If necessary, block lightly (see p. 136).

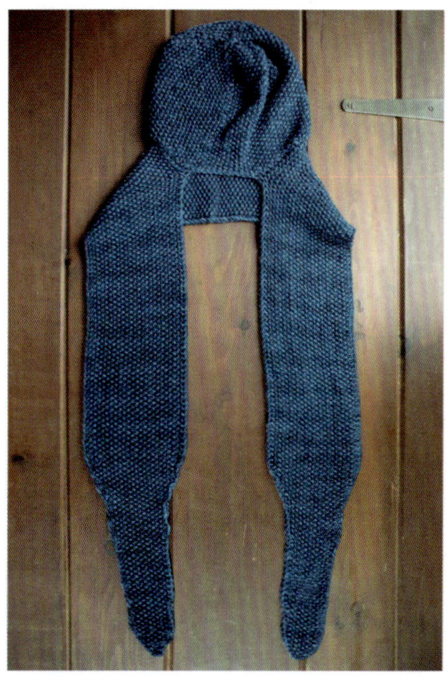

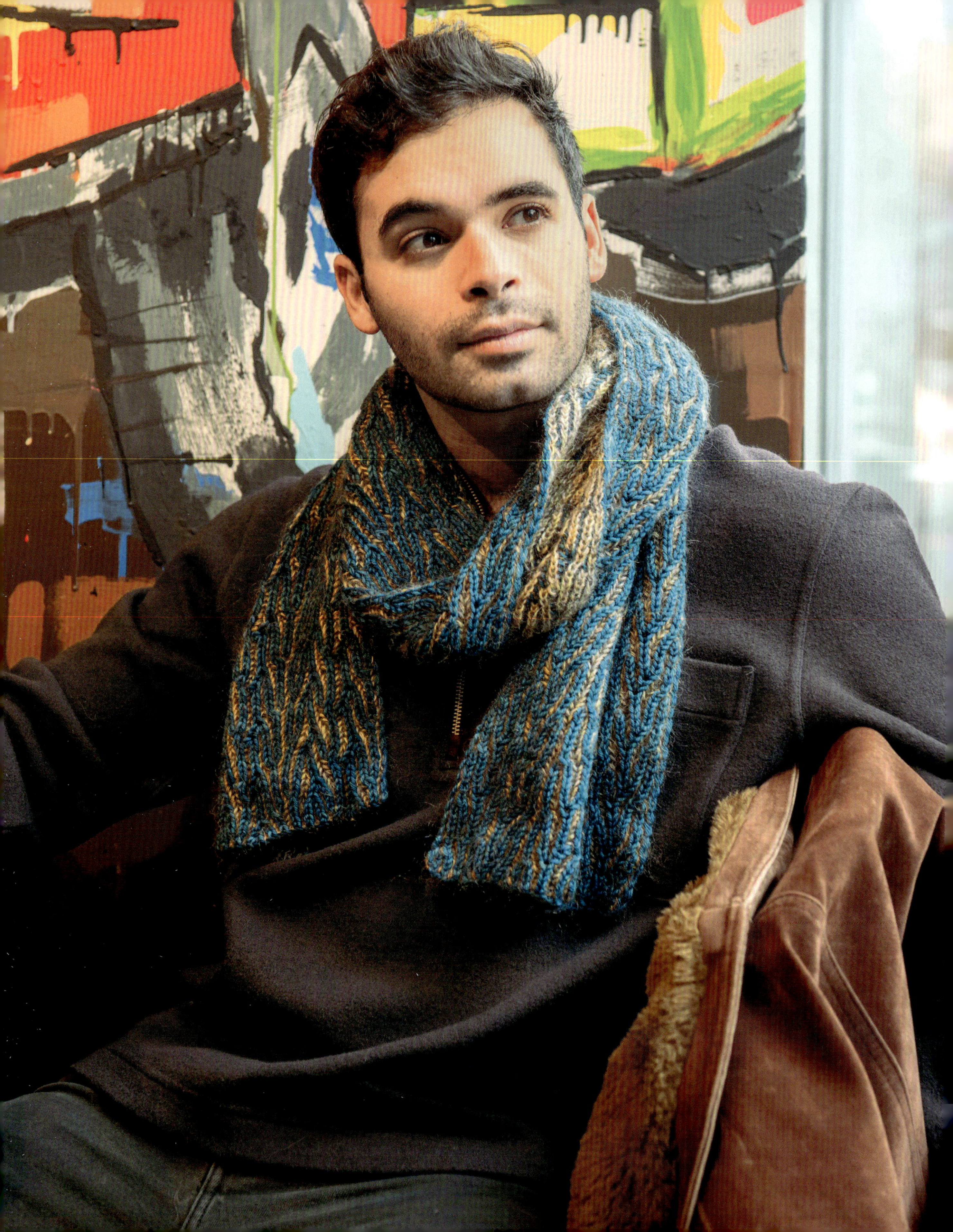

THEO'S MOHAIR AND MERINO SCARF

Inspired by *Self-Portrait or Portrait of Theo van Gogh*

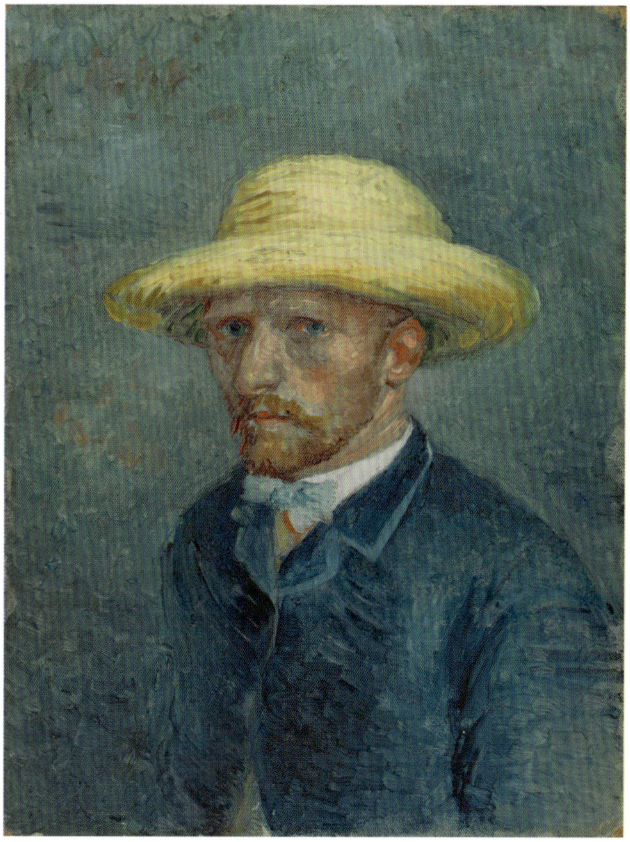

This painting was long thought to be a self-portrait of van Gogh, but it is also possible the painting is of his brother Theo. The brothers shared an uncanny resemblance. There is no way to know definitively who is portrayed, hence the double title. This dual-sided scarf pulls that idea of double into play, with the blues and greens from the garment and the deep background the subject sits against dominating the appearance of one side, and the tan and yellows from his straw hat dominating the appearance of the reverse. The textured pattern symbolizes van Gogh's visible strokes and use of layering colors.

For more information on van Gogh's *Self-Portrait or Portrait of Theo van Gogh*, see p. 139.

SIZES

One size

FINISHED MEASUREMENTS

8 in. / 20.5 cm wide and 66 in. / 167.5 cm long

YARN

MC: Malabrigo "Arroyo" 100% Superwash Merino Wool; Sport (100 g / 335 yd. / 306 m) #685 Greenish Blue – 1 skein

CC: Malabrigo "Mohair" 72% Mohair, 28% Silk; Lace(25 g / 229 yd. / 210 m) #660 Tigers Eye (held doubled) – 3 skeins

NEEDLES

- US size 6 / 4.0 mm, 16 in. / 40 cm long circular knitting needles

Or size needed to obtain gauge

NOTIONS

- Scissors
- Tapestry needle for weaving in ends

GAUGE

- 25 stitches and 20 rows = 4 in. / 10 cm over basic brioche stitch
- 22 stitches and 30 rows = 4 in. / 10 cm in stockinette stitch using MC

NOTES

- This scarf is worked flat, widthwise across the scarf.
- CC mohair is held doubled.
- Always slip stitches wyib unless otherwise noted.
- If you want to make your scarf wider or narrower, this pattern is a multiple of 16 + 3 stitches.
- As written, this pattern uses up almost all of your yarn. If you would like to make your scarf longer or wider, you will need more MC and CC yarn.

KNITTING INSTRUCTIONS

With MC, cast on 51 sts.

Setup Row 1A (WS, MC): Sl1, *sl1YO, P1* to end. Don't turn. Slide sts to other end of the needle.
Setup Row 1B (WS, CC): Sl1, *brk1, sl1YO* to last 2 sts, brk1, sl1. Turn.

Row 1A (RS, MC): Sl1, sl1YO, (*brk1, sl1YO* twice, brkYObrk, sl1YO, brkLdec, sl1YO, *brk1, sl1YO* 3 times) to last st, P1. Don't turn. Slide sts to other end of the needle.
Row 1B (RS, CC): Sl1, brp1, (*sl1YO, brp1* twice, sl1YO, P1, *sl1YO, brp1* 5 times) to last st, wyif sl1. Turn.

Row 2A (WS, MC): Sl1, *sl1YO, brp1* to last 2 sts, sl1YO, P1. Don't turn. Slide sts to other end of the needle.
Row 2B (WS, CC): Sl1, *brk1, sl1YO* to last 2 sts, brk1, sl1. Turn.

Row 3A (MC): Sl1, sl1YO, (brkRdec, sl1YO, brkYObrk, sl1YO, *brk1, sl1YO* 5 times) to last st, P1. Don't turn. Slide sts to other end of the needle.
Row 3B (CC): Wyif sl1, brp1, (sl1YO, brp1, sl1YO, P1, *sl1YO, brp1* 6 times) to last st, wyif sl1. Turn.

Row 4A (MC): Sl1, *sl1YO, brp1* to last 2 sts, sl1YO, P1. Don't turn. Slide sts to other end of the needle.
Row 4B (CC): Sl1, *brk1, sl1YO* to last 2 sts, brk1, sl1. Turn.

Row 5A (MC): Sl1, sl1YO, (*brk1, sl1YO* 5 times, brkYObrk, sl1YO, brkLdec, sl1YO) to last st, P1. Don't turn. Slide sts to other end of the needle.
Row 5B (CC): Wyif sl1, brp1, (*sl1YO, brp1* 5 times, sl1YO, P1, *sl1YO, brp1* twice) to last st, wyif sl1. Turn.

Row 6A (MC): Sl1, *sl1YO, brp1* to last 2 sts, sl1YO, P1. Don't turn. Slide sts to other end of the needle.
Row 6B (CC): Sl1, *brk1, sl1YO* to last 2 sts, brk1, sl1. Turn.

Row 7A (MC): Sl1, sl1YO, (*brk1, sl1YO* 3 times, brkRdec, sl1YO, brkYObrk, sl1YO, *brk1, sl1YO* twice) to last st, P1. Don't turn. Slide sts to other end of the needle.
Row 7B (CC): Wyif sl1, brp1, (*sl1YO, brp1* 4 times, sl1YO, P1, *sl1YO, brp1* 3 times) to last st, wyif sl1. Turn.

Row 8A (MC): Sl1, *sl1YO, brp1* to last 2 sts, sl1YO, P1. Don't turn. Slide sts to other end of the needle.
Row 8B (CC): Sl1, *brk1, sl1YO* to last 2 sts, brk1, sl1. Turn.

Rep Rows 1–8 until piece measures 66 in. / 167.5 cm long. End after working a Row 7B.

Cut CC.

Bind off with MC as follows: Sl1, K1, psso, *brp1, pass first st on RH needle over second st, K1, pass first st on RH needle over second st* to last st, k1, pass first st on RH needle over second st.

Break yarn and pull tail through remaining loop; pull tight to secure.

FINISHING

Weave in all tails (see p. 133).

If necessary, lightly block your scarf (see p. 136).

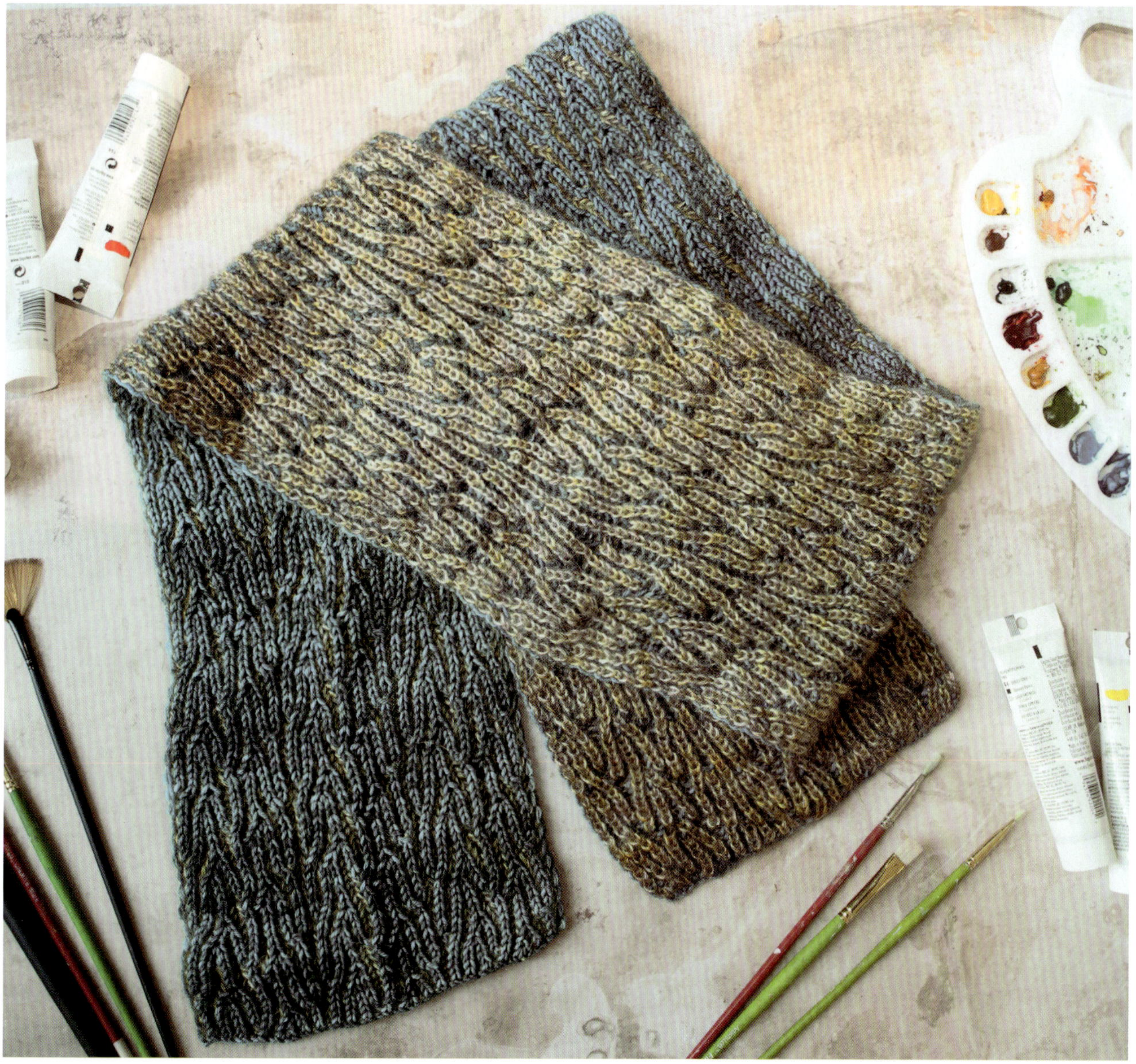

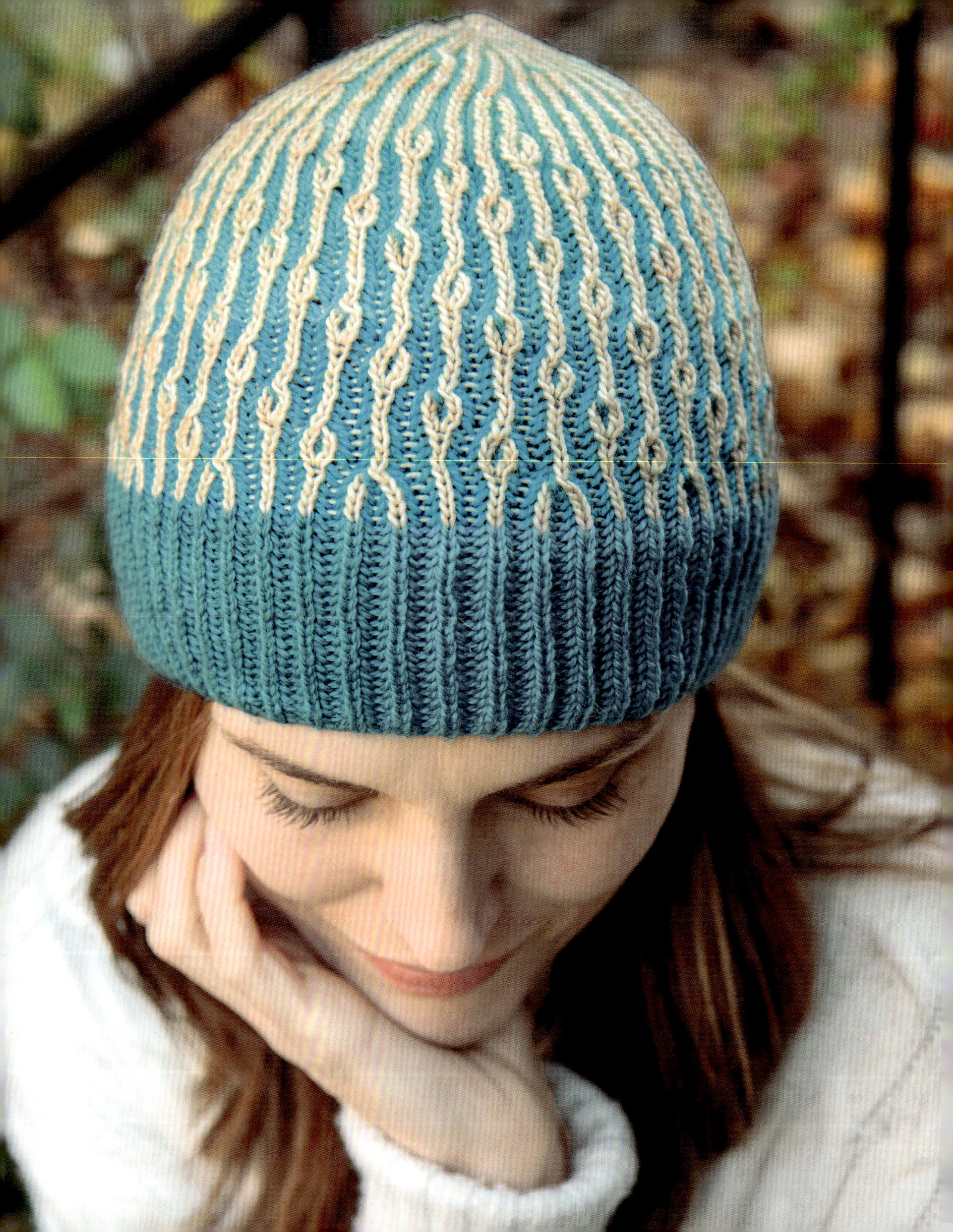

SKILL LEVEL 3

BRIOCHE HAT

Inspired by *Almond Blossom*

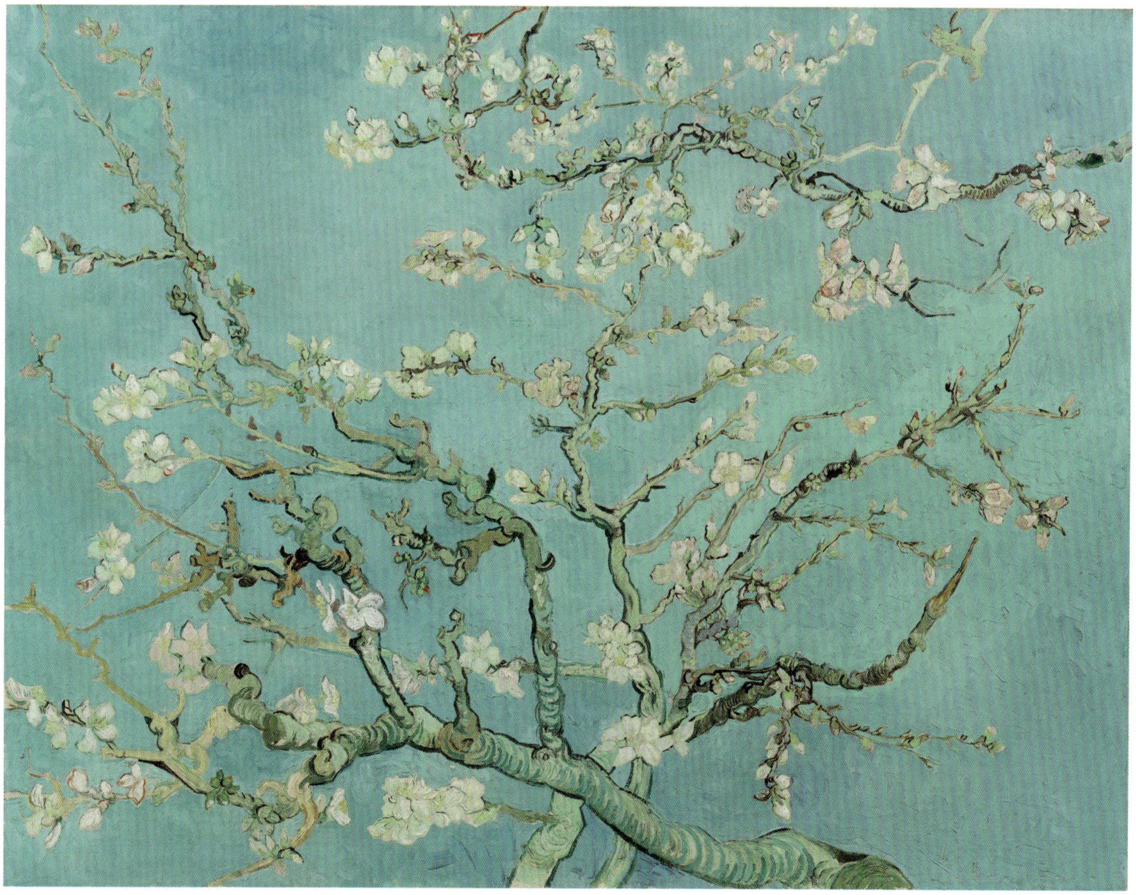

In creating another pattern for the *Almond Blossom* painting, I wanted to be sure to add a unique element and variation that would give knitted garments inspired by the same piece, completely different feels. I pulled the same colors and softness from the painting and used the ombré technique to incorporate the lightest turquoise at the crown of the hat and darker turquoise at the bottom just as the painting does. In contrast, while the silken shawl (see p. 15) focuses on horizontal lines, this hat is inspired by a vertical pattern. I added small loops to the vertical brioche pattern here to represent the white flowers against the blue sky.

For more information on van Gogh's *Almond Blossoms*, see p. 138.

SIZES

One size fits an average female adult sized head.

FINISHED MEASUREMENTS

8 in. / 20 cm wide, 8 in. / 20 cm tall, and 16 in. / 41 cm circumference unstretched

YARN

C1: Malabrigo "Mechita" 100% Superwash Merino Wool; Fingering (100 g / 420 yd. / 384 m) #704 Ivory – 1 skein

C2 – C5: Wonderland Yarns "Cheshire Cat Mini-Skein Pack" 100% SW Merino; Light Fingering Weight (142 g / 640 yd. / 585 m) #74 Caterpillar – 1 mini-pack set

NEEDLES

- US size 2 / 2.75 mm, 16 in. / 40 cm long circular knitting needles
- US size 2 / 2.75 mm, set of double pointed needles (DPNs)

Or size needed to obtain gauge

NOTIONS

- Scissors
- Stitch marker
- Tapestry needle for weaving in ends

GAUGE

- 28 stitches and 38 rows = 4 in. / 10 cm in 2-color brioche rib stitch
- 27 stitches and 40 rows = 4 in. / 10 cm in stockinette stitch using C2

NOTES

- If you want to make your hat larger or smaller, this pattern is a multiple of 8 stitches.
- Color C2 is the darkest color in the mini-skein pack and C5 is the second lightest color in the pack. The stripes are worked from darkest to lightest and only four of the mini-skeins are used.
- Changes to DPNS in the crown shaping when the circumference becomes too small for the circular needles.

KNITTING INSTRUCTIONS

With C2 and 16 in. / 40 cm circular needles, cast on 112 sts.

Place sm and join in the round being careful not to twist sts.

Setup Rnd: *K1, sl1YO* around.

Rnd 1A: *Sl1YO, brp1* around.
Rnd 1B: *Brk1, sl1YO* around.

Rep Rnds 1A and 1B until piece measures 2 in. / 5 cm from cast on. End after working Rnd 1B.

Cut C2.

BODY OF HAT

JJoin C3 on Rnd 1A; join C1 on Rnd 1B.

Rnd 1A (C3): *Sl1YO, brp1* around.
Rnd 1B (C1): *Brk1, sl1YO* around.

Rep Rnds 1A and 1B four *more* times.

Rnd 6A (C3): *Sl1YO, brp1* around.
Rnd 6B (C1): *BrkLdec, sl1YO, brkYObrk, sl1YO, brk1, sl1YO* around.

Rnd 7A (C3): Sl1YO, brp1, (sl1YO, P1, *sl1YO, brp1* 3 times) to last 6 sts, sl1YO, P1, *sl1YO, brp1* twice.
Rnd 7B (C1): *Brk1, sl1YO* around.

Rnd 8A (C3): *Sl1YO, brp1* around.
Rnd 8B (C1): *Brk1, sl1YO* around.

Rnd 9A (C3): *Sl1YO, brp1* around.
Rnd 9B (C1): *Brk1, sl1YO* around.

Rnd 10A (C3): *Sl1YO, brp1* around.
Rnd 10B (C1): *Brk1, sl1YO, brkRdec, sl1YO, brkYObrk, sl1YO* around.

Rnd 11A (C3): (Sl1YO, *brp1, sl1YO* twice, P1, sl1YO, brp1) around.
Rnd 11B (C1): *Brk1, sl1YO* around.

Rnd 12A (C3): *Sl1YO, brp1* around.
Rnd 12B (C1): *Brk1, sl1YO* around.

Rnd 13A (C3): *Sl1YO, brp1* around.
Rnd 13B (C1): *Brk1, sl1YO* around.

Rnd 14A (C3): *Sl1YO, brp1* around.
Rnd 14B (C1): *BrkYObrk, sl1YO, brk1, sl1YO, brkLdec, sl1YO* around.

Rnd 15A (C3): (Sl1YO, P1, *sl1YO, brp1* 3 times).
Rnd 15B (C1): *Brk1, sl1YO* around.

Rnd 16A (C3): *Sl1YO, brp1* around.
Rnd 16B (C1): *Brk1, sl1YO* around.

Rnd 17A (C3): *Sl1YO, brp1* around.
Rnd 17B (C1): *Brk1, sl1YO* around.

Rnd 18A (C3): *Sl1YO, brp1* around.
Rnd 18B (C1): *BrkRdec, sl1YO, brkYObrk, sl1YO, brk1, sl1YO* around.

Rnd 19A (C3): Sl1YO, brp1, (sl1YO, P1, *sl1YO, brp1* 3 times) to last 6 sts, sl1YO, P1, *sl1YO, brp1* twice.
Rnd 19B (C1): *Brk1, sl1YO* around.

Rnd 20A (C3): *Sl1YO, brp1* around.
Rnd 20B (C1): *Brk1, sl1YO* around.

Cut C3 and join C4.

Rnd 21A (C4): *Sl1YO, brp1* around.
Rnd 21B (C1): *Brk1, sl1YO* around.

Rnd 22A (C4): *Sl1YO, brp1* around.
Rnd 22B (C1): *Brk1, sl1YO, brkLdec, sl1YO, brkYObrk, sl1YO* around.

Rnd 23A (C4): (Sl1YO, *brp1, sl1YO* twice, P1, sl1YO, brp1) around.
Rnd 23B (C1): *Brk1, sl1YO* around.

Rnd 24A (C4): *Sl1YO, brp1* around.
Rnd 24B (C1): *Brk1, sl1YO* around.

Rnd 25A (C4): *Sl1YO, brp1* around.
Rnd 25B (C1): *Brk1, sl1YO* around.

Rnd 26A (C4): *Sl1YO, brp1* around.
Rnd 26B (C1): *BrkYObrk, sl1YO, brk1, sl1YO, brkRdec, sl1YO* around.

Rnd 27A (C4): (Sl1YO, P1, *sl1YO, brp1* 3 times).
Rnd 27B (C1): *Brk1, sl1YO* around.

Rnd 28A (C4): *Sl1YO, brp1* around.

(Pattern continues on next page)

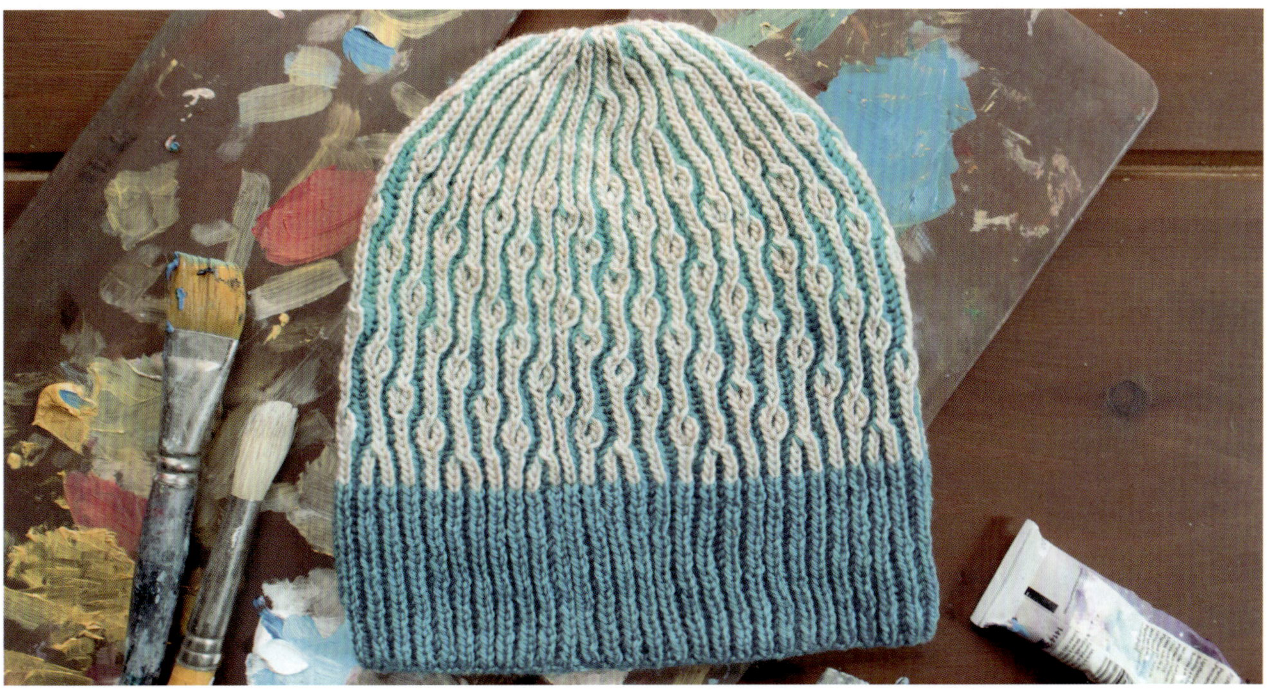

Rnd 28B (C1): *Brk1, sl1YO* around.

Rnd 29A (C4): *Sl1YO, brp1* around.
Rnd 29B (C1): *Brk1, sl1YO* around.

Rnd 30A (C4): *Sl1YO, brp1* around.
Rnd 30B (C1): *BrkLdec, sl1YO, brkYObrk, sl1YO, brk1, sl1YO* around.

Rnd 31A (C4): Sl1YO, brp1, (sl1YO, P1, *sl1YO, brp1* 3 times) to last 6 sts, sl1YO, P1, *sl1YO, brp1* twice.
Rnd 31B (C1): *Brk1, sl1YO* around.

Rnd 32A (C4): *Sl1YO, brp1* around.
Rnd 32B (C1): *Brk1, sl1YO* around.

Rnd 33A (C4): *Sl1YO, brp1* around.
Rnd 33B (C1): *Brk1, sl1YO* around.

Rnd 34A (C4): *Sl1YO, brp1* around.
Rnd 34B (C1): *Brk1, sl1YO, brkRdec, sl1YO, brkYObrk, sl1YO* around.

Rnd 35A (C4): (Sl1YO, *brp1, sl1YO* twice, P1, sl1YO, brp1) around.
Rnd 35B (C1): *Brk1, sl1YO* around.

Rnd 36A (C4): *Sl1YO, brp1* around.
Rnd 36B (C1): *Brk1, sl1YO* around.

Rnd 37A (C4): *Sl1YO, brp1* around.
Rnd 37B (C1): *Brk1, sl1YO* around.

Rnd 38A (C4): *Sl1YO, brp1* around.
Rnd 38B (C1): *BrkYObrk, sl1YO, brk1, sl1YO, brkLdec, sl1YO* around.

Rnd 39A (C4): (Sl1YO, P1, *sl1YO, brp1* 3 times).
Rnd 39B (C1): *Brk1, sl1YO* around.

Rnd 40A (C4): *Sl1YO, brp1* around.
Rnd 40B (C1): *Brk1, sl1YO* around.

Cut C4 and join C5.

Rnd 41A (C5): *Sl1YO, brp1* around.
Rnd 41B (C1): *Brk1, sl1YO* around.

CROWN DECREASING

Rnd 42A (C5): *Sl1YO, brp1* around.
Rnd 42B (C1): (BrkRdec, *sl1YO, brk1* 2 times, sl1YO) around—84 sts.

Rnd 43A (C5): *Sl1YO, brp1* around.
Rnd 43B (C1): *Brk1, sl1YO* around.

Rep Rnds 43A and 43B four *more* times.

Rnd 48A (C5): *Sl1YO, brp1* around.
Rnd 48B (C1): (BrkLdec, *sl1YO, brk1* 4 times, sl1YO) around—70 sts.

Work Rnds 43A and 43B a total of five times.

Rnd 54A (C5): *Sl1YO, brp1* around.
Rnd 54B (C1): (*Brk1, sl1YO* twice, brkLdec, sl1YO, brk1, sl1YO)—56 sts.

Work Rnds 43A and 43B a total of three times.

Rnd 58A (C5): *Sl1YO, brp1* around.
Rnd 58B (C1): (BrkRdec, *brk1, sl1YO* twice, sl1YO) around—42 sts.

Work Rnds 43A and 43B a total of two times.

Rnd 61A (C5): *Sl1YO, brp1* around.
Rnd 61B (C1): (Brk1, sl1YO, brkLdec, sl1YO) around—28 sts.

Work Rnds 43A and 43B one *more* time.

FINISHING

Cut C5 yarn leaving a tail to weave in. Cut C1 leaving a 10 in. / 25.5 cm tail. Using a tapestry needle, weave C1 tail through remaining live stitches and cinch tight. Weave in your ends (see p. 133).

If necessary, block lightly (see p. 136).

"IT'S A WONDERFUL THING
TO LOOK AT SOMETHING
AND FIND IT BEAUTIFUL,
TO REFLECT ON IT
AND HOLD IT FAST
AND THEN TO SAY,
I'M GOING TO DRAW THAT,
AND THEN TO WORK ON IT
UNTIL IT'S DONE."

—Vincent van Gogh to his brother Theo,
April 6, 1882

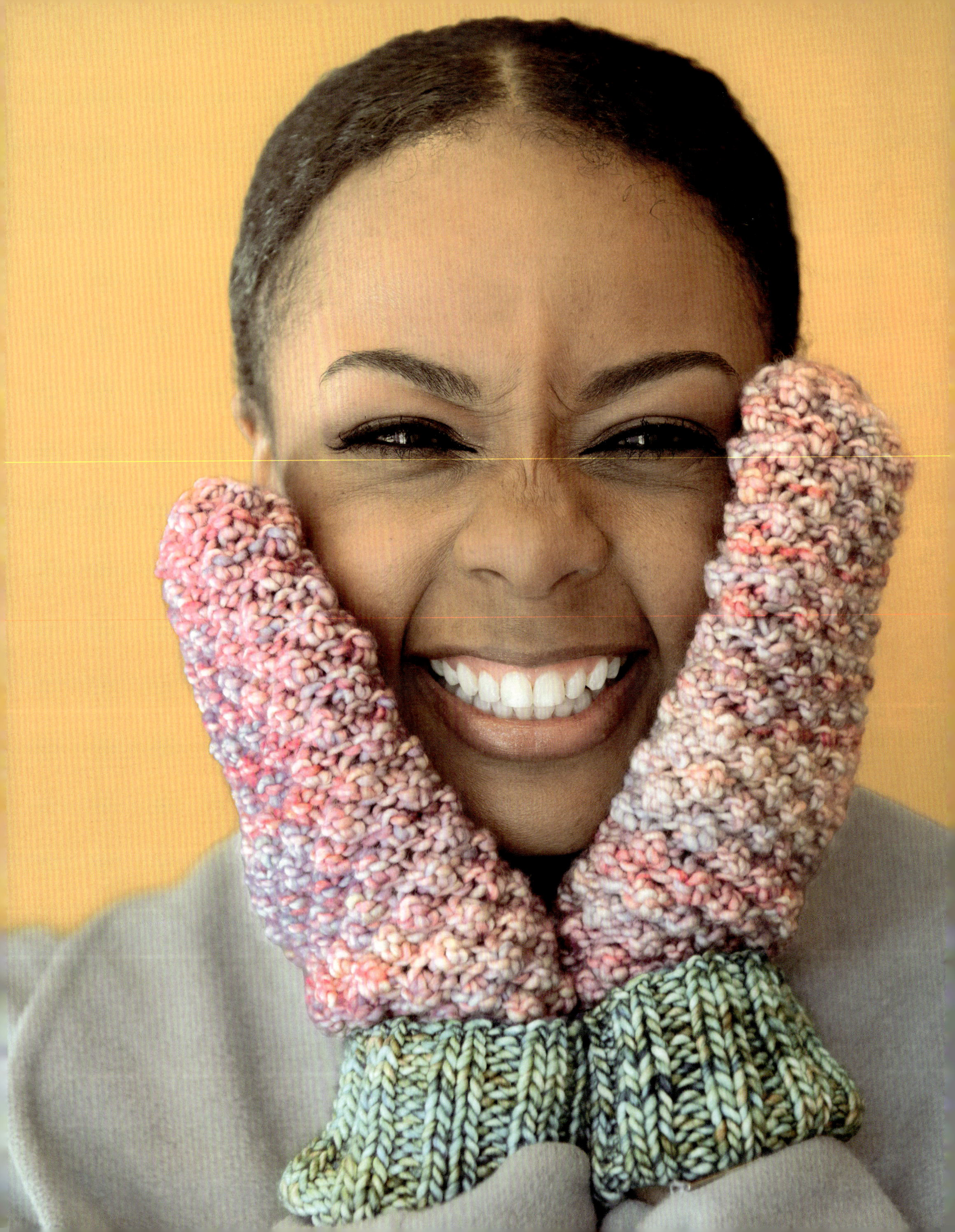

MITTENS OF AUVERS

Inspired by *Vase of Flowers*

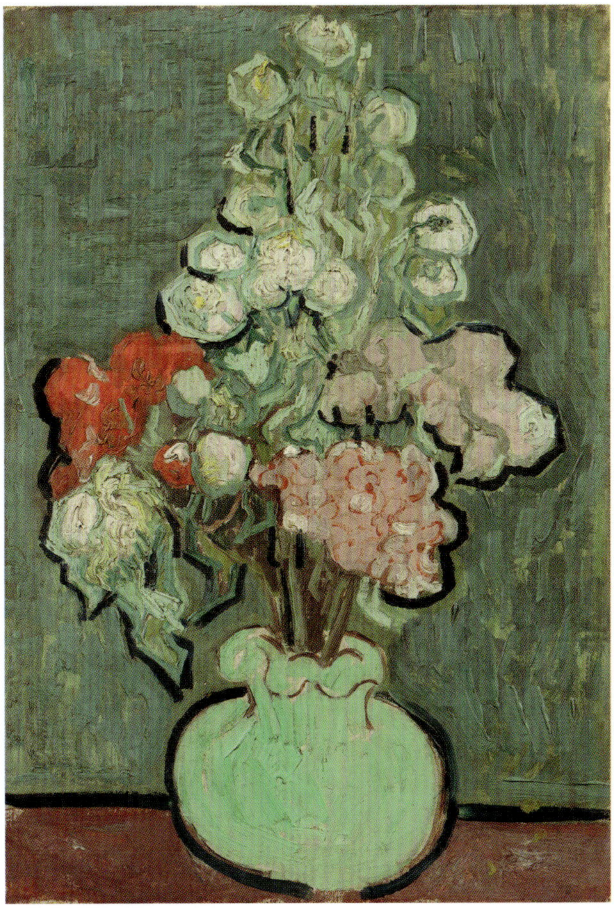

The color blocking of these soft knit mittens beautifully translates the vase and flowers of this painting. Van Gogh painted this particular subject with loose and rapid brushstrokes, and made the flowers only just recognizable, surrounding them with thick blue outlining. The cuffs of these mittens represent the green vase, and the tops represent the flowers and leaves. The various shades of green in the cuffs nod to both the lighter green of the vase and the darker greens seen in the background. I used a holy trinity stitch for the tops, which gives it the patterned and raised look it has. The holy trinity stitch helped represent the puffiness of the flower petals.

For more information on van Gogh's *Vase of Flowers*, see p. 139.

SIZES
Small (Large)

FINISHED MEASUREMENTS
8.5 (10.25) in. / 21.5 (26) cm circumference and 13 in. / 33 cm long (from bottom of cuff to top of mitten)

YARN
Malabrigo "Mecha" 100% Superwash Merino Wool; Bulky (100 g / 130 yd. / 119 m)

C1: #336 Taystee – 1 (1) skein

C2: #398 Rosalinda – 1 (2) skeins

NEEDLES
- US size 8 / 5.0 mm, set of double pointed needles (DPNs)
- US size 9 / 5.5 mm, set of double pointed needles (DPNs)

Or size needed to obtain gauge

NOTIONS
- Scissors
- Stitch marker
- Tapestry needle
- Scrap yarn

GAUGE
17 stitches and 24 rows = 4 in. / 10 cm in pattern stitch worked in the round on larger needle

NOTES
- The mittens are worked from the cuff up.
- Instructions are provided for size Small first, with size Large in parentheses. If only one set of instructions is provided, it applies to both sizes.
- If you want to make your mittens larger or smaller, this pattern is a multiple of 4 stitches. You will need more yarn if you make your mittens larger. Both mittens are worked the same.

KNITTING INSTRUCTIONS

MITTEN (MAKE TWO)
Using smaller needles and C1, CO 36 (44) sts.
Join to work in the rnd being careful not to twist. Place sm to note bor.

K2, P2 for 4 in. / 10 cm.

Cut C1. Change to C2 and larger needles.

Setup Rnd: Knit.

Rnd 1: Purl.
Rnd 2: *(P1, K1, P1) into next st, K3tog* around.
Rnd 3: Purl.
Rnd 4: *K3tog, (P1, K1, P1) into next st* around.

Rep Rnds 1–4 one *more* time.

GUSSET SHAPING
Rnd 9: The first st on your LH needle is a K3tog from the previous rnd. In each of the 3 sts that are below the st sitting on your LH needle is what you will be working into. With RH needle, lift the first st (the right-most st) of the K3tog onto your LH needle and purl it tbl. Lift the second st (the center st) of the K3tog onto your LH needle and purl it tbl. Lift the third stitch (the left-most st) of the K3tog onto your LH needle and purl it tbl. Into the first st on LH needle, pf&b. A total of 4 sts have been increased. P to end.

Rnd 10: *(P1, K1, P1) into next st, K3tog* around.
Rnd 11: Purl.
Rnd 12: *K3tog, (P1, K1, P1) into next st* around.

Rep Rnds 9–12 three *more* times—52 (60) sts.

Next Rnd: Place first 16 sts onto scrap yarn (these will be the base sts of the thumb), P to end—36 (44) sts.

HAND
Rnd 1: *(P1, K1, P1) into next st, K3tog* around.
Rnd 2: Purl.
Rnd 3: *K3tog, (P1, K1, P1) I to next st* around.
Rnd 4: Purl.

Rep Rnds 1–4 four *more* times.
Work Rnds 1–3 one *more* time.

Rnd 24: *K1, P3tog* around—18 (22) sts.
Rnd 25: Knit.
Rnd 26: *P2tog* around—9 (11) sts.

Cut yarn leaving a tail. Weave tail through remaining 9 (11) sts and cinch tight (see p. 133).

THUMB

(Both sizes are worked the same.)
Place 16 sts onto larger needles. Join C2.

Setup Rnd: Purl across 16 sts, pick up and knit 4 sts across the gap—20 sts. Join to work in the rnd. Place sm to note bor.

Rnd 1: *(P1, K1, P1) into next st, K3tog* around.
Rnd 2: Purl.
Rnd 3: *K3tog, (P1, K1, P1) into next st* around.
Rnd 4: Purl.

Rep Rnds 1–4 one + time.
Work Rnds 1–3 one *more* time.

Rnd 12: *K1, P3tog* around—10 sts.
Rnd 13: Knit.
Rnd 14: *P2tog* around—5 sts.

Cut yarn leaving a tail. Weave tail through remaining 5 sts and cinch tight (see p. 133).

Weave in all your ends (see p. 136).

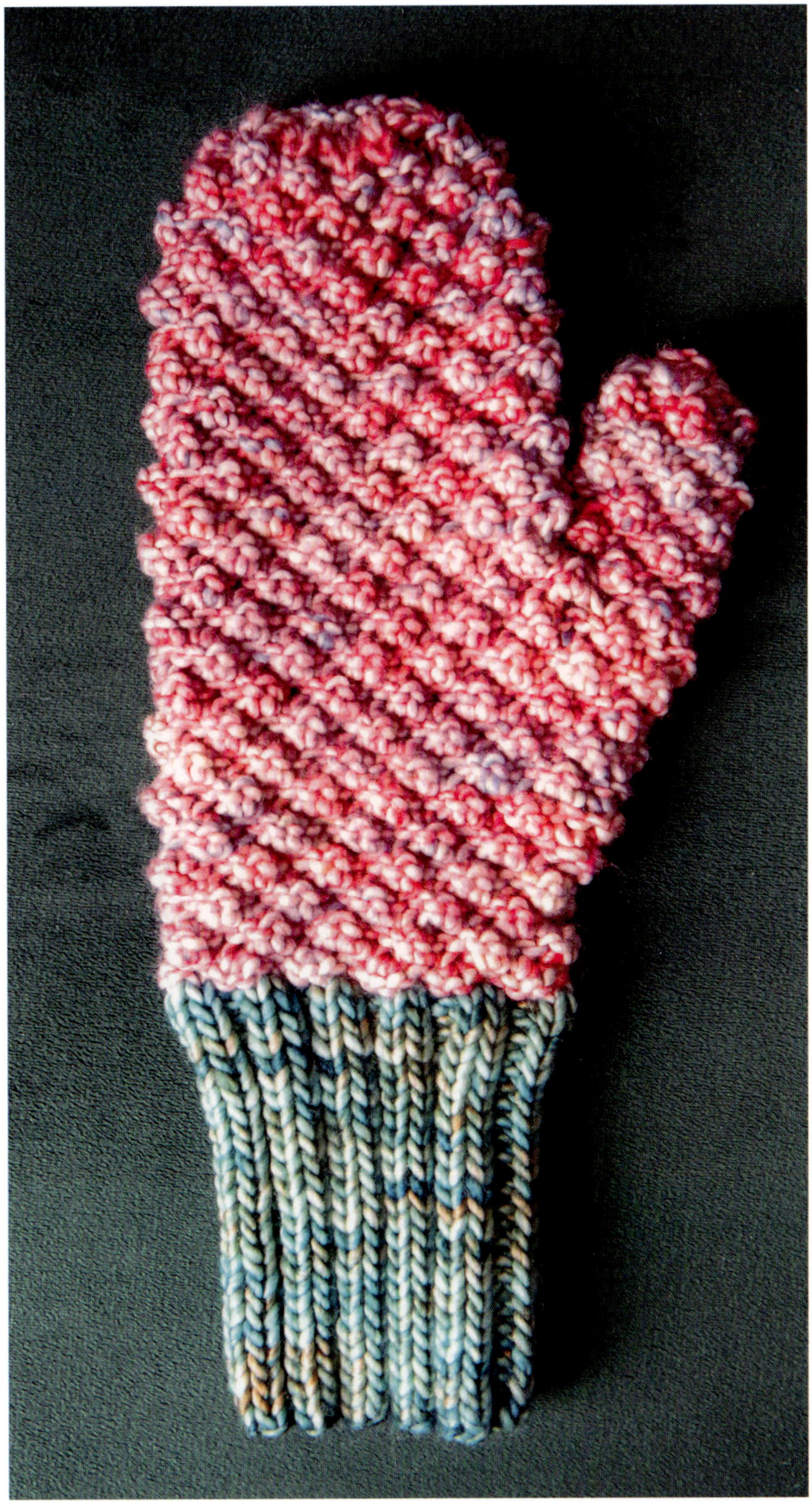

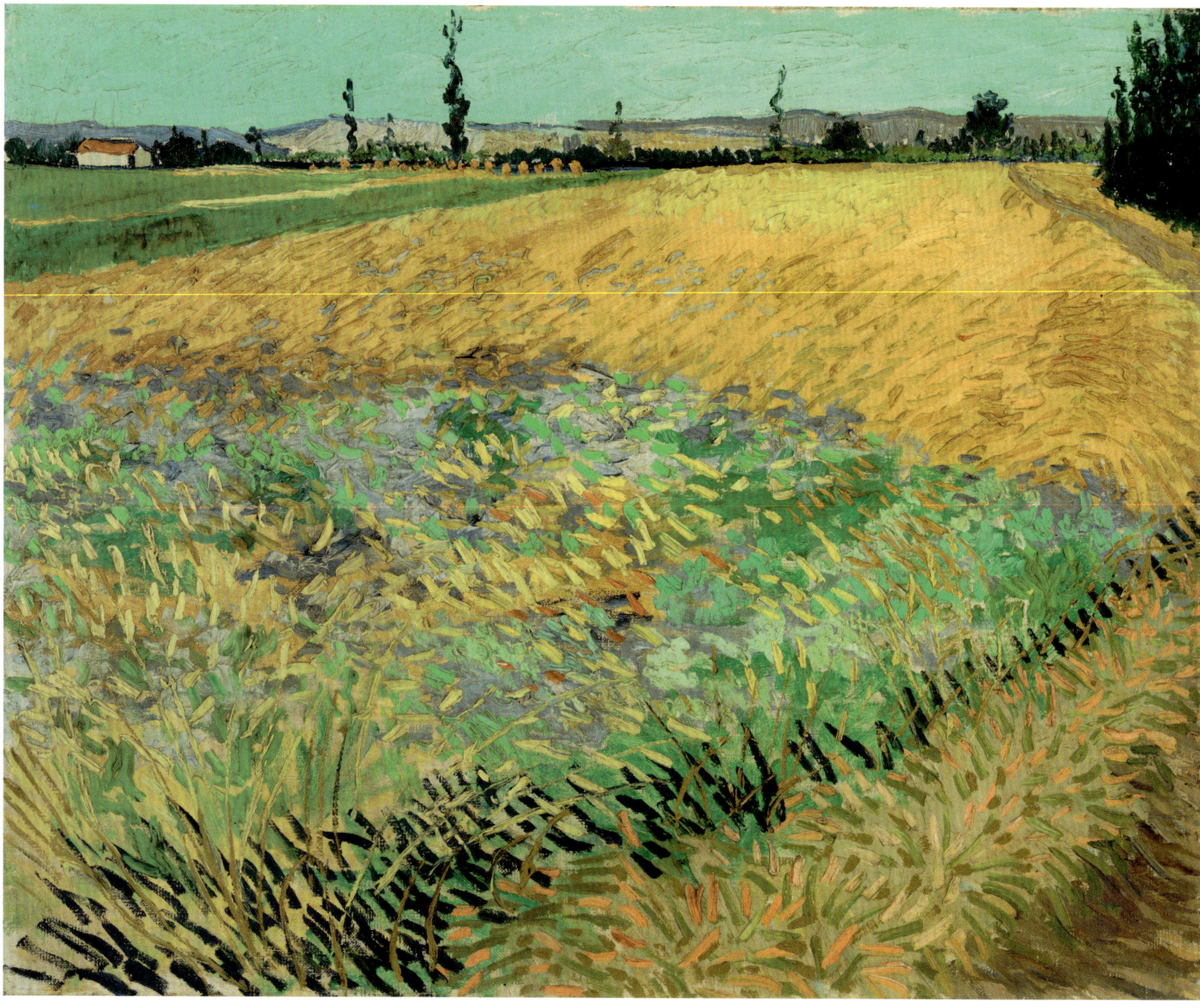

Wheatfield (p. 55)

“ARRANGING COLOURS
IN A PAINTING
TO MAKE THEM SHIMMER
AND STAND OUT
THROUGH THEIR CONTRASTS,
THAT'S SOMETHING
LIKE ARRANGING JEWELS
OR DESIGNING COSTUMES.”

—Vincent van Gogh to his sister Willemien,
September 14, 1888

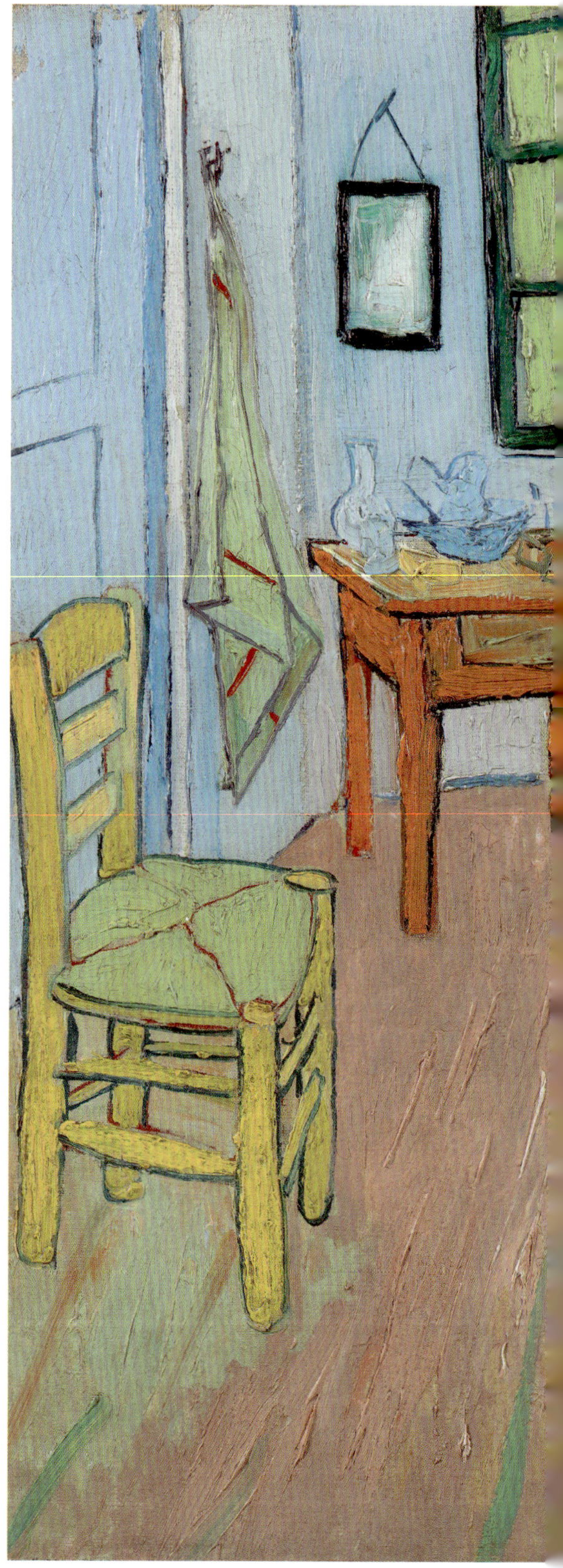

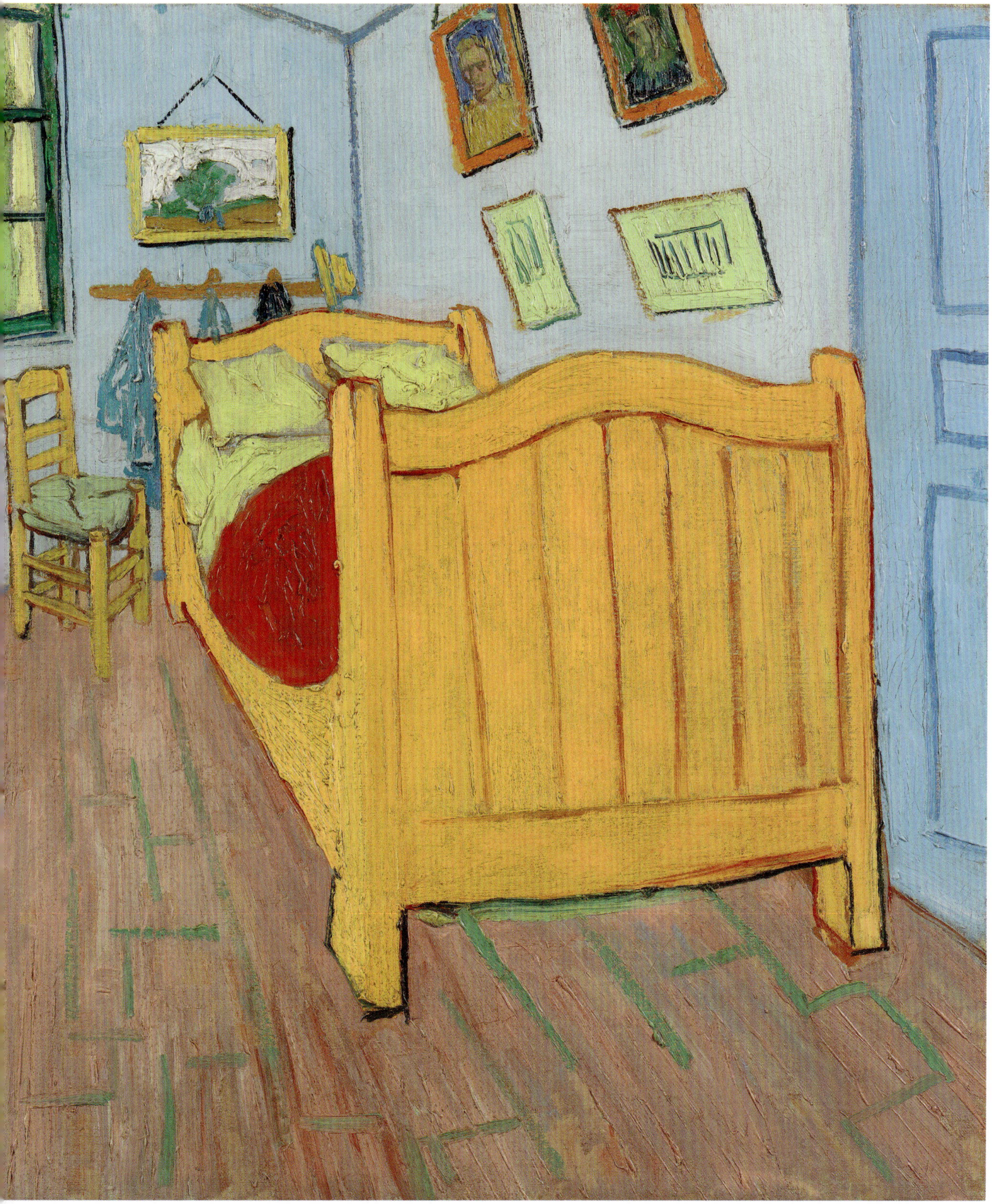

The Bedroom (p. 97)

INSPIRED DÉCOR

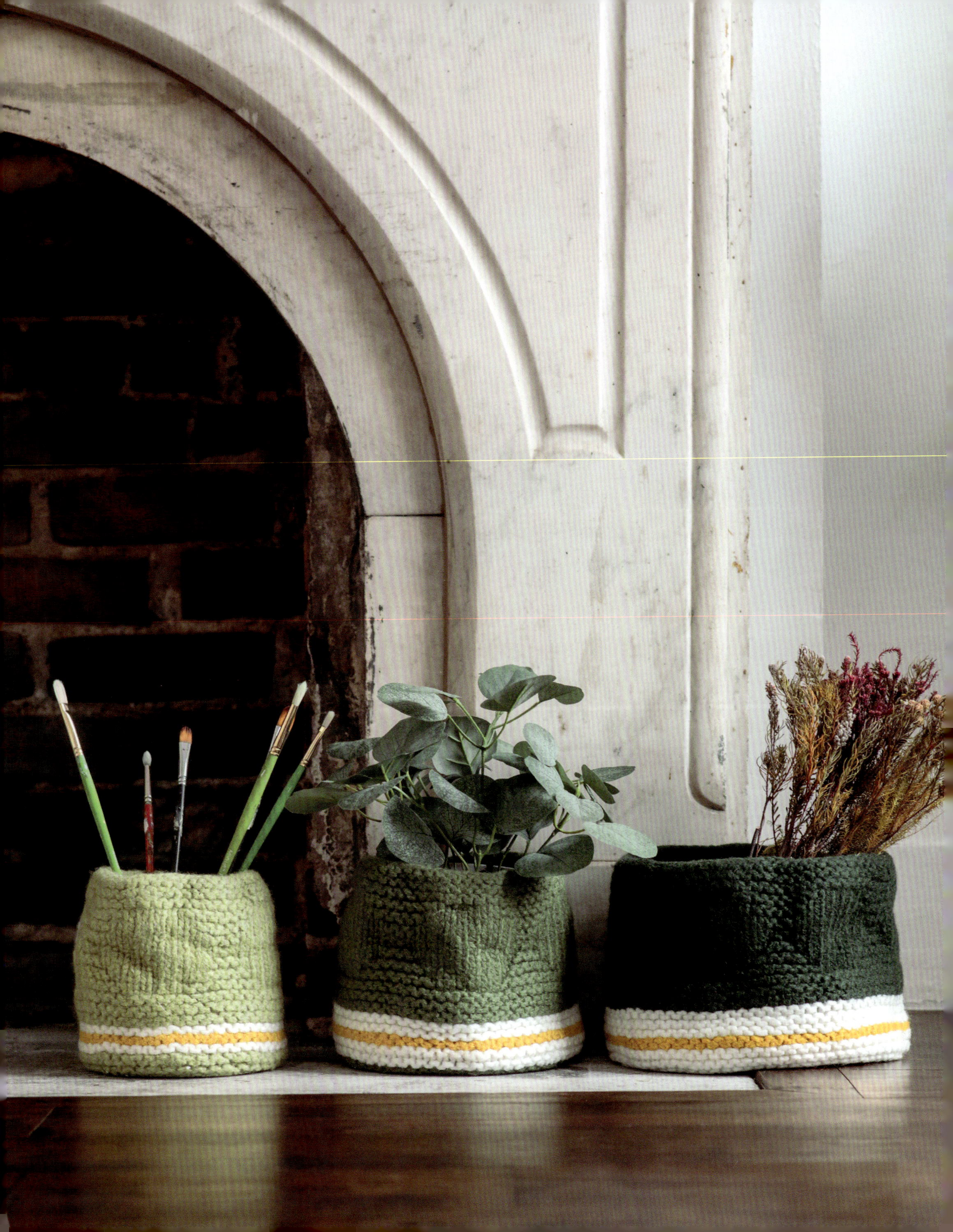

FELTED NESTING BASKETS

Inspired by *Wild Roses*

SKILL LEVEL **1**

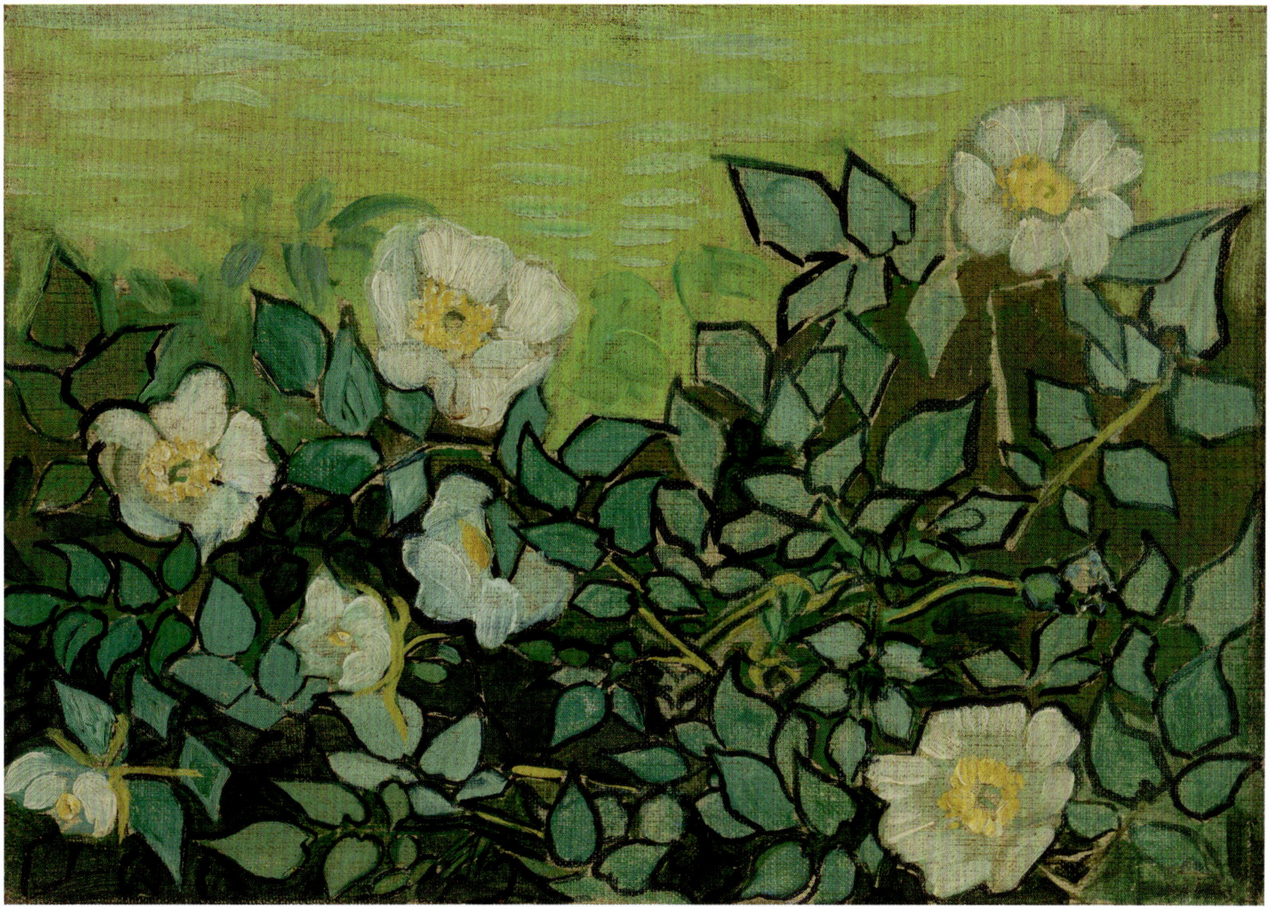

The serene feeling this painting may conjure is very different than the state of mind van Gogh found himself in while painting it. That is the beauty of art, whether created with paint or yarn; it inspires and gives of itself, offering peace where there may be none. These nesting baskets focus on the various greens used in the painting—light, medium, and dark—along with strong lines of white and yellow to represent the blooming roses. They are perfect for holding potted plants—wild roses, perhaps—or even useful for storage in various spaces of your home.

For more information on van Gogh's *Wild Roses*, see p. 139.

SIZES

Small (Medium, Large)

FINISHED MEASUREMENTS

7 (8, 9) in. / 18 (20.5, 23) cm in diameter and 6 (6.5, 7) in. / 15 (16.5, 18) cm tall

YARN

Knit Picks "Wool of the Andes Bulky Weight" 100% Peruvian Highland Wool; Bulky (100 g / 137 yd. / 125 m)

- **C1**: Green Tea Heather – 2 skeins
- **C2**: Fern – 2 skeins
- **C3**: Lumberjack – 2 skeins
- **C4**: White – 1 skein
- **C5**: Honey – 1 skein

NEEDLES

- US size 15 / 10 mm, 16 in. / 40 cm long circular knitting needles
- US size 15 / 10 mm, set of double pointed needles (DPNs)

Or size needed to obtain gauge

NOTIONS

- Scissors
- Stitch marker
- Tapestry needle for weaving in ends
- Lingerie bag (for felting)
- Mild liquid laundry detergent (for felting)

GAUGE

- 11 stitches and 12 rows = 4 in. / 10 cm in stockinette stitch worked in the round with two strands held together, taken before felting
- 10 stitches and 18 rows = 4 in. / 10 cm in stockinette stitch worked in the round with two strands held together, taken after felting

NOTES

- Baskets are knit using two strands of yarn held together throughout entire piece.

KNITTING INSTRUCTIONS

Using 2 strands of C1 (C2, C3) held doubled, CO 48 (60, 72) sts.

Join to work in the round being careful not to twist. Place sm to note bor.

Rnd 1: Purl.
Rnd 2: Knit.

Rep Rnds 1–2 2 two *more* times.

Rnd 7: *P7, K5* around.
Rnd 8: Knit.
Rnd 9: *K1, P5, K6* around.
Rnd 10: Knit.
Rnd 11: *K2, P3, K7* around.
Rnd 12: Knit.
Rnd 13: *K3, P1, K8* around.
Rnd 14: Knit.
Rnd 15: *K2, P3, K7* around.
Rnd 16: Knit.
Rnd 17: *K1, P5, K6* around.
Rnd 18: Knit.
Rnd 19: *P7, K5* around.
Rnd 20: Knit.

Work Rnds 1–2 two times, then work Rnd 1 one *more* time.

Cut yarn and join C4.

Rnd 26 (C4): Knit.
Rnd 27 (C4): Purl.

Rep Rnds 26–27 0 (1, 2) *more* time(s).

Don't cut C4. Join C5.

Next Rnd (C5): Knit.
Next Rnd (C5): Purl.

Cut C5.

Next Rnd (C4): Knit.
Next Rnd (C4): Purl.

Rep last 2 rnds 0 (1, 2) *more* time(s).

Cut C4. Join C1 (C2, C3).

Next Rnd: Knit.
Next Rnd: Purl.

BEGIN BOTTOM SHAPING

Continue with C1 (C2, C3). As you decrease stitches, switch to DPNs when you don't have enough stitches to fit around your circular needles.

Rnd 1: *K4, K2tog* around—40 (50, 60) sts.

Rnd 2: Purl.
Rnd 3: Knit.

Rep Rnds 2–3 two *more* times.

Rnd 8: Purl.
Rnd 9: *K3, K2tog* around—32 (40, 48) sts.
Rnd 10: Purl.
Rnd 11: Knit.
Rnd 12: Purl.
Rnd 13: *K2, K2tog* around—24 (30, 36) sts.
Rnd 14: Purl.

Rnd 15: *K1, K2tog* around—
16 (20, 24) sts.
Rnd 16: Purl.
Rnd 17: *K2tog* around—
8 (10, 12) sts.

Cut yarn leaving a 6 in. / 15 cm tail. Weave tail through remaining 8 (10, 12) sts and cinch tight (see p. 133).

FINISHING

Weave in tails (see p. 133).

Felt each basket in a separate lingerie bag (see p. 134).

Place damp baskets on a flat surface and mold to rounded shape. Let baskets dry completely before using.

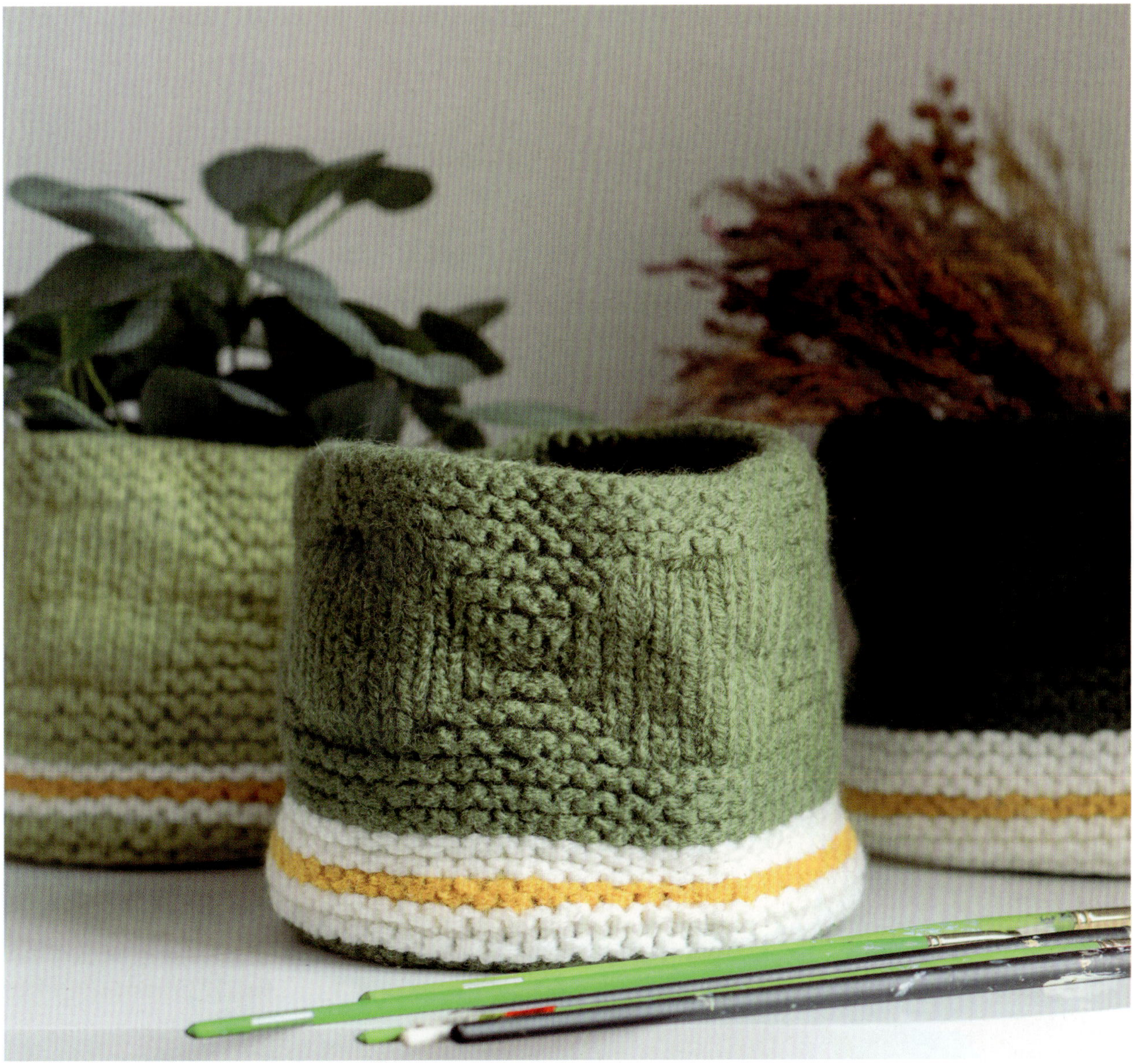

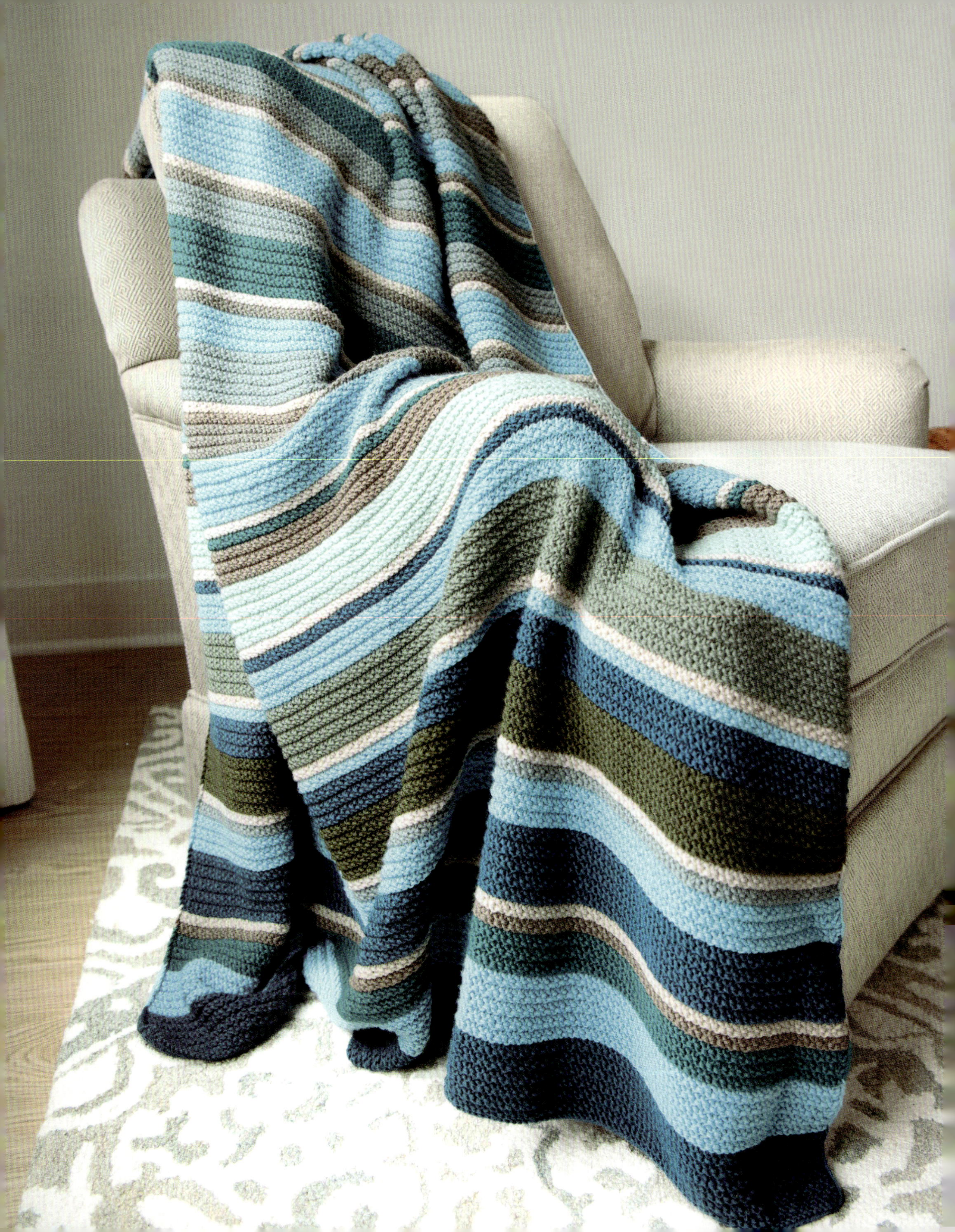

SKILL LEVEL 1

BLOSSOM BRANCH BLANKET

Inspired by *Almond Blossom*

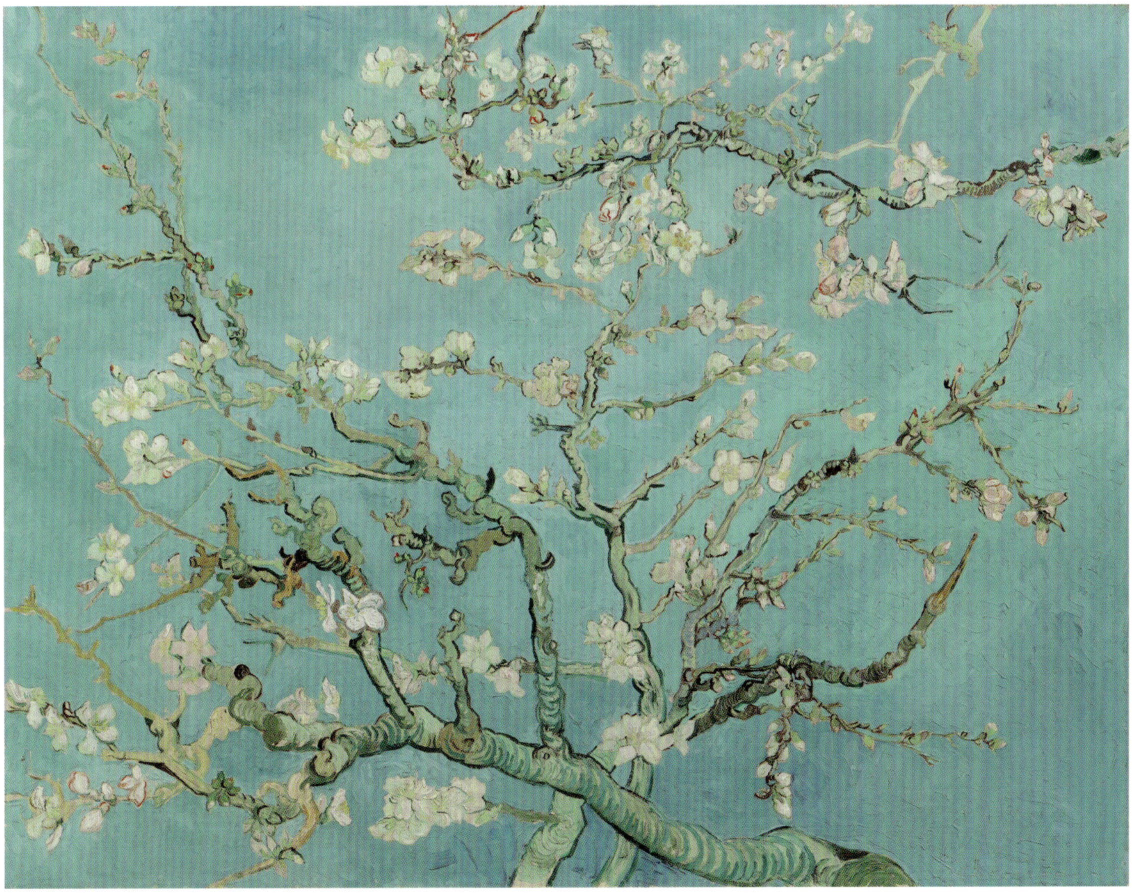

The splaying branches were my inspiration for this final *Almond Blossom* knit. I decided to make this piece a meeting of all the elements we've explored thus far from one of van Gogh's most infamous paintings. The painting is serene, and comforting, much like this blanket. I brought in more of the brown to represent the branches and origin of the almond blossoms. I focused on aligning the additional blues and white in a vertical line pattern, being sure to keep the presence of the flowers and the surrounding sky. This blanket makes for the perfect cozy throw to accent your décor.

For more information on van Gogh's *Almond Blossoms*, see p. 138.

SIZES

One size

FINISHED MEASUREMENTS

Approximately 46 in. / 117 cm wide and 65 in. / 165 cm long

YARN

Plymouth Yarn "Worsted Merino Superwash" 100% Superwash Fine Merino Wool; Worsted (100 g / 218 yd. / 199 m)

- C1: #62 Teal – 3 skeins
- C2: #89 Turquoise Heather – 5 skeins
- C3: #43 Greenlake – 2 skeins
- C4: #65 Fox – 1 skein
- C5: #33 Creme – 1 skein
- C6: #70 Slate – 2 skeins
- C7: #82 Natural Heather – 1 skein
- C8: #78 Pesto – 1 skein
- C9: #35 Sage – 1 skein
- C10: #52 Sea-Foam – 1 skein
- C11: #75 Gravel – 1 skein

NEEDLES

- US size 7 / 4.5 mm, 32 in. / 80 cm long circular knitting needles

Or size needed to obtain gauge

NOTIONS

- Scissors
- Tapestry needle for weaving in ends

GAUGE

20 stitches and 38 rows = 4 in. / 10 cm in Textured Stitch Pattern

NOTES

- Pattern is a multiple of 2 + 1 stitches. To make your blanket larger or smaller, add or subtract stitches in multiples of 2. If you make your blanket larger, you will need more yarn.
- Cut yarns between each striped section.

KNITTING INSTRUCTIONS

TEXTURED STITCH PATTERN

Row 1 (RS): Sl1, K to last st, P1.
Row 2 (WS): Sl1, K to last st, P1.
Row 3: Sl1, *K1, P1* to end.
Row 4: Sl1, *K1, P1* to end.

Using C1, CO 229 sts.

Setup Row (WS): Sl1, K to last st, P1.

Rep Rows 1–4 of Textured Stitch Pattern according to the chart on facing page.

When done with the chart, use C1 to bind off all sts.

FINISHING

Weave in tails (see p. 133).

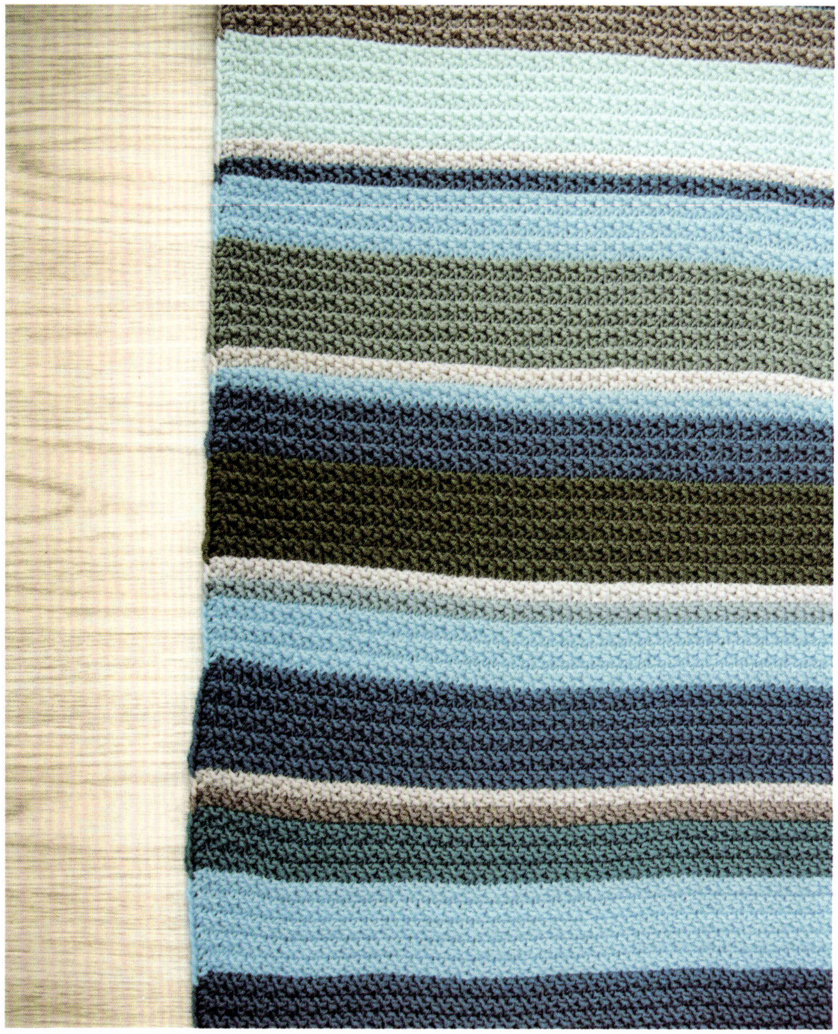

Follow the order of the color blocks to create the piece as pictured.

COLOR BLOCK	YARN COLOR	NUMBER OF TEXTURED STITCH PATTERN REPEATS
1	C1	6
2	C2	5
3	C3	3
4	C4	1
5	C5	1
6	C1	5
7	C2	3
8	C6	1
9	C7	1
10	C8	5
11	C1	3
12	C2	1
13	C5	1
14	C9	5
15	C2	3
16	C1	1
17	C7	1
18	C10	5
19	C4	3
20	C3	1
21	C5	1
22	C2	5
23	C11	3
24	C4	1
25	C7	1
26	C6	5
27	C2	3
28	C11	1
29	C5	1
30	C3	5
31	C6	3
32	C11	1
33	C7	1
34	C2	5

COLOR BLOCK	YARN COLOR	NUMBER OF TEXTURED STITCH PATTERN REPEATS
35	C7	1
36	C11	1
37	C6	3
38	C3	5
39	C5	1
40	C11	1
41	C2	3
42	C6	5
43	C7	1
44	C4	1
45	C11	3
46	C2	5
47	C5	1
48	C3	1
49	C4	3
50	C10	5
51	C7	1
52	C1	1
53	C2	3
54	C9	5
55	C5	1
56	C2	1
57	C1	3
58	C8	5
59	C7	1
60	C6	1
61	C2	3
62	C1	5
63	C5	1
64	C4	1
65	C3	3
66	C2	5
67	C1	6

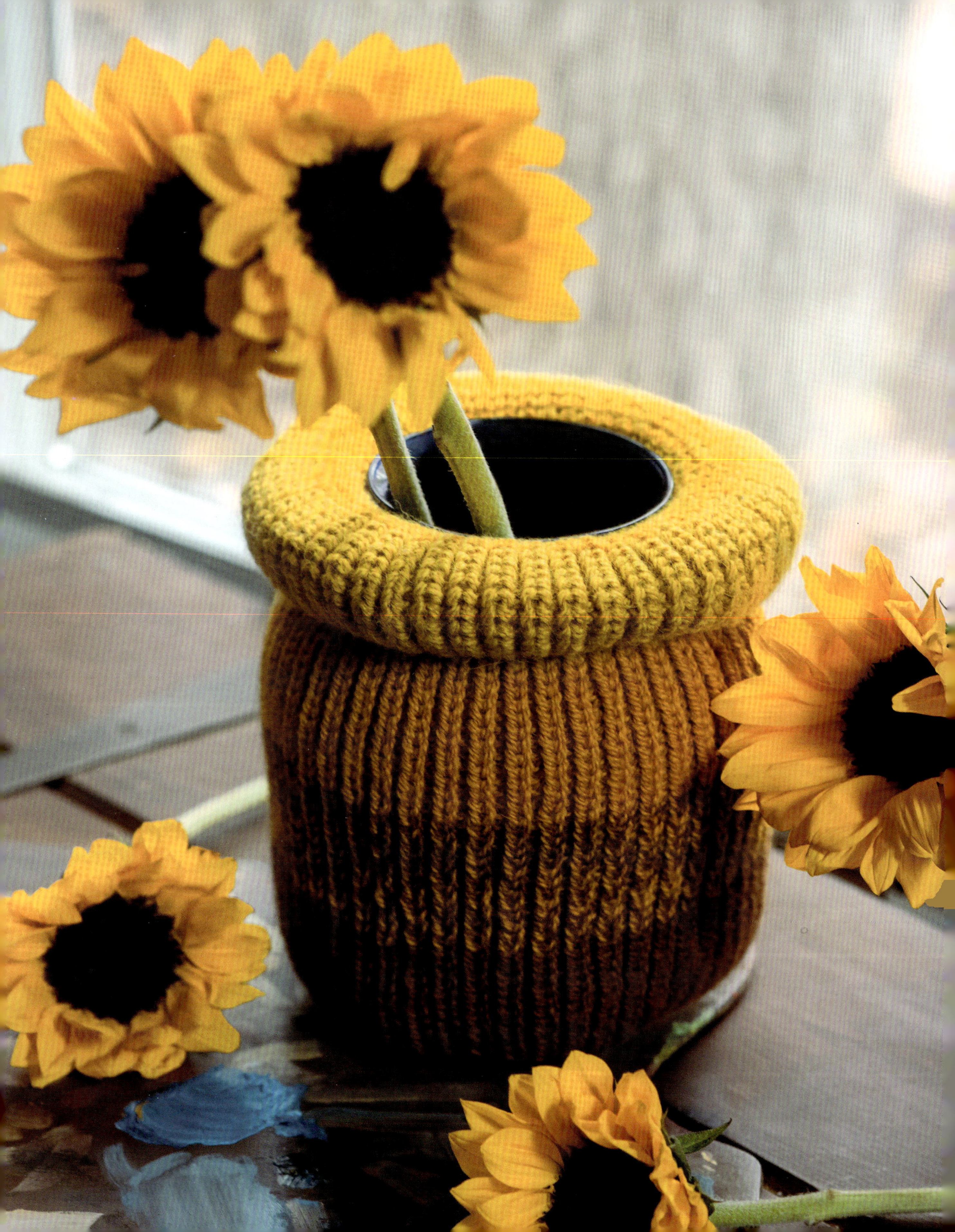

SKILL LEVEL 1

VASE COZY

Inspired by *Sunflowers*

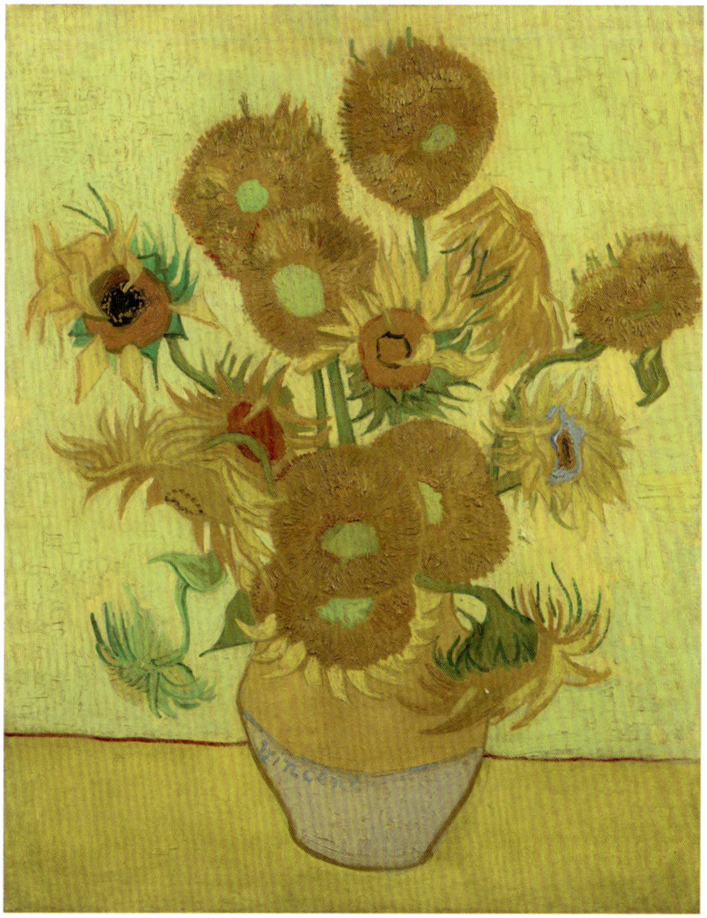

The still-life paintings of sunflowers that van Gogh painted have always been among my favorites. The effortlessness of his color palette allows a feeling of motion in a subject as simple as a vase full of sunflowers. I wanted to design a vase cozy that would brighten up any room and complement the beautiful flowers it holds. I pulled in the various shades of yellow we see in the flowers, vase, and background of this painting. I also pulled in deep, warm oranges and shades of brown to bring it all together. This cozy fits snugly onto a standard vase and can be folded down to accommodate a smaller one.

For more information on van Gogh's *Sunflowers*, see p. 139.

SIZES

One size

FINISHED MEASUREMENTS

Vase cozy is designed to fit around a vase that measures 22 in. / 56 cm at its widest circumference and 8.5 in. / 22 cm tall. Due to the stretchiness of this fabric, the circumference of your vase can vary by plus or minus 2 in. / 5 cm.

YARN

The Fibre Co. "Amble": 70% Easy-wash Merino wool; 20% Easy-wash Alpaca; 10% recycled Nylon; Fingering (100 g / 355 yd. / 325 m)

- **C1**: Catbells – 1 skein
- **C2**: Yellow Earl – 1 skein
- **C3**: Daffodil – 1 skein

NEEDLES

- US size 5 / 3.75 mm, 16 in. / 40 cm long circular knitting needles and set of double pointed needles (DPNs)
- US size 7 / 4.5 mm, 16 in. / 40 cm long circular knitting needles

Or size needed to obtain gauge

NOTIONS

- Scissors
- Stitch marker
- Tapestry needle for weaving in ends

GAUGE

22 stitches and 28 rows = 4 in. / 10 cm in stockinette stitch with two strands held together on smaller needles without blocking

NOTES

- Rather than dividing your skein into two halves, wind the yarn into a "cake" or a center pull ball that allows you to pull yarn from the inside and outside simultaneously. This allows you to work with two strands of one color at the same time without having to divide your skeins.

KNITTING INSTRUCTIONS

Using two strands of C1 held together and DPNs, CO 6 sts. Join to work in the round. Place sm to note bor.

Rnd 1: Knit.
Rnd 2: *kf&b* around—12 sts.
Rnd 3: Knit.
Rnd 4: *K1, M1L* around—24 sts.
Rnds 5–7: Knit.
Rnd 8: *K1, M1L* around—48 sts.
Rnds 9–14: Knit.
Rnd 15: *K2, M1L* around—72 sts.
Rnds 16–23: Knit.
Rnd 24: *K3, M1L* around—96 sts.

Change to smaller 16 in. / 40 cm circular needles.

Rnd 25: Knit.

Rnd 26: *K1, P1* around.
Rnd 27: *K1b, P1* around.

Rep Rnds 26–27 eleven *more* times.

Cut one strand of C1 and join one strand of C2.

Using one strand of C1 and one strand of C2, work Rnds 26 – 27 a total of 12 times.

Cut remaining strand of C1 and join second strand of C2.

Using two strands of C2, work Rnds 26–27 a total of 12 times.

Cut one strand of C2 and join one strand of C3.

Using one strand of C2 and one strand of C3, work Rnds 26–27 a total of 12 times.

Cut remaining strand of C2 and join second strand of C3.

Using two strands of C3, work Rnds 26–27 a total of 12 times.

Bind off all sts.

Using larger needles and one strand of C1, C2, and C3 all held together, work i-cord as follows:

CO 3 sts, do not turn.

Push sts to other end of the needle, K3, do not turn.

Repeat between * * until i-cord is long enough to wrap around your vase desired number of times.

Last Row: K3togtbl. Cut yarn leaving a tail to weave in later. Pull yarn through remaining loop and cinch closed (see p. 133).

FINISHING

Weave in all ends (see p. 133).

Fold top of piece down and wrap i-cord around vase. Finish off with a lightly tied square knot.

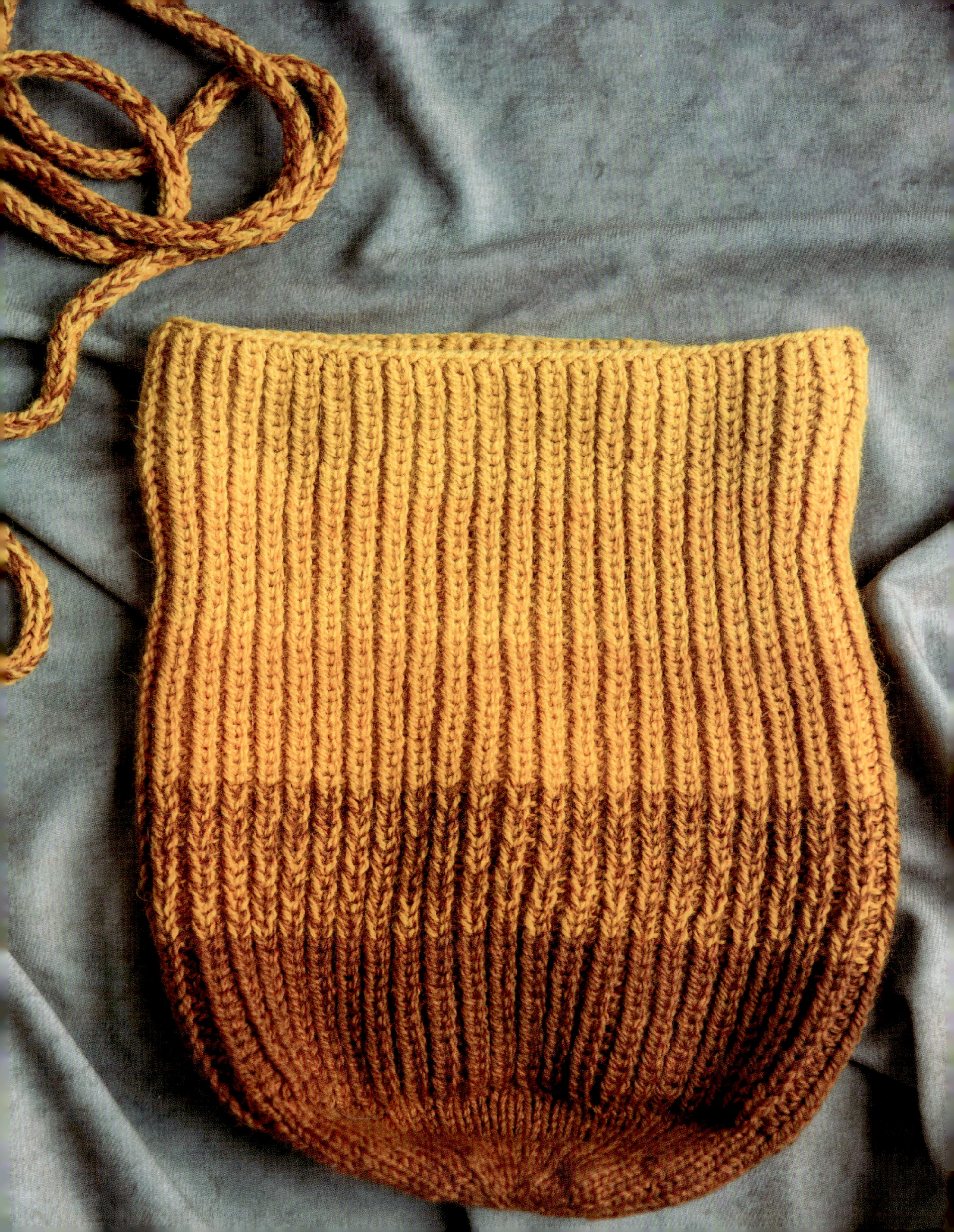

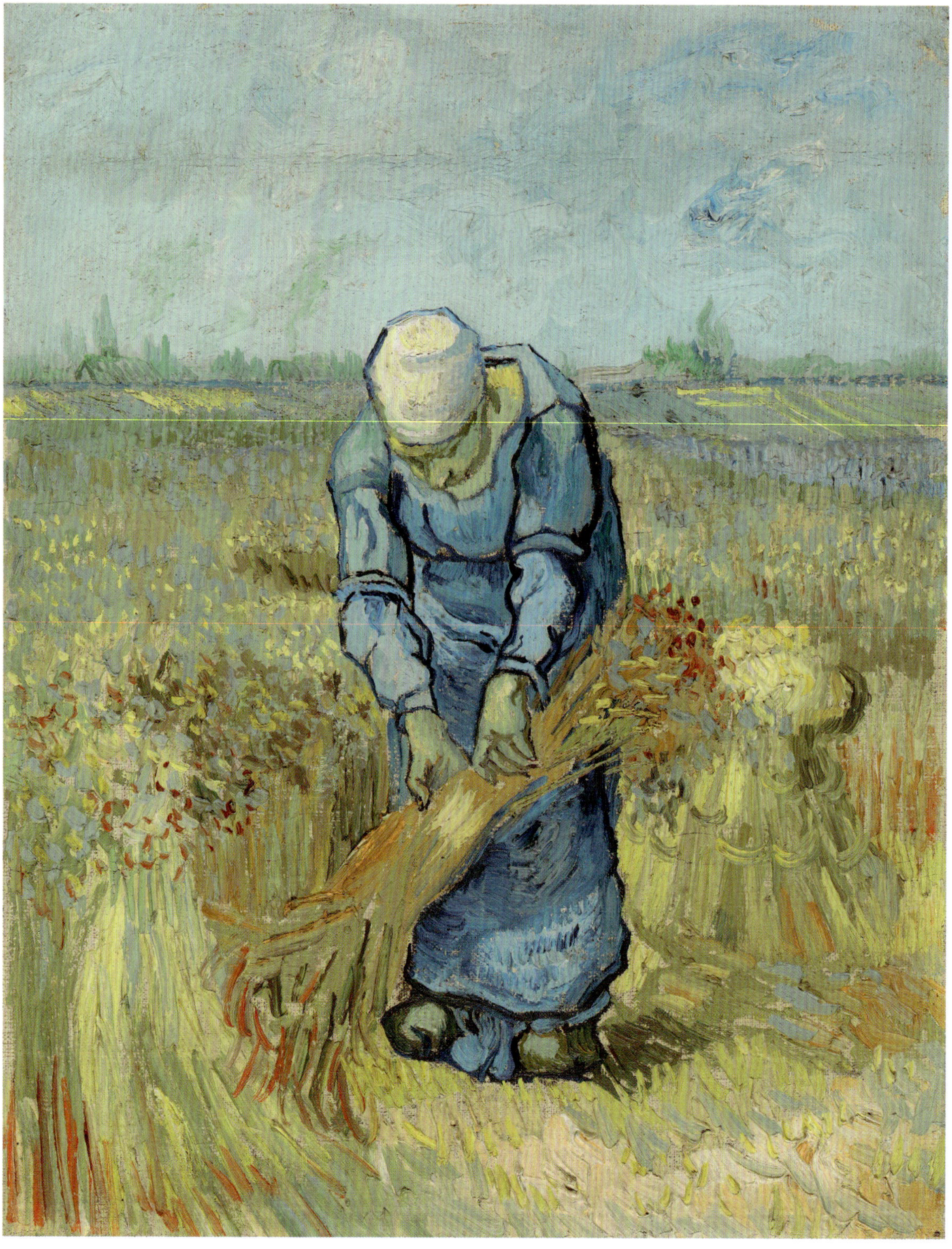

Peasant Woman Binding Sheaves (after Millet) (p. 27)

"I'M CONCERNED WITH THE WORLD ONLY IN THAT I HAVE A CERTAIN *OBLIGATION* AND *DUTY*, AS IT WERE—BECAUSE I'VE WALKED THE EARTH FOR 30 YEARS—TO LEAVE A CERTAIN SOUVENIR IN THE FORM OF DRAWINGS OR PAINTINGS IN GRATITUDE."

—Vincent van Gogh to his brother Theo,
August 7, 1883

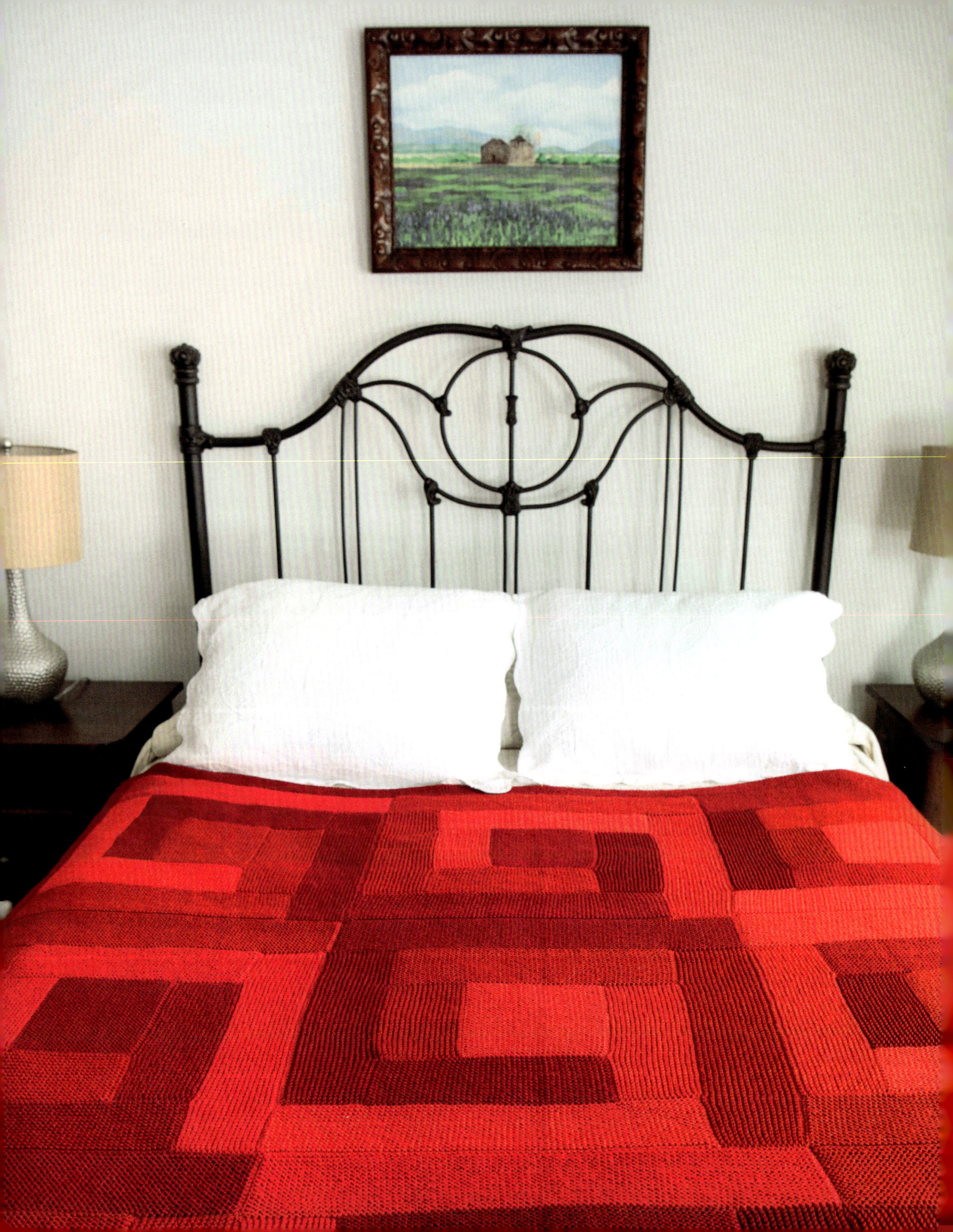

VINCENT'S BLANKET

Inspired by *The Bedroom*

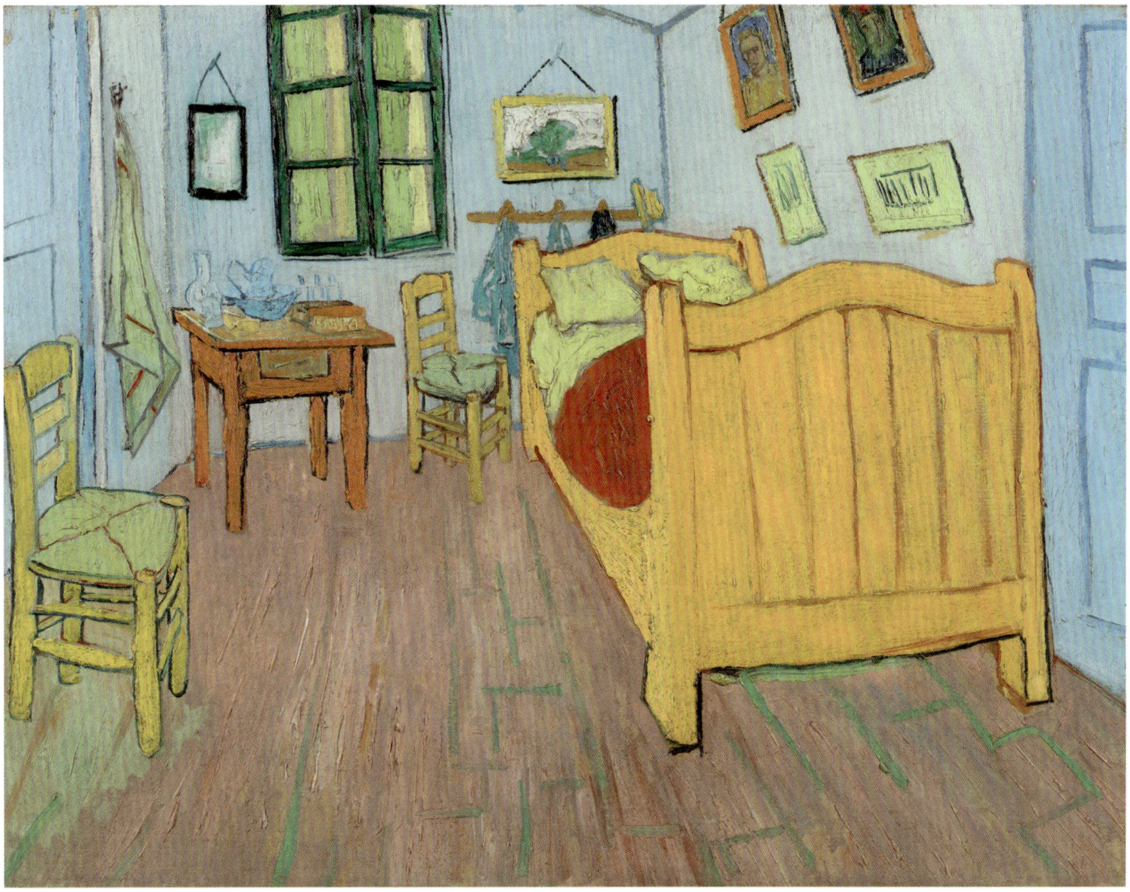

I like to think this three-by-three square blanket was pulled directly off the bed featured in this painting. This scene was van Gogh's room that he furnished and made his own during his time in Arles. Though you only see a small bit of the blanket or quilt, the vibrant red pulled my focus. I wondered what texture and pattern the actual blanket was and created my best guess. I chose the repetitive log cabin pattern for this because everything we see in this painting is blocky, rigid, and square, from the windowpane to the floorboards to the framed art on the wall, which is said to be van Gogh's work. A van Gogh within a van Gogh, if you will.

For more information on van Gogh's *The Bedroom*, see p. 138.

SIZES
One size

FINISHED MEASUREMENTS
Approximately 60 in. / 152 cm wide and 60 in. / 152 cm long

YARN
Cascade Yarns "220 Superwash" 100% Superwash Wool; DK / Light Worsted (100 g / 220 yd. / 200 m)

C1: #809 Really Red – 6 balls
C2: #1922 Christmas Red Heather – 6 balls
C3: #893 Ruby – 8 balls

NEEDLES
- US size 7 / 4.5 mm, 24 in. / 60 cm long circular knitting needles
- US size 7 / 4.5 mm, 40 in. / 100 cm long circular knitting needles

Or size needed to obtain gauge

NOTIONS
- Scissors
- Tapestry needle for weaving in ends

GAUGE
20 stitches and 40 rows = 4 in. / 10 cm in garter stitch

NOTES
- A total of nine large blocks will be knit separately, using the shorter needles for each one, and then seamed together at the end. The border will be knit using longer needles once all pieces have been seamed together.

KNITTING INSTRUCTIONS

All blocks are knit the same, but the color order changes.

Three A blocks are knit in this sequence: C1 (Section 1), C2 (Section 2), C3 (Section 3), C1 (Section 4), C2 (Section 5), C3 (Section 6), C1 (Section 7), C2 (Section 8), C3 (Section 9).

Three B blocks are knit in this sequence: C2 (Section 1), C3 (Section 2), C1 (Section 3), C2 (Section 4), C3 (Section 5), C1 (Section 6), C2 (Section 7), C3 (Section 8), C1 (Section 9) .

Three C blocks are knit in this sequence: C3 (Section 1), C1 (Section 2), C2 (Section 3), C3 (Section 4), C1 (Section 5), C2 (Section 6), C3 (Section 7), C1 (Section 8), C2 (Section 9) .

Entire border is worked using C3.

SECTION 1

Using shorter needles, CO 30 sts.

Row 1: Sl1, K to last st, P1.

Work Row 1 a total of 61 times (31 garter bumps).

Bind off all sts. Cut yarn.

SECTION 2

Rotate piece 90 degrees clockwise and using next color, pick up and knit 31 sts along the edge of Section 1.

Work Row 1 a total of 31 times—16 garter bumps.

Bind off all sts. Cut yarn.

SECTION 3

Rotate piece 90 degrees clockwise and using next color, pick up and knit 46 sts along the edge of Section 2 and the cast on edge of Section 1.

Work Row 1 a total of 31 times—16 garter bumps.

Bind off all sts. Cut yarn.

SECTION 4

Rotate piece 90 degrees clockwise and using next color, pick up and knit 46 sts along the edges of Sections 3 and 1.

Work Row 1 a total of 31 times—16 garter bumps.

Bind off all sts. Cut yarn.

SECTION 5

Rotate piece 90 degrees clockwise and using next color, pick up and knit 62 sts along the edge of Section 4, the bind off edge of Section 1 and the edge of Section 2.

Work Row 1 a total of 31 times—16 garter bumps.

Bind off all sts. Cut yarn.

(Pattern continues on p. 101)

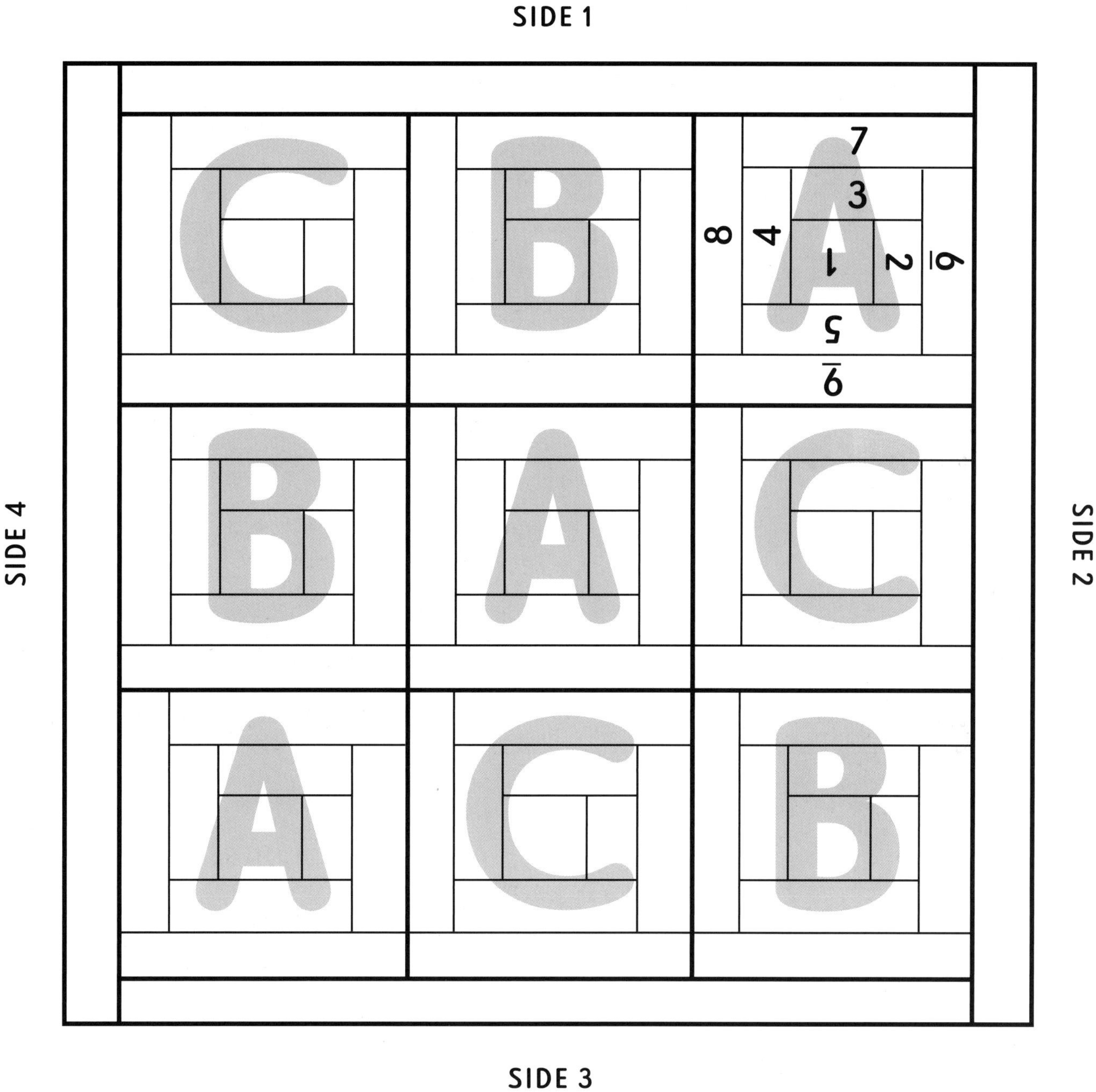
SIDE 1
SIDE 2
SIDE 3
SIDE 4
7
3
8
4
1
2
9
5
9

SECTION 6

Rotate piece 90 degrees clockwise and using next color, pick up and knit 62 sts along the edge of Section 5 and the bind off edge of Section 2.

Work Row 1 a total of 31 times—16 garter bumps.

Bind off all sts. Cut yarn.

SECTION 7

Rotate piece 90 degrees clockwise and using next color, pick up and knit 78 sts along the edge of Section 6, the bind off edge of Section 3 and the edge of Section 4.

Work Row 1 a total of 31 times—16 garter bumps.

Bind off all sts. Cut yarn.

SECTION 8

Rotate piece 90 degrees clockwise and using next color, pick up and knit 78 sts along the edge of Section 7, the bind off edge of Section 4 and the edge of Section 5.

Work Row 1 a total of times—16 garter bumps.

Bind off all sts. Cut yarn.

SECTION 9

Rotate piece 90 degrees clockwise and using next color, pick up and knit 94 sts along the edge of Section 8, the bind off edge of Section 5 and the edge of Section 6.

Work Row 1 a total of 31 times—16 garter bumps.

Bind off all sts. Cut yarn.

SEAMING

Seam all blocks together using mattress stitch (see p. 136) according to the chart on p. 99.

BORDER

Using C3 and longer needles, pick up and knit 282 sts along edge of Side 1.

Row 1: Sl1, K to last st, P1.

Work Row 1 a total of 15 times—8 garter bumps.

Bind off all sts. Cut yarn.

Using C3 and longer needles, pick up and knit 282 sts along edge of Side 3.

Row 1: Sl1, K to last st, P1.

Work Row 1 a total of 15 times—8 garter bumps.

Bind off all sts. Cut yarn.

Using C3 and longer needles, pick up and knit 298 sts along edge of Side 2 (this will include the edges of Sides 3 and 1).

Row 1: Sl1, K to last st, P1.

Work Row 1 a total of 15 times—8 garter bumps.

Bind off all sts. Cut yarn.

Using C3 and longer needles, pick up and knit 298 sts along edge of Side 4 (this will include the edges of Sides 1 and 3).

Row 1: Sl1, K to last st, P1.

Work Row 1 a total of 15 times—8 garter bumps.

Bind off all sts.

FINISHING

Weave in all tails (see p. 133).

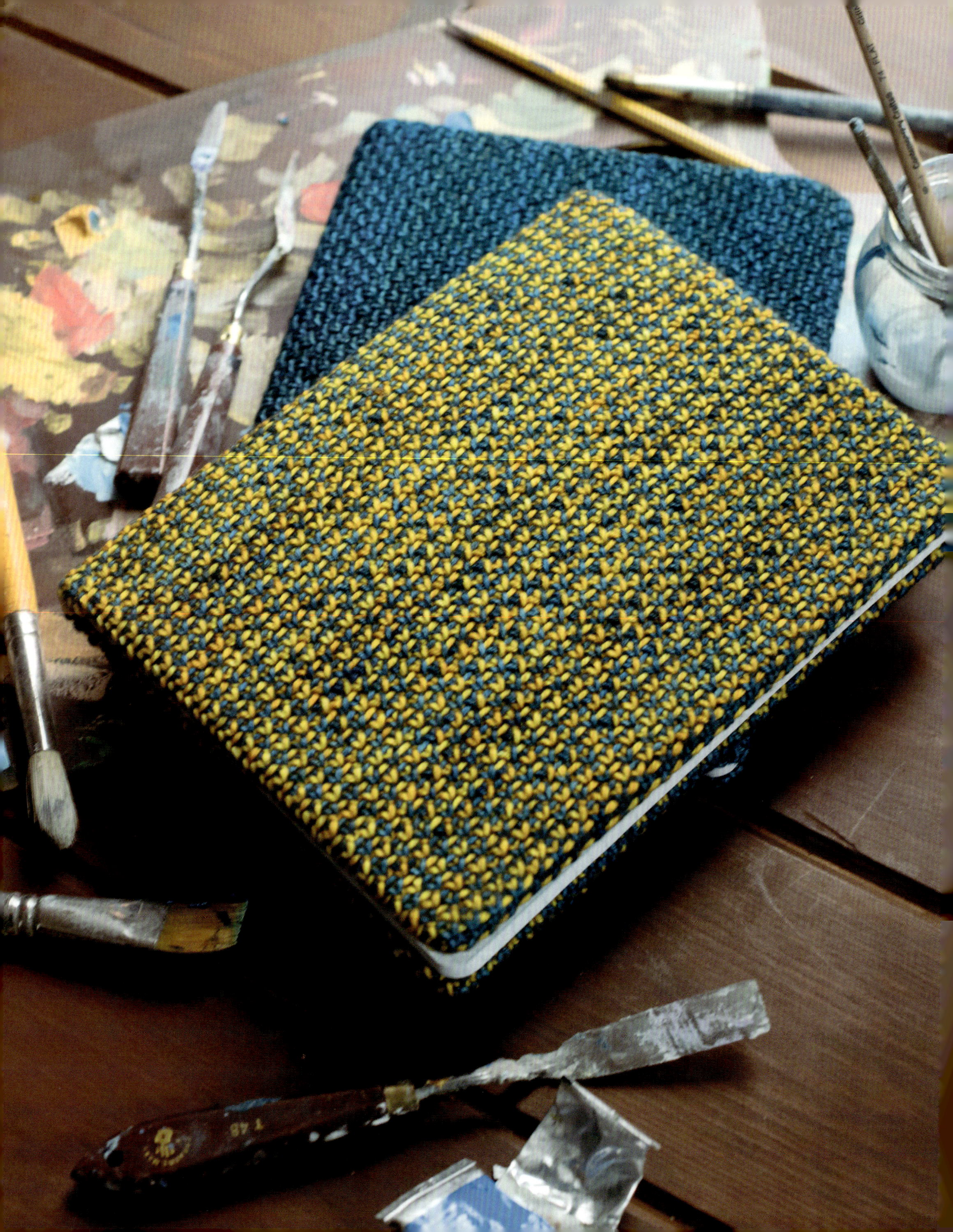

ART JOURNAL COVER

Inspired by *Self-Portrait with Straw Hat*

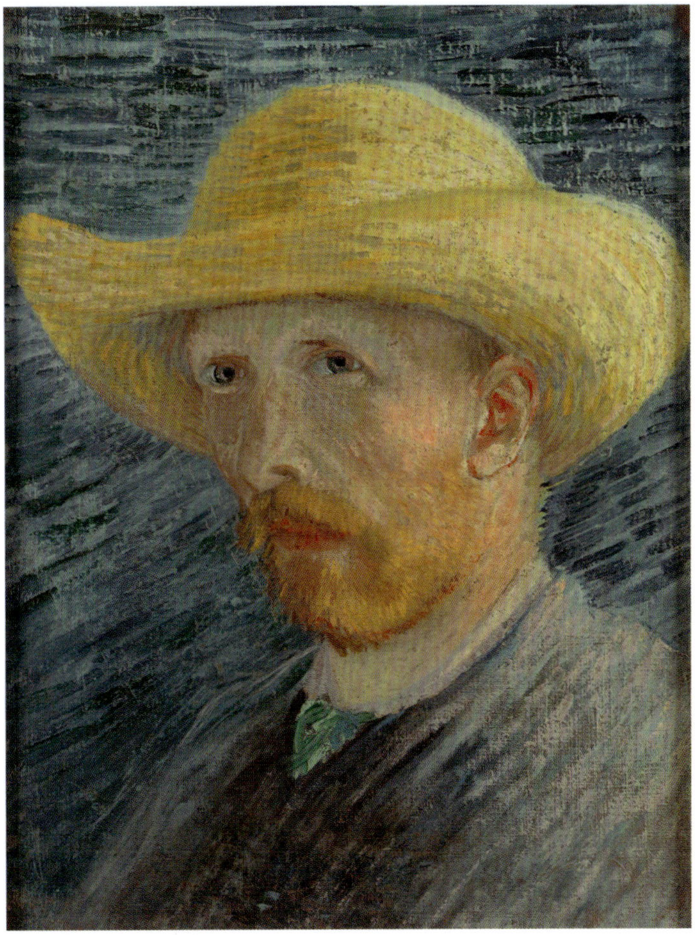

Pulling more deep blues and vibrant yellows from another of van Gogh's self-portraits, this journal cover is soft and can easily distinguish your personal journal from just any other notebook. Van Gogh was as prolific at journaling and letter writing as he was at painting. He was passionate about sharing his ideas and feelings with friends and family. I designed this journal cover so that you could have colorful and stylish journals that match your personality. This would be a safe place to write down your deepest thoughts, dreams, or even inspirations for new knitting sketches.

For more information on van Gogh's *Self-Portrait with Straw Hat*, see p. 139.

SIZES
One size

FINISHED FIT
Designed to fit an 8 in. / 20.5 cm width by 10 in. / 25.5 cm tall composition book

YARN
Madelinetosh "Tosh Vintage"
100% Superwash Merino Wool; Worsted (115 g / 200 yd. / 182 m)

C1: Cousteau – 1 skein

C2: Candlewick – 1 skein

You will need 2 full skeins of yarn for this project. If you want a single-colored journal cover, you will need 2 skeins of your selected color. If you want a two-colored journal cover, you will need 1 skein each of two different colors.

NEEDLES
- (2) US size 3 / 3.25 mm, 16 in. / 40 cm long circular knitting needles

Or size needed to obtain gauge

NOTIONS
- Locking stitch marker
- Scissors
- Stitch marker
- Tapestry needle for weaving in ends

GAUGE
- 25 stitches and 34 rows = 4 in. / 10 cm in stockinette stitch
- 22 sts and 32 rows = 4 in. / 10 cm in slip stitch pattern

NOTES
- The fabric for this project is knit tightly. You will be using a needle much smaller than the yarn suggests.
- Slip all stitches wyif unless otherwise noted.
- This pattern is written to be worked in the round using the 2 Circulars method. You can use the Magic Loop method if preferred.
- The journal cover can be made using one color or two colors. The pattern is written using two colors (C1 and C2). If you want a single-colored journal cover, ignore the color changes and work the entire piece in C1.

KNITTING INSTRUCTIONS
Using figure 8 cast on (see p. 130) and C1, CO 110 sts (55 sts on each needle). Place locking sm on fabric to note bor.

Setup Rnd (C1): Ktbl 55 sts on back needle, drop slipknot off back needle, ktfl 55 sts on second needle.

The pattern will now be worked contiguously across both needles.

Rnd 1 (C2): *K1, sl1* around.
Rnd 2 (C2): Knit.
Rnd 3 (C1): *Sl1, K1* around.
Rnd 4 (C1): Knit.

Rep Rnds 1–4 nineteen *more* times. When you have enough fabric to be able to knit in the round on one circular needle, you can switch to working with a single circular needle if desired. Be sure to place a sm to note your bor.

Work Rnd 1 one *more* time with C2.

Rnd 82 (C2): K3, *K1, P1* over next 48 sts, K to end.
Rnd 83 (C1): *Sl1, K1* 2 times, *P1, K1* over next 48 sts, *sl1, K1* to end.
Rnd 84 (C1): K4, *P1, K1* over next 48 sts, K to end.
Rnd 85 (C2): K1, sl1, K2, *P1, K1* over next 48 sts, *K1, sl1* to end.
Rnd 86 (C2): K4, *P1, K1* over next 48 sts, K to end.
Rnd 87 (C1): *Sl1, K1* 2 times, *P1, K1* over next 48 sts, *sl1, K1* to end.
Rnd 88 (C1): K3, BO 49 sts, K to end of rnd, slm, with C2, K1, sl1, P1, turn.

You will now be working back and forth, flat, over 61 sts. Keep your bor sm where it is and slip it as indicated.

ROWS FOR OPENING
Row 1 (WS, C2): Wyib sl1, P2, slm, *wyib sl1, P1* to end.
Row 2 (RS, C2): Wyib sl1, K to sm, slm. With C1: sl1, K1, P1.
Row 3 (C1): Wyib sl1, P2, slm, *P1, wyib sl1* to last 2 sts, P2.
Row 4 (C1): Wyib sl1, K to sm, slm. With C2: K1, sl1, P1.
Row 5 (C2): Wyib sl1, P2, slm, *wyib sl1, P1* to end.
Row 6 (C2): Wyib sl1, K to sm, slm, do not turn.

Next Row (RS, C1): Sl1, K1, sl1, CO 49 sts using knitted cast on (See p. 131). Do not turn. Join to work in the round being careful that there are no twists in your cast on sts. K1, *K1, sl1* to 1 st before sm, K1–110 sts.

SECOND HALF

Rnd 1 (C1): K3, *K1, P1* over next 48 sts, K to end.

Rnd 2 (C2): K1, sl1, K1, *K1, P1* over next 48 sts, K1, *K1, sl1* to end.

Rnd 3 (C2): K3, *K1, P1* over next 48 sts, K to end.

Rnd 4 (C1): Sl1, K1, sl1, *K1, P1* over next 48 sts, *K1, sl1* to last st, K1.

Rnd 5 (C1): K3 *K1, P1* over next 48 sts, K to end.

Rnd 6 (C2): K1, sl1, K1, *K1, P1* over next 48 sts, K1, *K1, sl1* to end.

Rnd 7 (C2): Knit.

Rnd 8 (C1): *Sl1, K1* around.

Rnd 9 (C1): Knit.

Rnd 10 (C2): *K1, sl1 * around.

Rep Rnds 7–10 nineteen *more* times.

Work Rnds 7–8 one *more* time.

Cut C2.

Bring second circular needle back in. Slip 55 sts onto second needle. Kitchener stitch bind off (see p. 132) with C1.

FINISHING

Weave all your tails in carefully (see p. 133).

Carefully put covers of your composition book journal into the sleeve. If book pops open a little, very lightly spray the outside seam of fabric with water (don't get your paper wet). Lay on a flat surface and place a couple of books on top and let dry overnight.

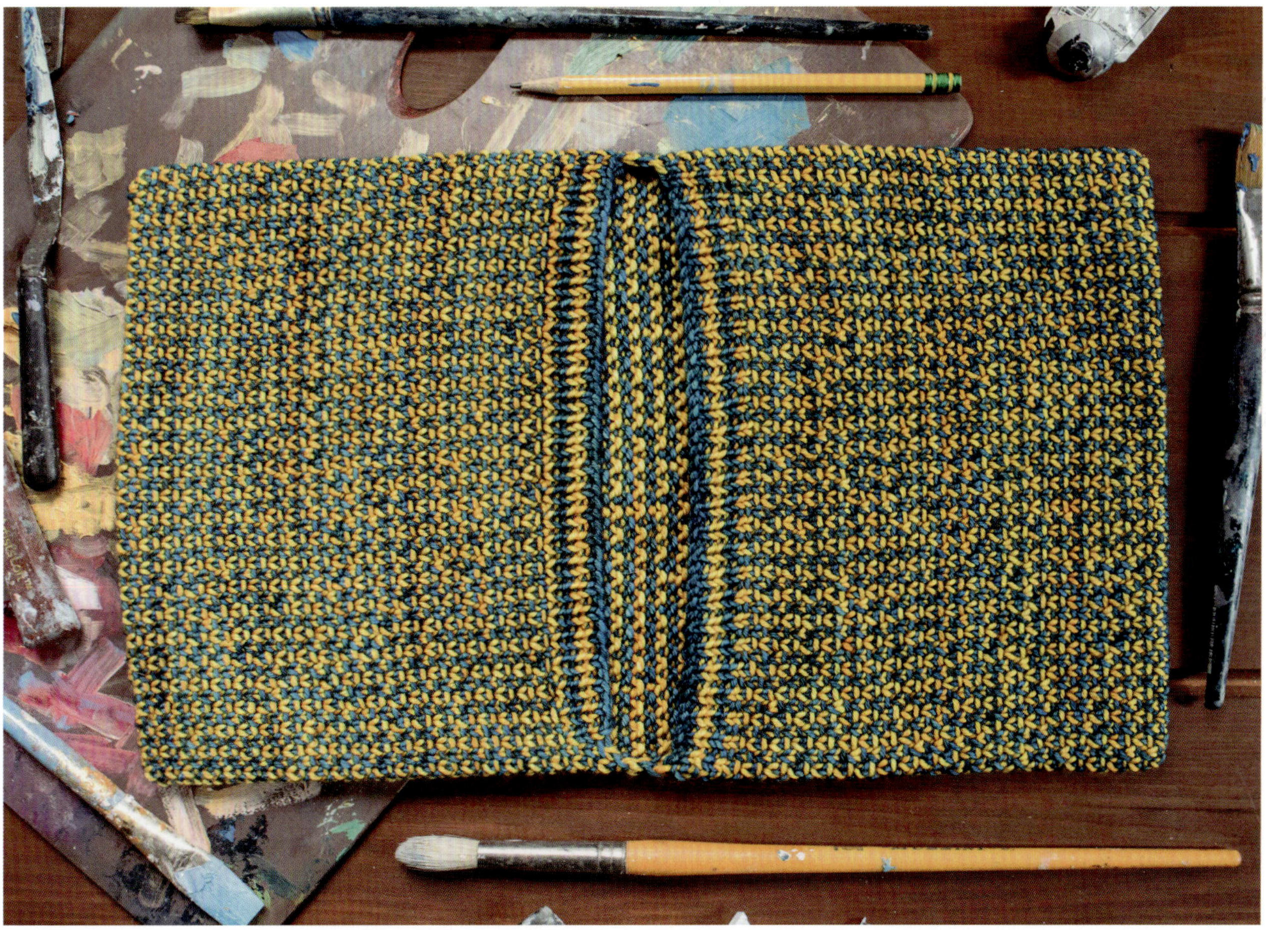

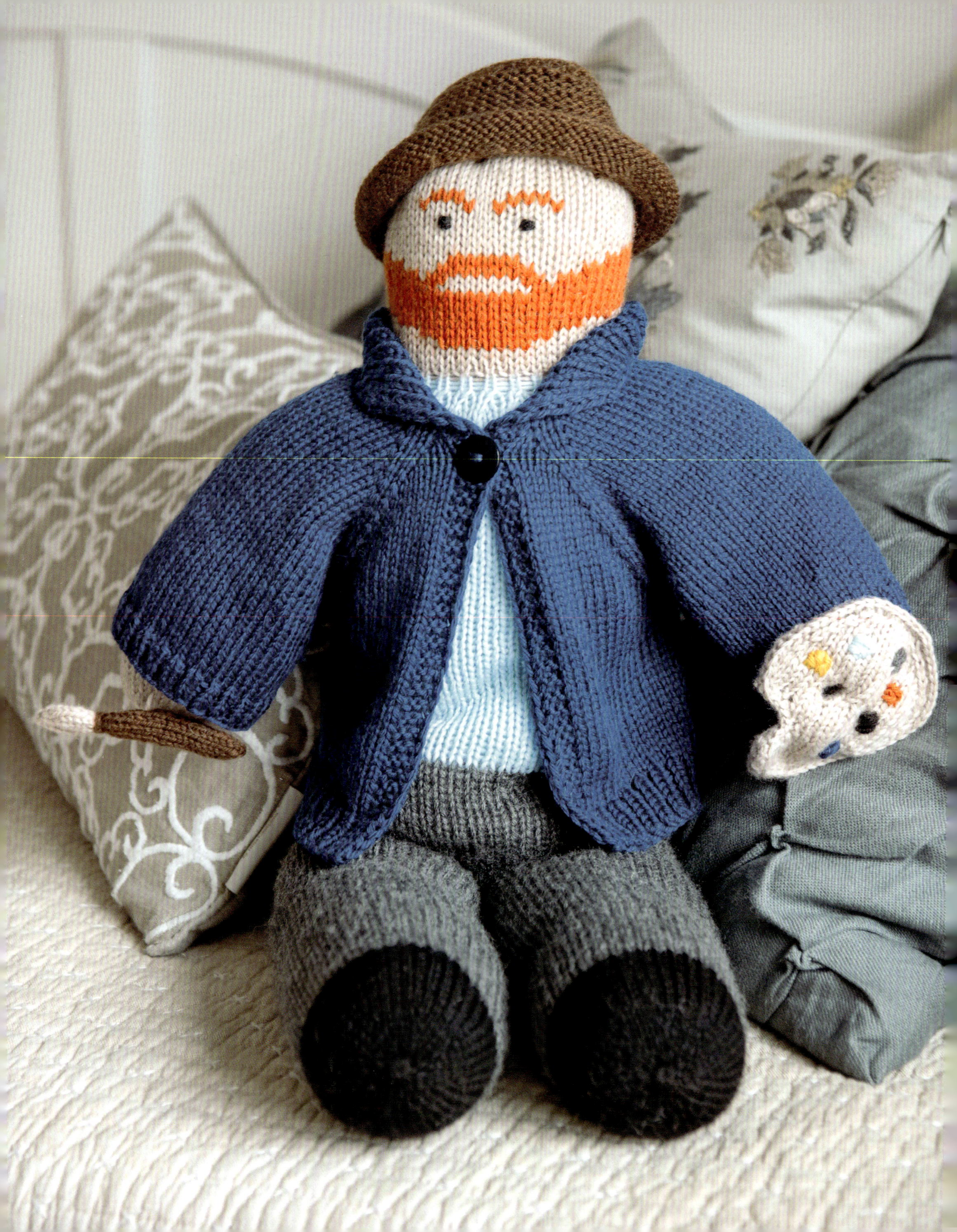

SKILL LEVEL 3

VAN GOGH DOLL

Inspired by *Self-Portrait as a Painter*

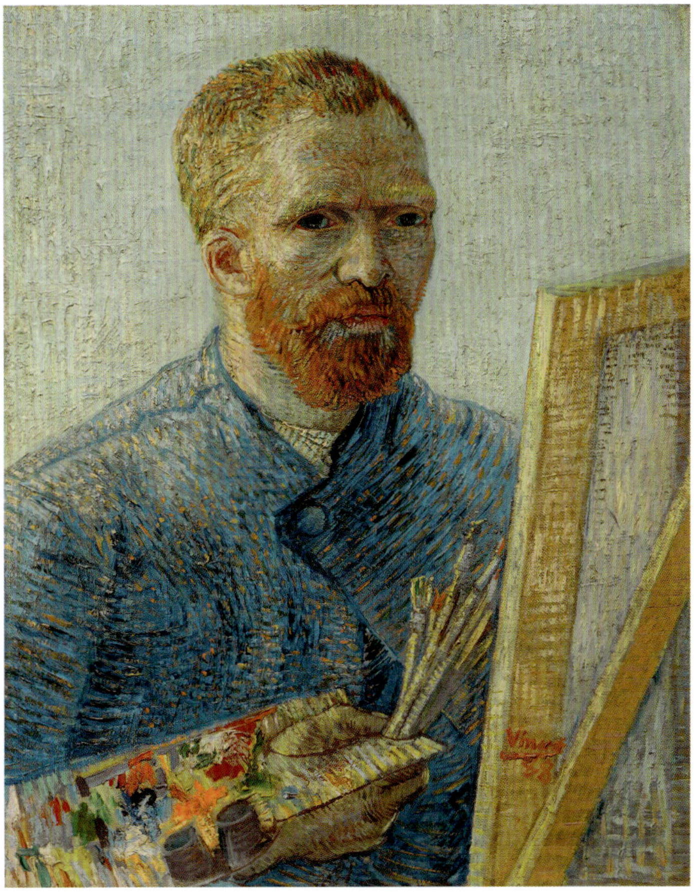

This self-portrait was the very last work van Gogh produced during his time in Paris. He intensified certain features in the painting, like his red beard. He also featured more prominent wrinkles along his forehead and the corners of his mouth to signify the age and stress he had from his time in Paris. This adorable doll is my rendition of van Gogh, the painter. The doll is dressed in van Gogh's signature blue smock, has his vibrant red hair, and holds on to a simple painter's palette and brush. This more playful design can be a great collectible item for yourself or a loved one, or a toy for a little one in your life.

For more information on van Gogh's *Self-Portrait as a Painter*, see p. 139.

SIZES

One size

FINISHED MEASUREMENTS

22 in. / 56 cm tall

YARN

Knit Picks "Swish DK" 100% Fine Superwash Merino Wool; DK (50 g / 123 yd / 112 m)

- C1: Nutmeg Heather – 1 ball
- C2: Arctic – 2 balls
- C3: Black – 1 ball
- C4: Cobblestone Heather – 1 ball
- C5: Dusk – 2 balls
- C6: Pinecone Heather – 1 ball
- C7: Allspice – 1 ball

NEEDLES

- US size 5 / 3.75 mm, 16 in. / 40 cm long circular knitting needles
- US size 5 / 3.75 mm double pointed needles (DPNs)

Or size needed to obtain gauge

NOTIONS

- Scissors
- Stitch marker
- Tapestry needle
- Fiberfill
- 1¾ in. / 19 mm button
- Sewing needle and thread (optional)
- Scrap yarn
- Blunt tapestry needle for duplicate stitching

GAUGE

20 stitches and 28 rows = 4 in. / 10 cm in stockinette stitch

NOTES

- The arms and legs are worked separately in the round. They are joined almost seamlessly to the body, with minimal sewing needed to close small gaps. The head is worked seamlessly onto the body.
- The face details are added using duplicate stitch.
- The hat, jacket, paintbrush, and palette are worked separately and attached to the completed doll.
- Use a spare DPN to push fiberfill into the extremities of the body.
- If the holes on the button are large enough to accommodate a tapestry needle and project yarn, use those to attach. If the holes are too small, a sewing needle and thread may be used.
- Change from DPNs to circular needles and back to DPNs when needed.

KNITTING INSTRUCTIONS

LEFT ARM

Using C1 and DPNs, CO 8 sts. Join to work in the rnd being careful not to twist. Place sm to note bor.

Rnds 1–2: Knit.
Rnd 3: *K1, M1L* around—16 sts.
Rnd 4: Knit.
Rnd 5: *K2, M1L* around—24 sts.
Rnd 6: Knit.
Rnd 7: *K3, M1L* around—32 sts.
Rnds 8–12: Knit.

Cut C1, join C2.

Knit 30 rnds.

**

Next Rnd: K22, BO 4 sts, K to end of rnd—28 sts .
Next Rnd: K22. Cut yarn leaving a 12" / 30.5 cm tail.

Place all live sts onto scrap yarn. Set Left Arm aside for now.

RIGHT ARM

Work as for Left Arm to **.

Next Rnd: K6, BO 4 sts, K to end of rnd—28 sts.
Next Rnd: K6. Cut yarn leaving a 12 in. / 30.5 cm tail.

Place all live sts onto scrap yarn. Set Right Arm aside for now.

LEFT LEG

Using C3 and DPNs, CO 8 sts. Join to work in the rnd being careful not to twist. Place sm to note bor.

Rnds 1 – 2: Knit.
Rnd 3: *K1, M1L* around—16 sts.
Rnd 4: Knit.
Rnd 5: *K2, M1L* around—24 sts.
Rnd 6: Knit.
Rnd 7: *K3, M1L* around—32 sts.
Rnd 8: Knit.
Rnd 9: *K4, M1L* around—40 sts.
Rnds 10—17: Knit.

Cut C3, join C4.

Knit 50 rnds.

***

Next Rnd: K27, BO 6 sts, K to end of rnd—34 sts.
Next Rnd: K27. Cut yarn leaving a 12 in. / 30.5 cm tail.

Place all live sts onto scrap yarn. Set Left Leg aside for now.

RIGHT LEG

Work same as for Left Leg up to the ***.

Next Rnd: K7, BO 6 sts, K to end of rnd—34 sts. Remove sm and turn work.
Next Row (WS): P34. Turn work.

JOIN LEGS

K34 across Right Leg. Place sm to note bor. Place Left Leg sts onto needles. Holding both legs so that the bound off stitches are facing each other, knit across 34 sts of Left Leg. You are now working around both legs to create the hips. K to end of rnd—68 sts.

HIPS

Knit 20 rnds.

BODY

Cut C4, join C2.

Knit 30 rnds.

Next Rnd: K15, BO 4 sts, K29, BO 4 sts, K29 (slip bor sm when you come to it)—60 sts.

Place Left Arm sts onto needles. Holding the arm so the bound off stitches are facing the bound off sts of the body, knit across 28 sts of the Left aArm, attaching it to the body.

Knit across 30 front of body sts.

Place Right Arm sts onto needles. Holding the arm so the bound off stitches are facing the bound off sts of the body, knit across 28 sts of the Right Arm, attaching it to the body.

Knit across remaining 15 sts on back. You are at your bor sm and arms are joined—116 sts.

Knit 15 rnds.

Next Rnd: *K2, K2tog*—87 sts.
Next Rnd: Knit.
Next Rnd: *K1, K2tog*—58 sts.
Next Rnd: Knit.
Next Rnd: *K2tog* around—29 sts.
Next 2 rnds: Knit.

Cut C2, join C1.

HEAD

Rnds 1-2: Knit.
Rnd 3: *K1, M1L* around—58 sts.

Knit 30 rnds.

At this point, sew up the holes at the BO edges at the underarms and between the legs. Weave in all your tails. Stuff your doll with fiberfill until it is a density of your liking.

Next Rnd: *K2tog* around—29 sts.
Next Rnd: Knit.
Next Rnd: *K2tog* to last st, K1—15 sts.
Next Rnd: Knit.

JACKET

Using C5, CO 67 sts.

Collar:
Row 1 (RS): Sl1, *K1, P1* to end.
Row 2 (WS): Sl1, *P1, K1* to last 2 sts, P2.

Rep Rows 1–2 five *more* times.
Work Row 1 one *more* time.

Next Row (WS): Sl1, P4, pm, *P19, pm* 3 times, P5.

Row 1 (RS): Sl1, *K to 1 st before sm, M1R, K1, slm, K1, M1L* 4 times, K to last st, P1—8 sts inc.
Row 2 (WS): Sl1, K3, P to last 4 sts, K3, P1.

Rep Rows 1–2 fifteen *more* times—195 sts.

Your stitch count should be: 21/51/51/51/21.

Next Row (RS): (Remove all sm when you get to them) sl1, K20, place next 51 sleeve sts onto scrap yarn, K51 across back, place next 51 sleeve sts onto scrap yarn, K20, P1—93 sts.

Next Row (WS): Sl1, K3, P to last 4 sts, K3, P1.
Next Row (RS): Sl1, K to last st, P1.

Rep last 2 rows nine *more* times.

Next Row (WS): Sl1, *P1, K1* to last 2 sts, P2.
Next Row (RS): Sl1, *K1, P1* to end.

Rep last 2 rows two *more* times.

Bind off in pattern.

Sleeves:
(work both alike)

Put 51 live sleeve sts onto needles.
With RS facing and using C5, knit across 51 sts. Pick up and knit 1 st at underarm—52 sts. Join to work in the rnd. Place sm to note bor.

Knit 16 rnds.

Next Rnd: *K1, P1* around.

Rep last rnd three *more* times.

Bind off in pattern.

(Pattern continues on next page)

HAT

Using C6, CO 5 sts.

Row 1 (RS): Sl1, K to last st, P1.
Row 2 (WS): Sl1, kf&b, K to last 2 sts, kf&b, P1—2 st inc.

Rep Rows 1–2 five *more* times—17 sts.

Row 13: Sl1, K to last st, P1.
Row 14: Sl1, K to last st, P1.

Rep Rows 13–14 nine *more* times.

Row 33: Sl1, K to last st, P1.
Row 34: Sl1, K2tog, K to last 3 sts, SSK, P1—2 sts dec.

Rep Rows 33–34 five *more* times—5 sts.

BODY OF HAT

Setup Rnd: Sl1, K4, rotating piece clockwise, pick up and knit 47 sts around piece. Place sm to note bor—52 sts.

Rnd 1: Purl.
Rnd 2: Knit.

Rep Rnds 1–2 eleven *more* times.

Rnd 25: *K2, M1L* around—78 sts.
Rnd 26: Knit.
Rnd 27: *K6, M1L* around—91 sts.
Knit 8 rnds.
Bind off.

FACE

Using the chart on p. 112 and C7, duplicate stitch beard, eyebrows, and hair onto the head of your doll. Using C3, duplicate stitch the eyes.

Whip stitch hat in place on top of doll's head.

PAINTBRUSH

Using C6 and DPNs, CO 4 sts. Join to work in the rnd being careful not to twist. Place sm to note bor.

Rnds 1–2: Knit.
Rnd 3: *K1, M1L* around—8 sts.
Knit 20 rnds.

Cut C6 leaving a 6 in. / 15 cm tail. Join C1.

Rnd 24: Knit.
Rnd 25: *K2, M1L* around—12 sts.
Knit 4 rnds.
Rnd 30: *K1, K2tog* around—8 sts.
Rnd 31: Knit.
Rnd 32: *K2tog* around—4 sts.
Rnd 33: Knit.

Weave tail through remaining live sts and cinch closed (see p. 133).

Using longer C6 tail, wrap around 3 times. Tie off.

PAINTERS PALETTE

Front:
Using C1, CO 3 sts.

Row 1 (and all WS Rows unless otherwise noted): Purl.
Row 2 (RS): K1, M1R, K to last st, M1L, K1—5 sts.
Row 4: *K1, M1R* twice, K1, *M1L, K1* twice—9 sts.
Row 6: *K1, M1R* twice, K5,

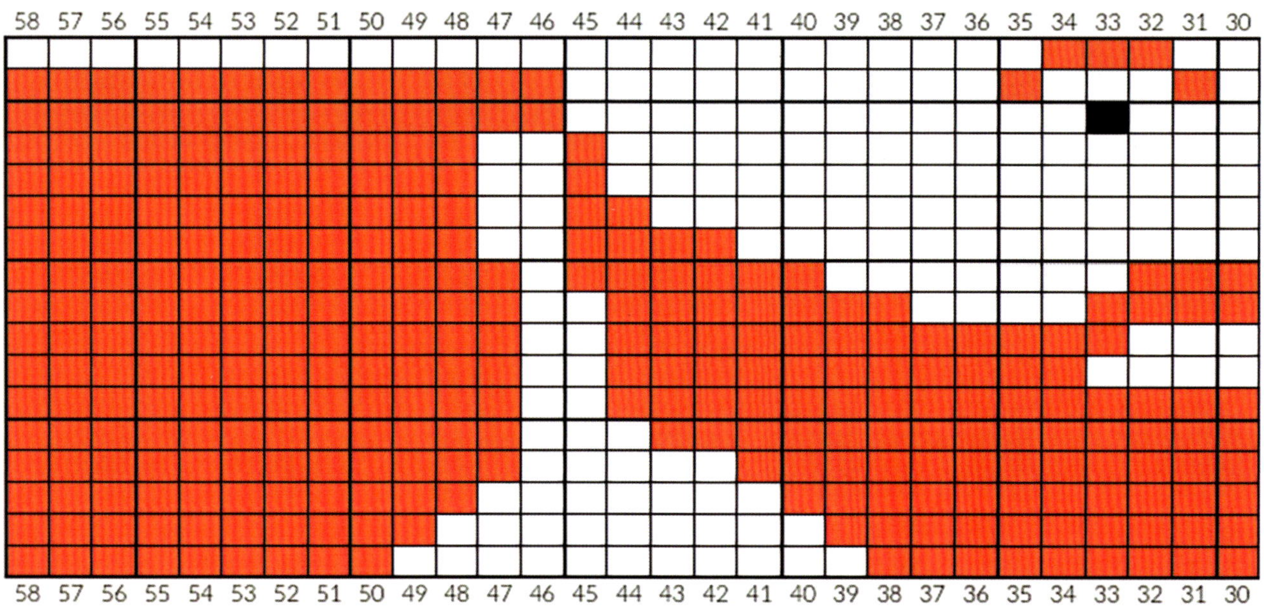

M1L, K1 twice—13 sts.
Row 8: K1, M1R, K11, M1L, K1—15 sts.
Row 10: Knit.
Row 11: BO 1 st, P3tog, pass 1 st on RH needle over st just made (binding off 1), P2tog, pass 1st st on RH needle over st just made, P to end—9 sts.
Row 12: *K1, M1R* twice, K to end—11 sts.
Row 14: K1, M1R, K to last st, M1L, K1, using backward loop cast on, CO 3 sts—16 sts.
Row 16: K to last st, M1L, K1—17 sts.
Row 18: K1, M1R, K7, K2tog, YO twice, SSK, K4, M1L, K1—19 sts.
Row 19: P8, P1tbl, P to end
Row 20: Knit.
Row 22: K1, SSK, K to last 3 sts, K2tog, K1—17 sts.
Row 24: K1, SSK, K to last 3 sts, K2tog, K1—15 sts.
Row 26: K1, SSK, K to last 3 sts, K2tog, K1—13 sts.
Row 28: K1, *SSK* twice, K3, *K2tog* twice, K1—9 sts.
Row 29: Purl.
Bind off.

Using scrap yarn colors, stitch blobs of paint onto front piece of painter's palette.

Back:
Work as for Front to the end of Row 10.

Row 11: Purl.
Row 12: BO 1 st, SSSK, pass 1 st on RH needle over at just made (binding off 1), SSK, pass 1st st on RH needle over st just made, K to end—9 sts.
Row 14: K to last 2 sts, *M1L, K1* twice—11 sts.
Row 15: P to end, using backward loop cast on, CO 3 sts—14 sts.
Row 16: K4, M1R, K to last st, M1L, K1—16 sts.
Row 18: K1, M1R, K to end—17 sts.
Row 20: K1, M1R, K4, K2tog, YO twice, SSK, K7, M1L, K1—19 sts.
Row 22: P11, P1tbl, P to end.
Row 23: Knit.
Row 22: K1, SSK, K to last 3 sts, K2tog, K1—17 sts.
Row 24: K1, SSK, K to last 3 sts, K2tog, K1—15 sts.
Row 26: K1, SSK, K to last 3 sts, K2tog, K1—13 sts.
Row 28: K1, *SSK* twice, K3, *K2tog* twice, K1—9 sts.
Row 29: Purl.

Bind off.

Place WS of Front and Back Palettes together. Using whip stitch and C1, stitch around palette to close up the sides and the thumbhole.

FINISHING

Put jacket on and sew button in place.

Weave in all remaining tails (see p. 133).

Attach paintbrush and painter's palette to hands.

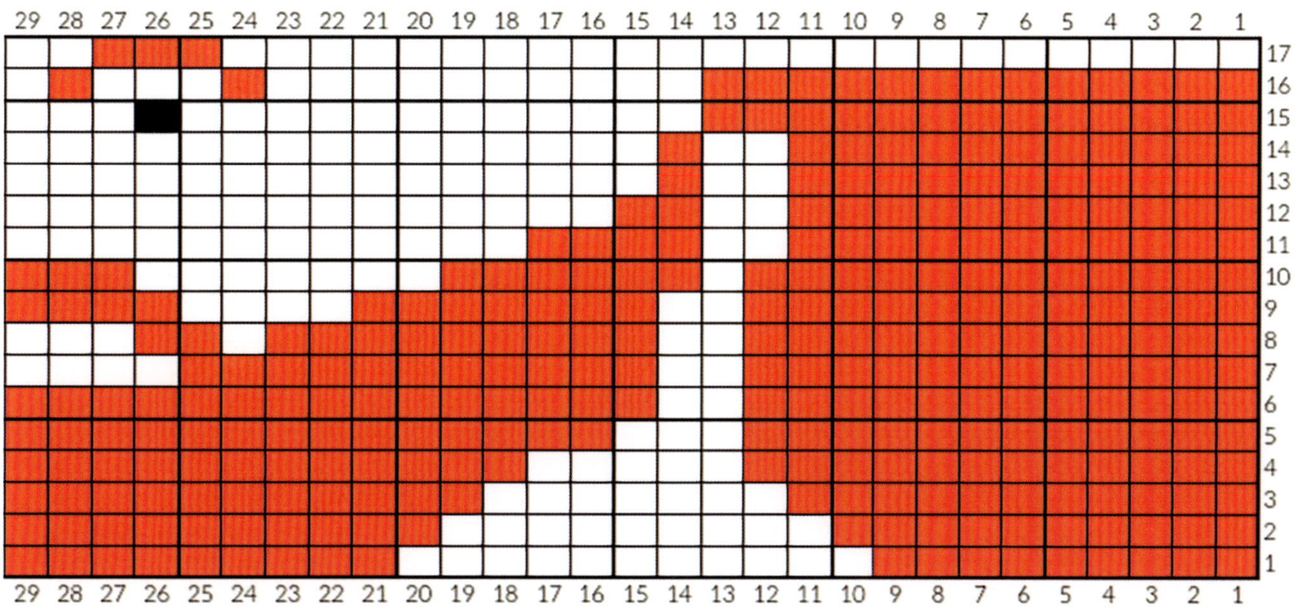

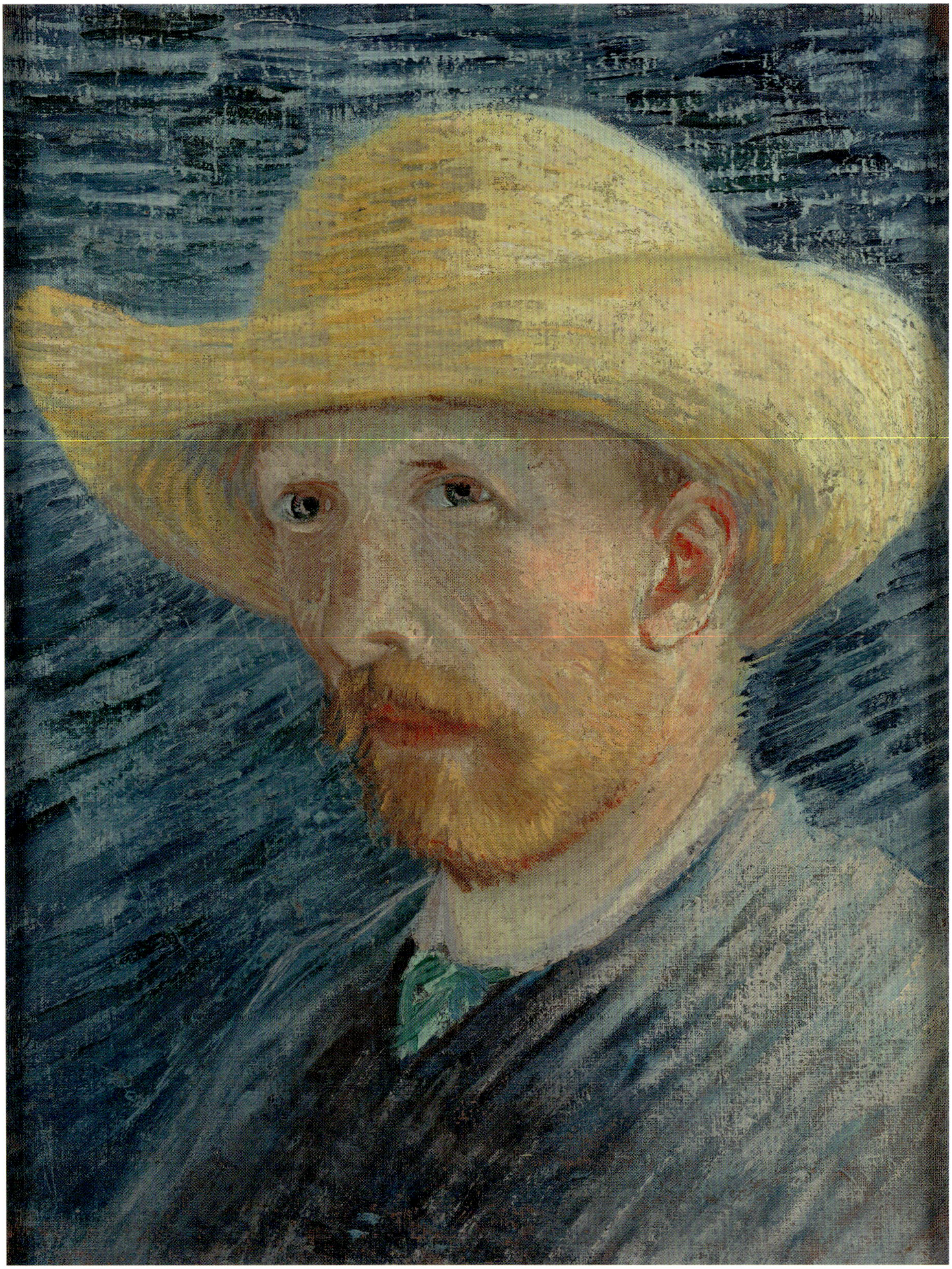

Self-portrait with Straw Hat (p. 103)

"PEOPLE WILL SAY—
AND I'M QUITE WILLING
TO BELIEVE IT—
THAT IT'S DIFFICULT
TO KNOW ONESELF—
BUT IT'S NOT EASY
TO PAINT ONESELF EITHER."

—Vincent van Gogh to his brother Theo,
September 5 and 6, 1889

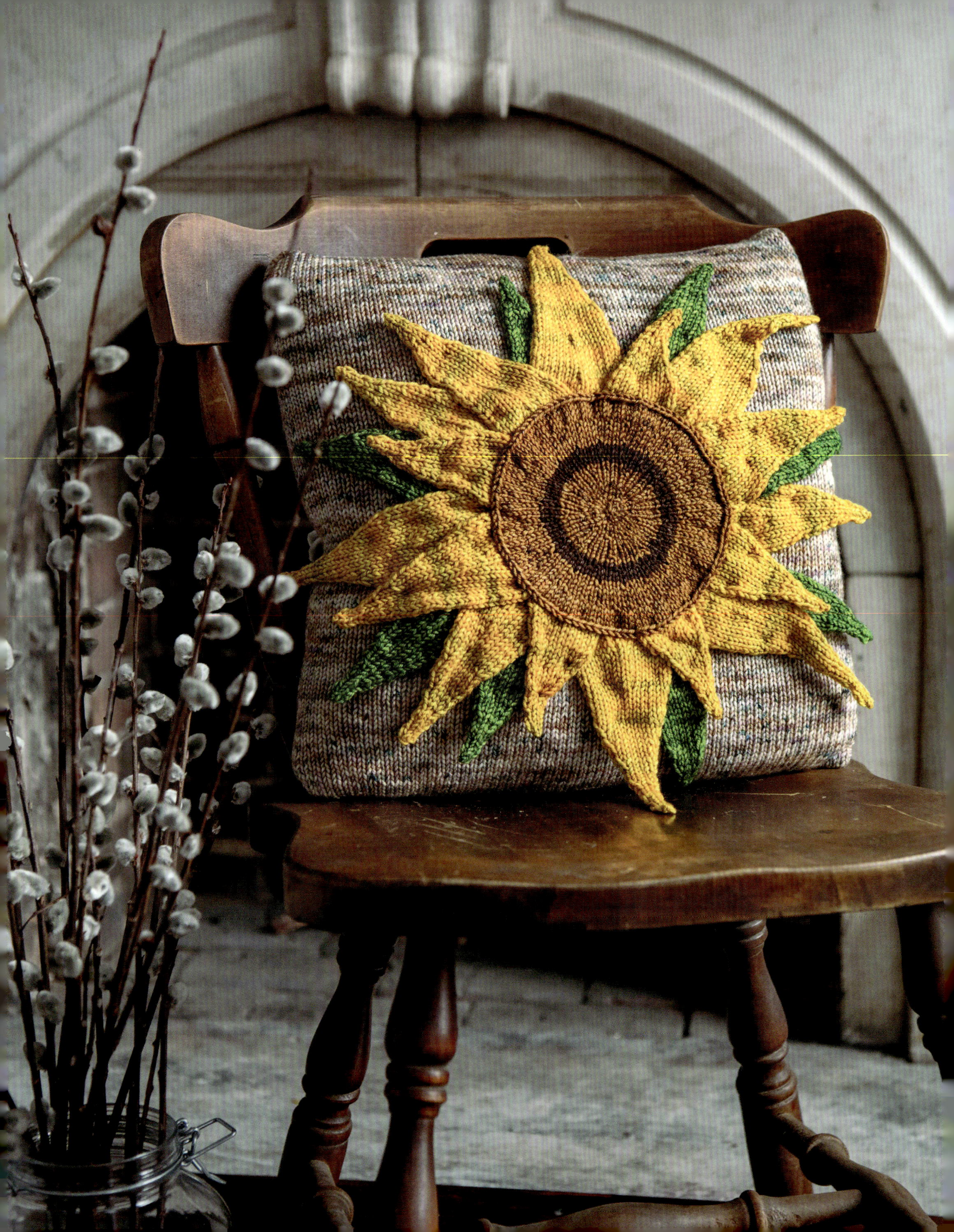

SUNFLOWER CUSHION

Inspired by *Sunflowers*

SKILL LEVEL **2**

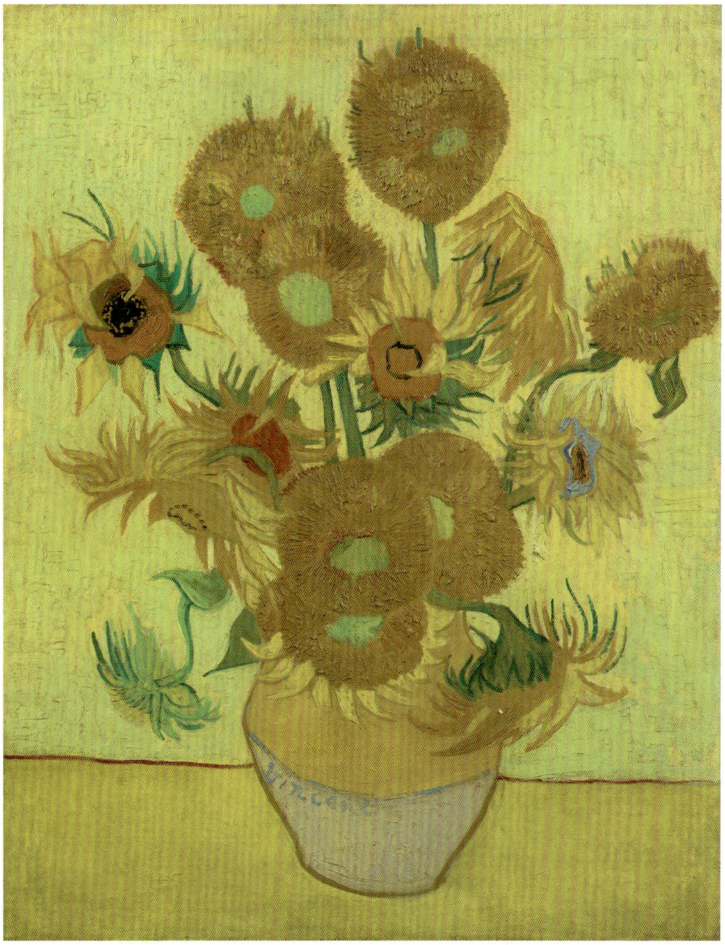

Van Gogh wrote in one of his many archived journal entries that sunflowers held special significance to him, as they communicated gratitude. Van Gogh's paintings of sunflowers are surely among his most famous. This pillow pattern was an ode to his most famous works and a special show of gratitude for his art. I focused on the pointed-tip shapes present in a few of the sunflower petals and leaves along the perimeter of the vase in the painting. I included a special touch of his signature on the back of the pillow to mimic the corner signature of one of his original works.

For more information on van Gogh's *Sunflowers*, see p. 139.

SIZES

One size

FINISHED MEASUREMENTS

16 in. / 40.5 cm square

YARN

Madelinetosh "Vintage" 100% Superwash Merino Wool; Worsted (100 g / 200 yd. / 182 m)

- **C1**: Mars Rover – 3 skeins
- **C2**: Rye Bourbon – 1 skein
- **C3**: Ristretto – 1 skein
- **C4**: Candlewick – 1 skein
- **C5**: Jade – 1 skein

NEEDLES

- (2) US size 7 / 4.5 mm, 16 in. / 40 cm long circular knitting needles
- US size 7 / 4.5 mm double pointed needles (DPNs)

Or size needed to obtain gauge

NOTIONS

- Locking stitch markers
- Round stitch marker
- Scissors
- Scrap yarn
- Tapestry needle for weaving in ends
- Blunt tapestry needle for duplicate stitching
- 16 in. / 40.5 cm square pillow form

GAUGE

20 stitches and 28 rows = 4 in. / 10 cm in stockinette stitch lightly blocked and unstretched

NOTES

- Pillow front and back are knit first. Duplicate stitch is then worked on the back piece to apply the signature. Three sides of the pillow are seamed and then petals, leaves, and flower center are knit separately and stitched on to the front. To make stitching the pieces on easier, temporarily insert the pillow form after three sides have been sewn up. Once everything has been stitched on and tails are woven in, then the fourth side of the pillow is seamed to close up the pillow.
- To make sewing the individual pieces on easier, it is recommended to block all of the petals, leaves, and the center piece so that they are mostly flat.

KNITTING INSTRUCTIONS

FRONT

Using C1, first circular needle, and provisional cast on (see p. 131), CO 80 sts.

Starting with a Purl row, work in st. st for 16 in. / 40.5 cm. End after working a Purl row.

Do not bind off. Cut yarn leaving a 10 ft. / 3 m tail to be used later when seaming the top and side of your pillow. Leave sts on first circular needle.

BACK

When casting on for the Back of your pillow, leave a tail about 10 ft. / 3 m long to be used later when seaming up the bottom and side of your pillow.

Using C1, second circular needle, and provisional cast on, CO 80 sts.

Starting with a Purl row, work in st. st for the same number of rows worked for the Front piece. End after working a Purl row.

Do not bind off. Cut yarn leaving a 4 in. / 10 cm tail. Leave sts on second circular needle.

STITCH THE SIGNATURE

Using duplicate stitch (see p. 135) and C3, follow the chart on p. 122 and stitch "Vincent" graphic onto the RS of the Back of pillow. Center the chart in the middle bottom half of the pillow, using picture as reference.

SEAM THE PILLOW

With RS facing each other, use the front tail and three-needle bind off (see p. 132) along the top of the pillow to join the Front and Back. Do not cut this tail.

Pull out provisional cast ons and put Front of pillow sts on one needle and Back of pillow sts on second needle. With RS facing each other, use the back cast on tail and three-needle bind off along the bottom of the pillow. Do not cut this tail.

Using mattress stitch (see p. 136) and the remainder of the long tail adjacent to one side edge, seam up one side of your pillow (either side is fine).

(Pattern continues on p. 119)

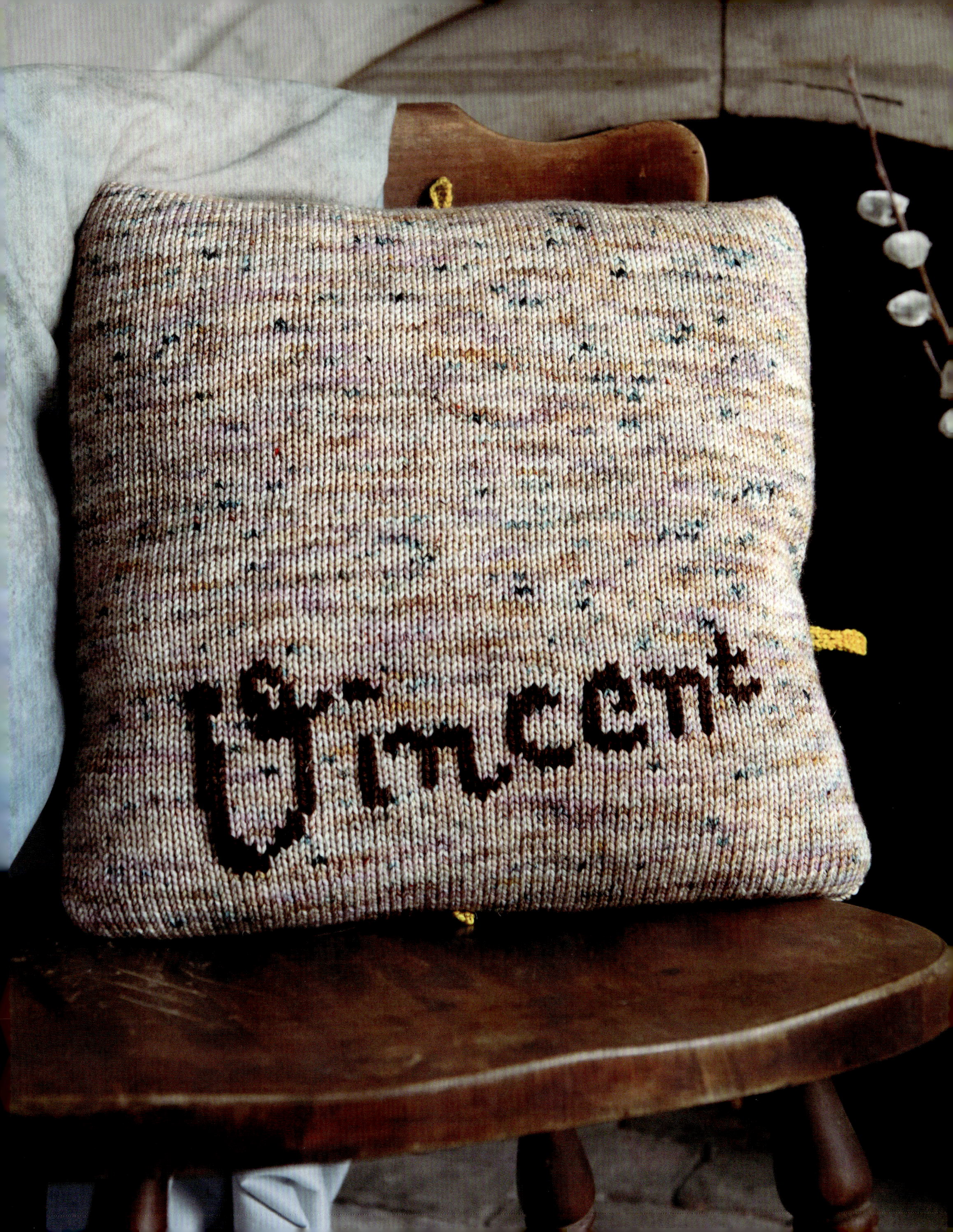
Vincent

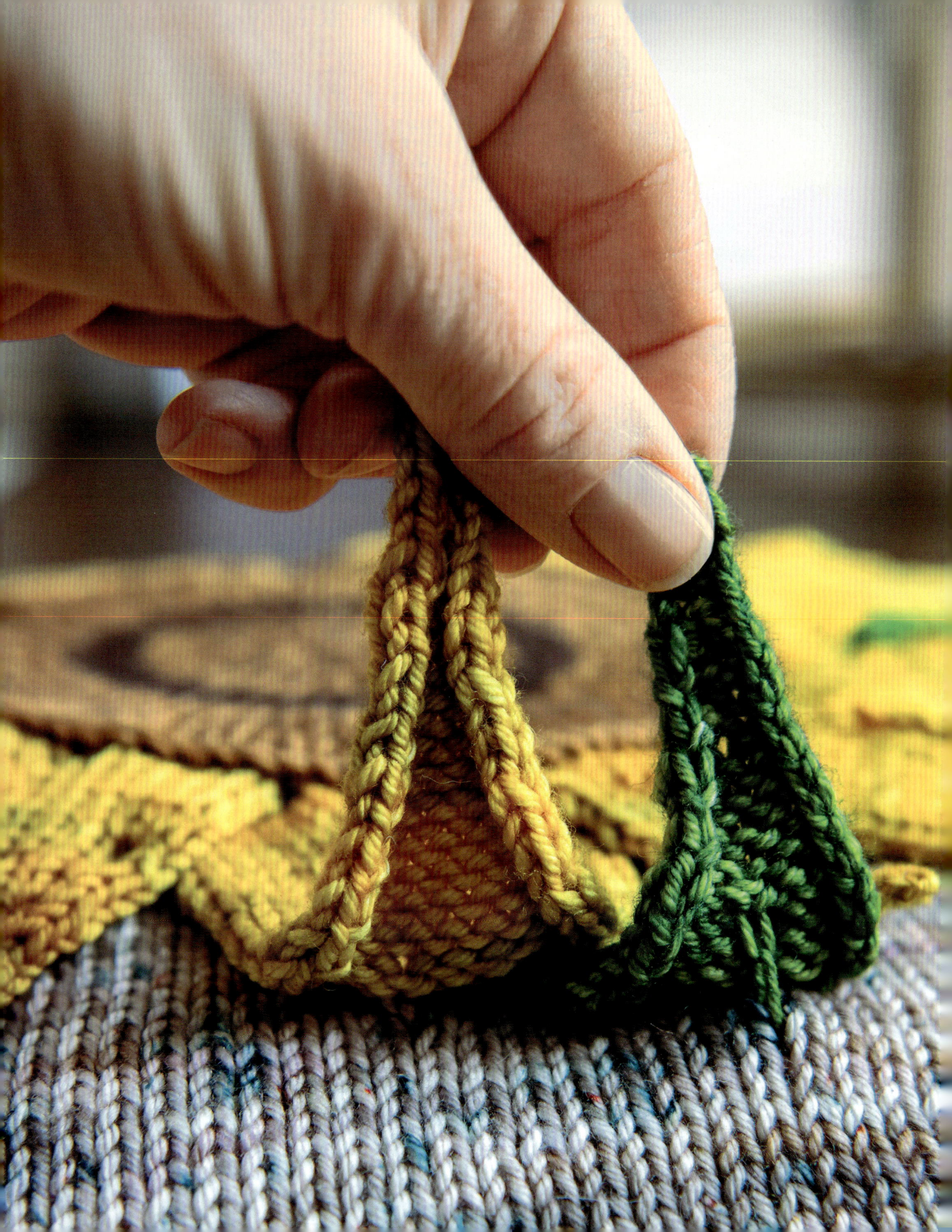

Place pillow form into pillow and use locking stitch markers to temporarily close the other side. This will make it easier to sew on the flower pieces.

CENTER OF SUNFLOWER

Using C2 and DPNs, CO 6 sts. Join to work in the rnd being careful not to twist. Place sm to note bor.

Rnd 1: Knit.
Rnd 2: Knit.
Rnd 3: *K1, M1L* around—12 sts.
Rnds 4–5: Knit.
Rnd 6: *K2, M1L* around—18 sts.
Rnd 7: Knit.
Rnd 8: *K2, M1L* around—27 sts.
Rnds 9–12: Knit.
Rnd 13: *K3, M1L* around—36 sts.

Join C3. Do not cut C2.

Rnds 14–15 (C3): Knit.
Rnd 16 (C3): *K2, M1L* around—54 sts.
Rnd 17 (C3): Knit.

Cut C3. Finish flower center using C2.

Rnds 18–19: Knit.
Rnd 20: *K3, M1L* around—72 sts.
Rnds 21–23: Knit.
Rnd 24: *K2, M1L* around—108 sts.
Rnds 25–27: Knit.

Bind off loosely. Cut yarn leaving a 20 in. / 51 cm tail to be used to sew center onto pillow.

PETALS AND LEAVES

Always leave a 20 in / 51 cm tail when casting on. These will be used to tack down your petals to the pillow.

LARGE

Make 5 in C4.

CO 17 sts.

Starting with a Purl row, work 9 rows in st. st.
Row 10 (RS): K7, sl2K1p2sso, K7—15 sts.
Work 7 rows in st. st.
Row 18: K6, sl2K1p2sso, K6—13 sts.
Work 5 rows in st. st.
Row 24: K1, SSK, K7, K2tog, K1—11 sts.
Work 3 rows in st. st.
Row 28: K1, SSK, K5, K2tog, K1—9 sts.
Work 3 rows in st. st.
Row 32: K1, SSK, K3, K2tog, K1—7 sts.
Work 5 rows in st. st.
Row 38: K1, SSK, K1, K2tog, K1—5 sts.
Work 5 rows in st. st.
Row 44: K1, sl2K1p2sso, K1—3 sts.
Work 5 rows in st. st.
Row 50: Sl2K1p2sso—1 st.
Row 51: P1.
Break yarn and pull tail through remaining loop; pull tight to secure.

MEDIUM

Make 6 in C4.
Make 5 in C5.

CO 15 sts.

Starting with a Purl row, work 7 rows in st. st.
Row 8 (RS): K6, sl2K1p2sso, K6—13 sts.
Work 5 rows in st. st.
Row 14: K5, sl2K1p2sso, K5—11 sts.
Work 5 rows in st. st.
Row 20: K1, SSK, K5, K2tog, K1—9 sts.
Work 5 rows in st. st.
Row 26: K1, SSK, K3, K2tog, K1—7 sts.
Work 3 rows in st. st.
Row 30: K1, SSK, K1, K2tog, K1—5 sts.
Work 3 rows in st. st.
Row 34: K1, sl2K1p2sso, K1—3 sts.
Work 3 rows in st. st.
Row 38: Sl2K1p2sso—1 st.
Row 39: P1.
Break yarn and pull tail through remaining loop; pull tight to secure.

SMALL

Make 5 in C4.
Make 3 in C5.

CO 13 sts.

Starting with a Purl row, work 5 rows in st. st.
Row 6 (RS): K5, sl2K1p2sso, K5—11 sts.
Work 5 rows in st. st.
Row 12: K1, SSK, K5, K2tog, K1—9 sts.
Work 3 rows in st. st.
Row 16: K1, SSK, K3, K2tog, K1—7 sts.
Work 3 rows in st. st.
Row 20: K1, SSK, K1, K2tog, K1—5 sts.

(Pattern continues on next page)

Work 3 rows in st. st.
Row 24: K1, sl2K1p2sso, K1—3 sts.
Work 3 rows in st. st.
Row 28: sl2K1p2sso—1 st.
Row 29: P1.
Break yarn and pull tail through remaining loop; pull tight to secure.

ASSEMBLE SUNFLOWER

Line up the middle of the sunflower center to the center of the pillow Front. This will help guide you to tack down your petals and leaves in the center of the pillow. Do not fully sew down the middle of the sunflower to the pillow Front; just tack it down in a few places, or use locking markers to keep it in place while you attach the petals and leaves.

One at a time, tack down petals and leaves according to the schematic on the facing page, positioning the edges under the edge of the middle of the sunflower as follows: use the CO tail and whip stitch base of petal or leaf to the pillow. Once the base of all leaves and petals have been tacked down, lightly tack down the rest of the petals and leaves. Only tack them down about three-fourths of the way up each piece so the tops of the leaves and petals can flap freely. Once all leaves and petals have been tacked down, sew around outside center of sunflower to secure it to the pillow.

FINISHING

Weave in any remaining tails (except remaining long tail; see p. 133).

Using mattress stitch (see p. 136) and the remainder of the long tail adjacent to the unseamed edge, close up the final side of the pillow. Weave in last tail.

"IF ONE TRULY LOVES NATURE, ONE FINDS BEAUTY EVERYWHERE."

—Vincent van Gogh to his brother Theo,
April 30, 1874

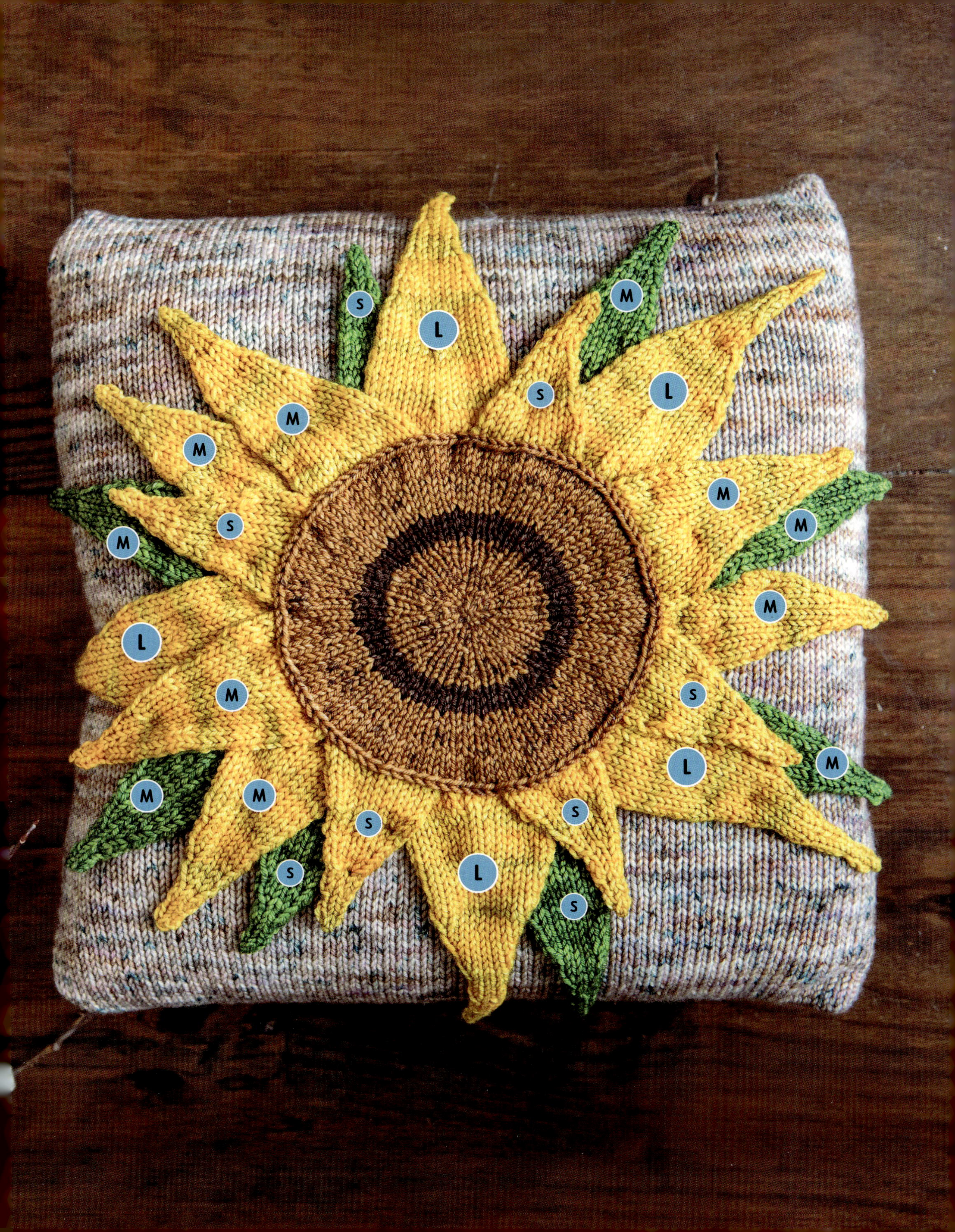
M
S
L
S
L
M
M
M
S
M
M
M
L
S
M
M
L
M
M
S
S
S
L
S

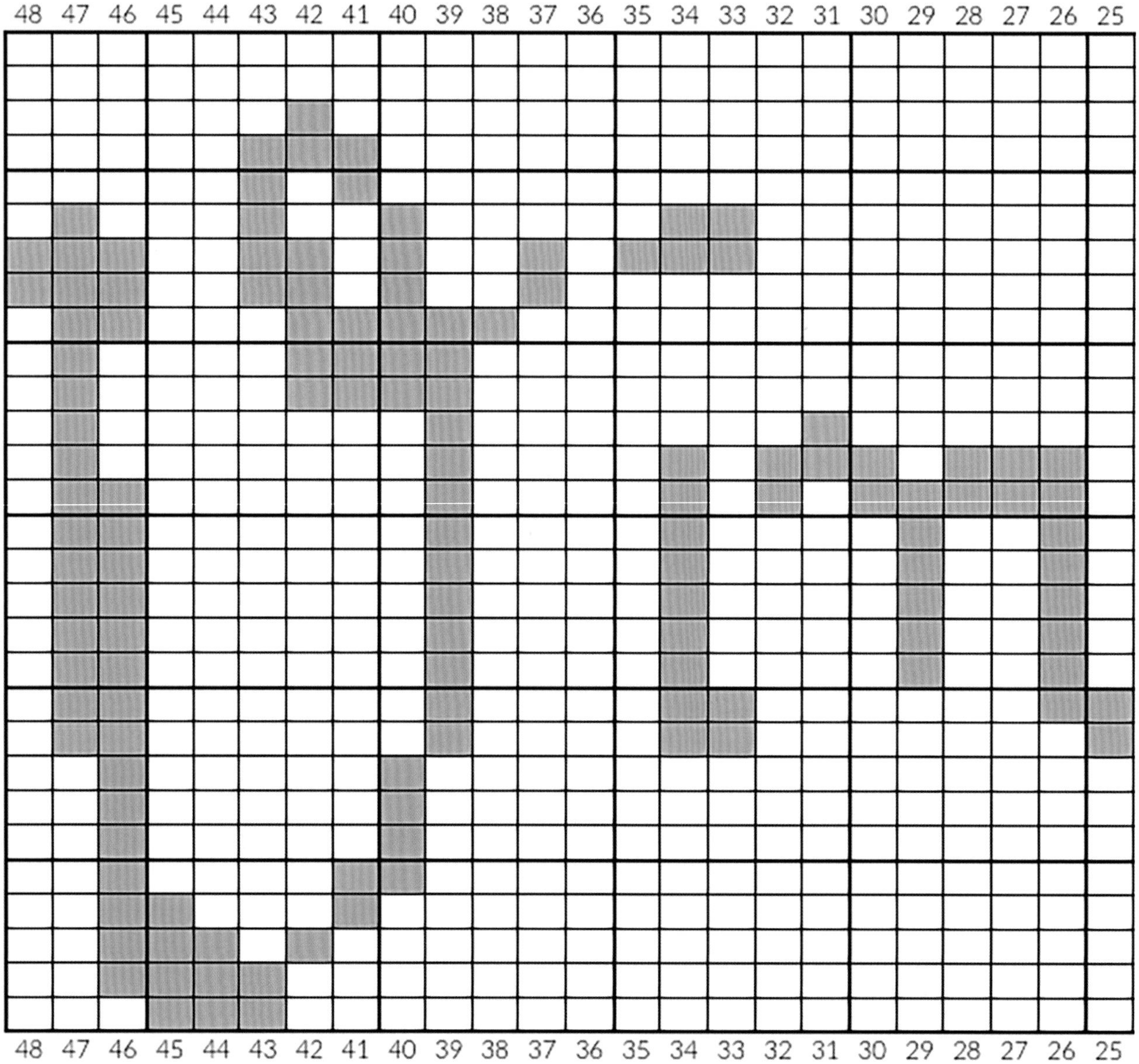
48 47 46 45 44 43 42 41 40 39 38 37 36 35 34 33 32 31 30 29 28 27 26 25
48 47 46 45 44 43 42 41 40 39 38 37 36 35 34 33 32 31 30 29 28 27 26 25

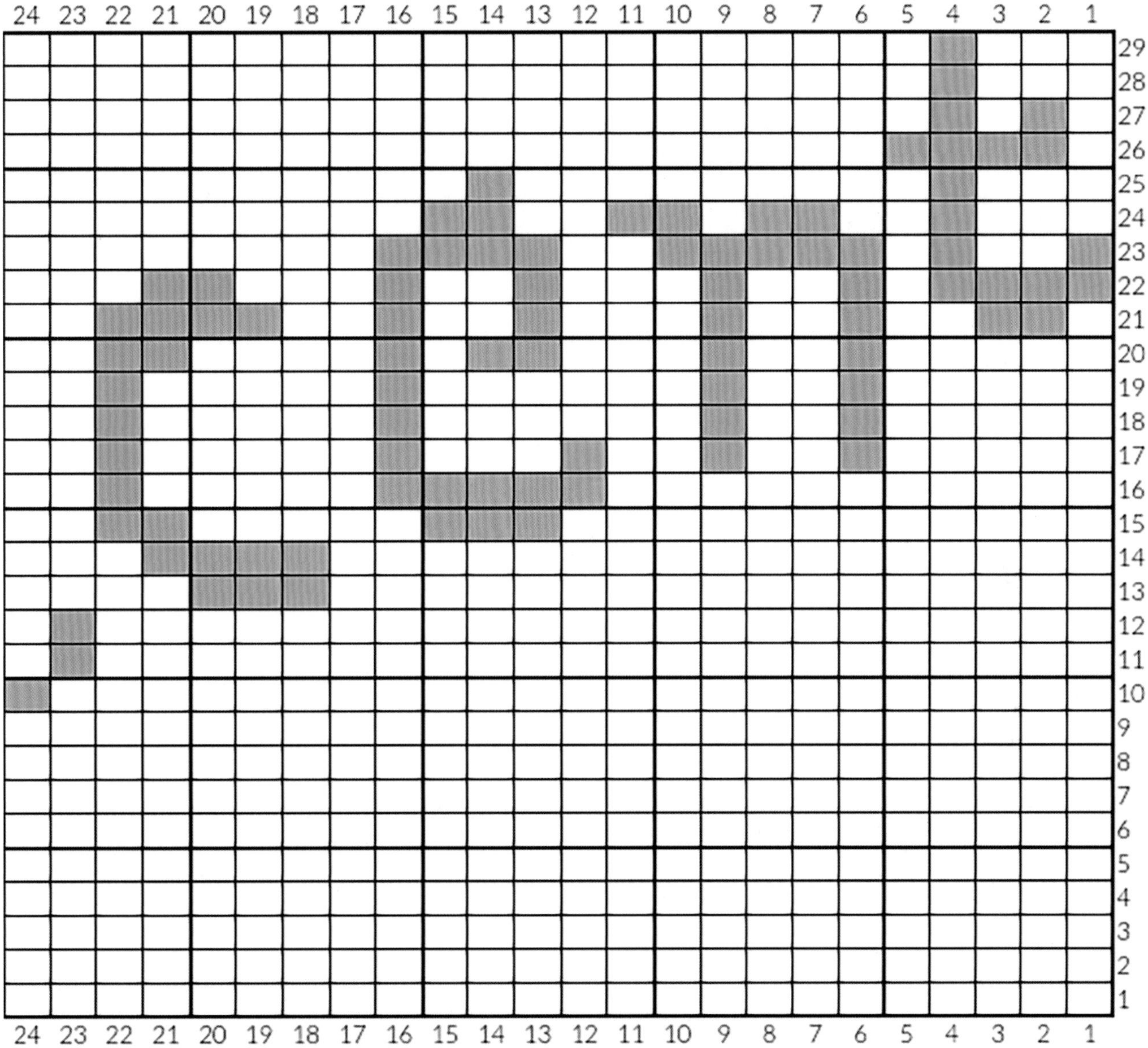

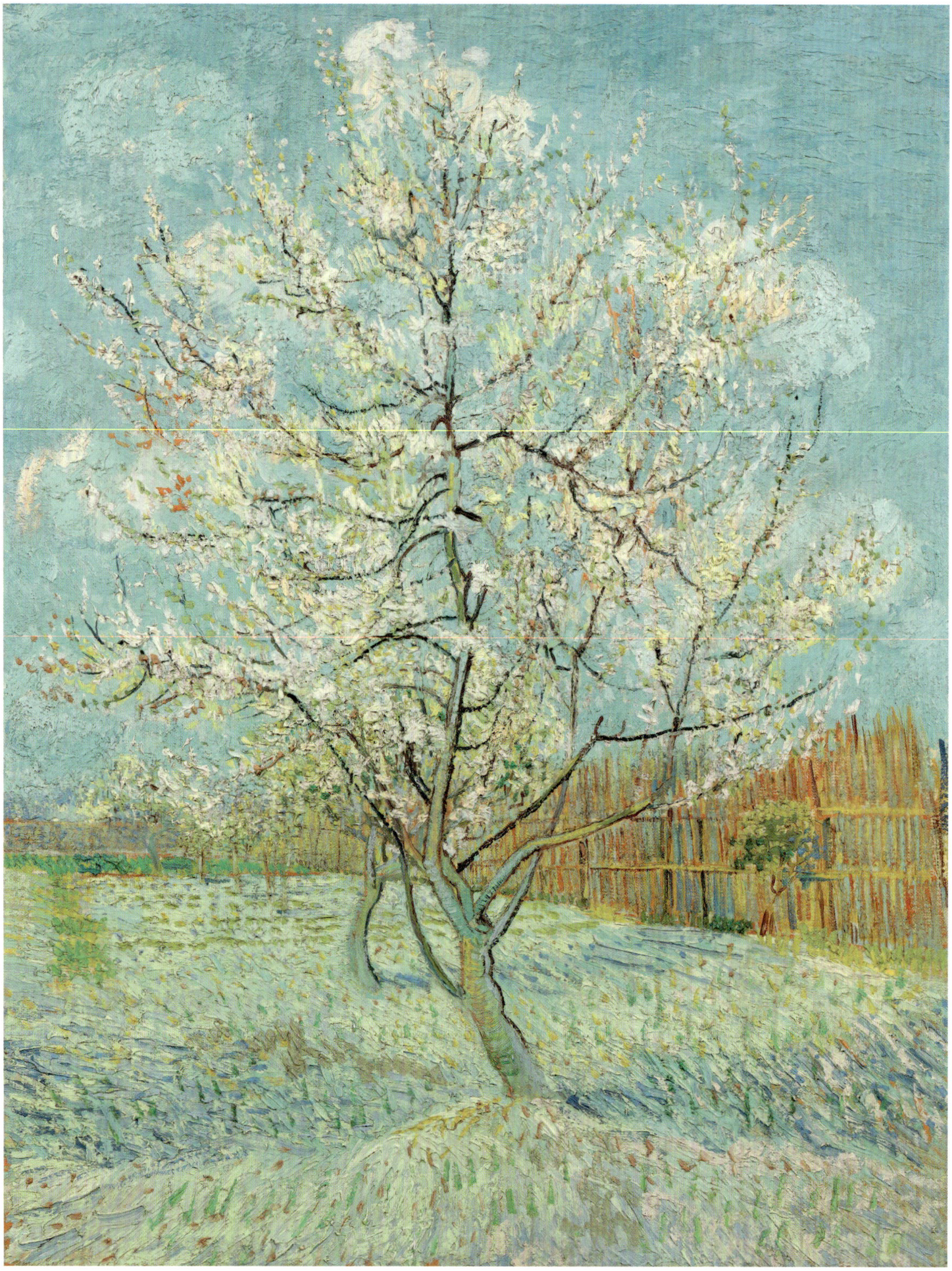

The Pink Peach Tree (p. 15)

"IN MY VIEW I'M OFTEN VERY RICH, NOT IN MONEY, BUT RICH ... BECAUSE I'VE FOUND MY WORK—HAVE SOMETHING WHICH I LIVE FOR HEART AND SOUL AND WHICH GIVES INSPIRATION AND MEANING TO LIFE."

—Vincent van Gogh to his brother,
March 11, 1883

RESOURCES

GLOSSARY

Cast Ons

LONG TAIL CAST ON

Leave a tail long enough to cast on the required number of stitches. This is about one wrap of the needle per stitch. Create a slip knot and place it onto the needle. Holding the needle in your right hand (the left needle is not used for this cast on), be sure the tail is coming off the front of the needle (closest to you) and working yarn is coming off the back of the needle (furthest from your body). Using your left hand, pinch your thumb and index finger together and place them below the needle and between the two yarns coming off the needle. Grab both strands of yarn with your remaining three free fingers and close up your hand so that both strands are snug in your palm. With your palm facing you, open your thumb and index finger to make a backward L. The tail is going over your thumb and the working yarn is going over your index finger. This is your setup position. Be sure you keep your other three fingers tight around the two strands of yarn in your palm.

Using the right needle, bring the tip of the needle toward you and over the top of the front tail. Moving away from your body, scoop the front tail up (your needle tip should touch the meat of your palm and be pointed away from your body) and continue to move toward your index finger. Going over the top of the yarn coming off the right side of your index finger, scoop up the back strand. Bring the tip of needle back toward your body and through the loop coming off your thumb. Drop the loop off your thumb and tighten the stitch. One stitch is cast on. Return to your setup position (double-check the tail is still coming off the front and working yarn is coming off the back) and repeat between the * * until the required number of stitches are on the needle.

CABLE CAST ON

This method of casting on is generally used when casting on stitches in the middle of a project.

To work this cast on in the middle of a project, the working tail needs to be coming off of the left needle. *Using the right needle, put the tip of the needle between the first two stitches on the left needle from front to back. Wrap yarn around the needle as you would for a knit stitch. Pull the needle and loop between the two stitches and place the loop onto the left needle.* One stitch is cast on. Repeat between * * until the required number of stitches have been cast on.

If there are not already stitches on the needle, start with a slipknot on the left needle. Knit into the stitch as normal, but do not slip the left stitch off the needle. Bring the newly knit stitch up and onto the left needle. Then cast on the rest of the stitches needed by repeating between the * * above.

Tip: Do not tighten the yarn after placing the newly knit stitch on the left needle until the right needle has been placed between the first two stitches to make the next stitch. Once the right needle is between the first two stitches on the left needle, pull the working yarn snug.

BACKWARD LOOP CAST ON

This method of casting on is generally used when casting on stitches in the middle or end of a project row or round. To work this cast on, the working tail can be on the right or the left needle, but new stitches will always be cast onto the needle that the working yarn is coming off of. *Using the working yarn, create a cursive "e" loop with the yarn. The working yarn should be crossing in front of the yarn coming directly off the needle. Slip a cursive "e" loop up onto the needle and pull snug.* Repeat between * * until the required number of stitches have been cast on.

Tip: If the stitch doesn't stay on the needle, the working yarn was not in front of the yarn coming directly off of the needle.

FIGURE 8 CAST ON

To work this cast on, two circular needles will be needed. Hold one needle tip from each of the two needles in the left hand so they are parallel to each other and have a small gap between them. Make a slipknot and tighten it up around the needle furthest from your body (this is the "back" needle). *Holding the working yarn in your right hand, bring the working yarn up between both needles, move the yarn away from you over the top of the back needle, then under the back needle and up between both needles, and finally over the top of the front needle.* Two stitches have been cast on—one stitch on the back needle and one stitch on the front needle. The slipknot does not count as a stitch. Repeat between * * until the desired number of stitches have been cast on. There needs to be the same number of stitches on the front needle as the back needle. Do not count the slipknot!

Once the required number of stitches have been cast on, push all stitches from the front needle down onto the cable, being careful they do not fall off and making sure the last front stitch doesn't fall off. Clip a locking marker to the right edge of the cast on stitches to indicate the beginning of the round.

Grab the other end of the back needle. Using this needle, begin working across the back needle stitches according to the pattern.

Provisional Cast Ons

CROCHET CHAIN PROVISIONAL CAST ON

Using scrap yarn and a crochet hook roughly the same size as the project needle, create a chain of stitches. Chain 8 to 10 more stitches than required for the cast on. Place a knot in the tail to mark the end of your crochet chain. (This will be referenced later.)

Hold the working needle in your right hand and the crochet chain in your left hand. The first stitch should be picked up three or four stitches away from the end of the chain to give you something to hold onto. Begin working from the end opposite the end with the knot in it.

Roll the chain over so the middle bump of the chain is on top.

Using the working needle, go into the bump on the crochet chain from front to back. Wrap the working yarn around the needle as if to knit and pull through the chain bump. One stitch has been cast on. Repeat between * * until the required number of stitches have been cast onto the right needle.

To undo the provisional cast on when ready to work these stitches, pull out the last crochet chain stitch worked. (This is the chain at the end where the knot was placed.) Carefully unzip the chain one stitch at a time and place live stitches onto the needle. Be sure to work this step slowly and only unzip one stitch at a time and immediately get that stitch onto the needle.

KNITTED CAST ON

To work this cast on in the middle of a project, the working tail needs to be coming off of the left needle. *Using the right needle, put the tip of the needle into the first stitch on the left needle. Wrap the yarn around the needle as you would for a knit stitch. Pull the loop through and place it onto the left needle.* One stitch is cast on. Repeat between * * until the required number of stitches have been cast on.

Bind Offs

PASS OVER BIND OFF

This is a simple bind off that is used when an edge does not need to be stretchy. It is easy to work this bind off too tight, so take care not to pull the yarn tight during this bind off. You can use this method to bind off all of the stitches knitwise or purlwise, or a combination of knits and purls, such as when binding off a ribbed fabric. If the pattern does not say which stitches to bind off in (as an example, pattern might say "continuing in 1x1 ribbing, work pass over bind off across all stitches"), then work knit stitches for the bind off.

To work this bind off: Work the first stitch (one stitch on the right needle). *Work the next stitch (two stitches on the right needle). Using the tip of the left needle, lift the right-most stitch up and over the second stitch from right to left and off the needle (one stitch remains on the right needle).* One stitch is bound off. Repeat between * * until you have one stitch remaining on the right needle and no stitches remaining on the left needle.

Cut the yarn leaving a tail and bring the right needle up toward the sky until the end of the tail pulls completely through the last stitch. All stitches have been bound off.

Note that if you are binding off in the middle of a piece, the pattern might not have you cut the yarn and you will continue to work the stitches that remain on your needle.

SEWN BIND OFF

A sewn bind off is a wonderful bind off to use when an edge needs to have stretch. Use this method when working any kind of ribbed edge that needs to stretch and bounce back in place. Sewn bind off works beautifully on 2x2 and 1x1 ribbing around necks or cuffs to give stretch, but doesn't flare the fabric out.

To work this bind off, cut the yarn 2.5 times the length of the edge of the piece. For example, if a sweater cuff measures 8 in. / 20 cm in circumference, cut the yarn leaving a tail about 20 in. / 51 cm long.

Using a blunt tapestry needle, thread the tail into the needle and work as follows across all stitches: *Go into the first two stitches on the left needle purlwise, pull the yarn tail all the way through. Go into the first stitch on the left needle knitwise and drop that stitch off the needle, pull the yarn tail all the way through.* Repeat between * * until there is one stitch remaining on the left needle. Go into the last stitch purlwise and drop off the needle.

THREE-NEEDLE BIND OFF

A three-needle bind off can only be worked when there are two sets of live stitches sitting on needles. There also needs to be the same number of live stitches on each needle.

To work this bind off, the public sides of the pieces (RS) need to be facing each other (imagine the public sides of the piece are kissing each other); the non-public sides of the pieces (WS) are facing out. The two needles that have live stitches on them are held in the left hand with the needles parallel to each other—one needle is in front and closest to your body and the second needle is next to it, but in back and away from your body—and the tips facing to the right.

Using a third needle, go into the front leg of the first stitch on the front needle and then into the front leg of the first stitch on the back needle. Wrap the yarn around the third needle as if to knit and pull the loop through both the back and front stitches. Drop the first stitch on the front and back needle off the left needles.

There is now one stitch on the right needle. Repeat between * * once. There are now two stitches on the right needle. Using the tip of one of the left needles, lift the right-most stitch up and over the second stitch from right to left and off the needle (one stitch remains on the right needle). One stitch is bound off. Repeat between * * again and pass over again. Continue this until all stitches on the left needles have been worked and only one stitch remains on the right needle. Cut the yarn leaving a tail and bring the right needle up toward the sky until the end of the tail pulls completely through last stitch. All stitches have been bound off.

Kitchener Stitch

Sometimes known as grafting, the Kitchener stitch invisibly joins two sets of live stitches.

To work this bind off, the public sides of the pieces (RS) need to be facing out; the private sides of the pieces (WS) are facing each other.

Place each set of stitches to be joined on two separate needles. There needs to be the same number of stitches on each needle. Needles will be held in the left hand parallel to each other—one needle is in front and closest to your body and the second needle is next to it, but in back and away from your body—and the tips facing to the right. The working yarn should be coming off the end of the front needle.

Be careful not to pull the working yarn too tight. Stitches can be snugged up after all stitches are off the needles. Thread the tail into a tapestry needle.

Step 1: Insert the tapestry needle purlwise through the first stitch on the front needle. Pull the yarn through leaving the stitch on the front needle.

Step 2: Insert the tapestry needle knitwise through the first stitch on the back needle and pull the yarn through. Leave the stitch on the back needle.

Step 3: Insert the tapestry needle knitwise through the first stitch on the front needle. Slip the stitch off the front needle and pull the yarn through.

Step 4: Insert the tapestry needle purlwise through the next stitch on the front needle and pull the yarn through. Leave the stitch on the front needle.

Step 5: Insert the tapestry needle purlwise through the first stitch on the back needle. Slip the stitch off the back needle and pull the yarn through.

Step 6: Insert the tapestry needle knitwise through the next stitch on the back needle and pull the yarn through. Leave the stitch on the back needle.

Repeat Steps 3–6 until the yarn has been threaded through the last stitch of each needle once.

To finish: Insert the tapestry needle knitwise into the last stitch on the front needle. Slip the stitch off the front needle and pull the yarn through. Next, insert the tapestry needle purlwise into the last stitch on the back needle. Slip the stitch from the needle, and pull the yarn through.

Go back along the stitches just made and gently tighten them up so that they match the tension of the stitches above and below them. Don't pull anything too tight and take time to be sure this row looks clean.

Weave in ends on the wrong side to secure.

Picking Up and Knitting Stitches

This method is used when stitches need to be created, but they need to come directly off of an existing knit piece. To pick up stitches, only the right needle will be used.

Place the tip of the right needle into the fabric where a stitch needs to be picked up. Wrap the working yarn around the needle like a knit stitch and pull a loop through the fabric. One stitch has been picked up. Repeat between * * until the required number of stitches have been picked up.

Tip: When picking up stitches, one stitch is picked up for every one stitch along a horizontal edge (it's a 1:1 stitch ratio). When picking up along a vertical edge, stitches are picked up at a variable ratio based on the fabric. If you are picking up along the edge of a stockinette stitch armhole opening, you will pick up three stitches for four rows (a 3:4 ratio). If you are picking up along a garter stitch edge, you will pick up one stitch for two rows (a 1:2 ratio).

Cinching Closed the Top of a Hat

When closing up the top of a hat, there should be a small number of stitches on the needles (around 6 to 12 depending on the yarn weight). To have a clean and secure top of the hat closure, cut the yarn leaving about a 12 in. / 30 cm tail. Thread the tail into a blunt tip tapestry needle. Working clockwise, insert the tapestry needle tip into the stitch to the left of the stitch the yarn is coming off of. This would be the next stitch knit if continuing to knit in the round. Insert the tapestry needle through all remaining live stitches clockwise once. All of the stitches are now off the needles. Don't pull tight. Weave the tapestry needle through all stitches one more time, being careful not to snag the stitches or the yarn you just wove through. Once the yarn has been pulled through all live stitches twice, carefully pull the tail snug until the hole in the center tightens up and the yarn won't pull anymore. Weave the tapestry needle clockwise through all stitches two or three more times. It does not matter if the yarn or stitches are slightly snagged at this point. Once the tail has been woven through all of the stitches four or five times, cut the tail flush with the fabric.

Weaving in Tails

When weaving in tails, always weave through the non-public (WS) side of the work. If there is not a non-public side of the work (as in a reversible scarf), then either side will work but weave all tails into the same side. Weave in all of your tails, but don't trim them flush with the fabric yet. Once the entire piece is knit and has been blocked and dried, then cut the tails carefully. Be sure to triple-check that the tail has been woven in before cutting it.

Wrap and Turn Short Rows—on Stockinette Stitch (W&T)

Wrap and turn is a method of working short rows. This means you don't work to the end of the row/round of your piece. You will stop partway across the row, work a wrap, and then turn the piece to continue working in the opposite direction. A w&t eliminates a hole from appearing where the turn was made.

To work a w&t on the knit

side: Knit the number of stitches the pattern states. With the yarn held to the back, slip the next stitch to the right needle purlwise, move the yarn to the front between the needles, slip the stitch back to the left needle purlwise. Return the yarn to the back by moving it between the needles to the purl side. Turn the work.

To work a w&t on the purl side: Purl the number of stitches the pattern states. With the yarn held to the front, slip the next stitch to the right needle purlwise, move the yarn to the back between the needles, slip the stitch back to the left needle purlwise. Return the yarn to the front by moving it between the needles to the purl side. Turn the work.

Picking up wrapped stitches on the knit side: work to the wrapped stitch. Using the left needle, scoop up the wrapped stitch from the bottom up so that it is sitting on the left needle. Work the wrap together with the stitch to its left as you would a K2tog.

Picking up wrapped stitches on the purl side: work to the wrapped stitch. Slip the wrapped stitch to the right needle purlwise. Using the left needle, scoop up the wrapped stitch from the bottom up so that it is sitting on the left needle. Return the slipped stitch to the left needle. Work the wrap together with the slipped stitch as you would a P2tog.

Wrap and Turn Short Rows—on Garter Stitch (w&t)

To work a w&t on either side of the fabric: Knit the number of stitches the pattern states. With the yarn held to the back, slip the next stitch to the right needle purlwise, move the yarn to the front between the needles, slip the stitch back to the left needle purlwise. Leave the yarn on the front side. Turn work. The stitch will appear half-wrapped and will be in position to knit the next row after the work is turned.

Picking up wrapped stitches on either side of the fabric: work to the wrapped stitch. Using the left needle, scoop up the wrapped stitch from the bottom up so that it is sitting on the left needle. Work the wrap together with the stitch to its left as you would a K2tog.

Adding Fringe

It is easiest to add fringe using a crochet hook that is a little larger than the ball band calls for. Be sure that all fringe is added while looking at the same side of the fabric.

To add fringe, first cut pieces of yarn according to the measurements given in the pattern. Fringe must be at least one piece of yarn (which is folded over in half to create two pieces of fringe hanging off the piece) or can be multiple strands of yarn. For example, if there are 4 strands of yarn, once they are folded over and attached, there will be 8 pieces of fringe hanging off the piece.

To attach fringe: Fold the yarn in half so the two cut ends meet. Insert the crochet hook into where the fringe should be placed from front to back. Place the loop of yarn (at the fold) on the hook and pull the hook through the piece slightly. Use the crochet hook to grab both tails and pull through the loop on the hook. Remove the hook and pull both tails equally tight to secure the fringe to the edge of the piece.

Once all pieces of the fringe are added, lightly trim them to be roughly the same length.

Felting

Felting is when non-superwash animal fiber yarn is agitated to create a denser fabric. This process shrinks the size of your finished piece and connects the fibers of your yarn together. The size of your piece will shrink much more in row height than in stitch width. Once an item has been felted, stitches cannot be changed. Felting is a permanent process, so make sure it's right before dropping it in the washing machine!

To felt a finished piece, insert it into a lingerie bag or a pillowcase closed with a hair tie. Put in the washing machine either by itself or with a grubby pair of jeans to expedite the process. (Be sure the dye from the jeans does not bleed in the water.) Use a small amount of mild laundry detergent and hot water. Run the washing machine for a full cycle. You can sporadically stop the machine to check the progress of the felting. The longer a piece is washed, the more it will felt until it can felt no more.

Once the piece is felted to your liking, remove it from the lingerie bag or pillowcase and form it to the desired shape. Let the piece air-dry in a cool dry place. Be sure the entire piece is dry before putting it to use.

Carrying Yarn Up

When working a piece where the pattern states to carry the yarn up the side, this is because that yarn will be used again very soon. The unused color will hang out at the edge of the work until it is ready to be used again. A float across the back will be created if the yarn is not carried up on rows/ rounds where it isn't being worked.

When carrying yarn up the side, work the first stitch as the pattern states (this is usually a knit, purl, or slipped stitch) and then wrap the unused color around the working color once. Drop the unused color and continue as the pattern states. It does not matter if the unused color is wrapped clockwise or counterclockwise, but it is recommended to always wrap the same direction throughout the piece.

Joining to Work in the Round

When working in the round, a proper join is important. Whether working on DPNs or on a circular needle, it is extremely important that there are no twists in the work before creating the join.

For a clean and proper join, cast on one extra stitch to the required cast on number. Push all stitches up to the tips of the needles. The very first stitch cast on should be on the left needle, and the last stitch cast on along with the working yarn should be coming off the right needle. Check the braid of the cast on to be sure there are no twists in it. The entire braid of the cast on should be facing into the center of the needles.

If the very first stitch of the pattern is a knit stitch, join as follows: with the working yarn being held in the back, slip the extra cast on stitch over to the left needle and immediately knit two together.

If the very first stitch of the pattern is a purl stitch, join as follows: with the working yarn being held in the front, slip the extra cast on stitch over to the left needle and immediately purl two together. Pull the working yarn and tail snug and continue in the pattern as stated.

Take time after the first round to double-check that the braid of the cast on is still facing into the center of the needles and there are no twists on the needle.

Duplicate Stitch

This technique is used to "draw" stitches on top of existing stitches using yarn and a blunt tapestry needle. Duplicate stitch is a type of colorwork, but is worked after the main project piece is knit, not during the knitting process (like with intarsia and Fair Isle).

Thread the yarn that will be used to stitch the design onto a blunt tip tapestry needle. Leave the yarn attached to the ball of yarn, but pull out a long tail to work with.

Starting with the tapestry needle on the non-public (WS) of the work, push the needle to the public (RS) of the work between the legs and below the stitch to be covered. Pull the yarn through the fabric.

If the stitches to be covered are to the left of the tapestry needle, work as follows: *insert the tapestry needle from right to left (tip of needle is facing left) behind both legs of the stitch above the stitch to be covered and end on the front. (Tapestry of the work needle is parallel to the fabric.) Insert the needle back in where the yarn was first pulled to the public side (RS) of the work. The needle is now on the non-public (WS) of the work. Bring the needle between the legs and below the next stitch to be covered. Pull the yarn through the fabric.* Repeat between * * covering stitches according to the pattern graph.

If stitches to be covered are to the right of the tapestry needle, work as follows: *insert the tapestry needle from left to right (tip of needle is facing right) behind both legs of the stitch above the stitch to be covered and end on the front of the work. (Tapestry needle is parallel to the fabric.) Insert the needle back in where the yarn was first pulled to the public side (RS) of the work. The needle is now on the non-public (WS) of the work. Bring the needle between the legs and below the next stitch to be covered. Pull the yarn through the fabric.* Repeat between * * covering stitches according to the pattern graph.

When you run out of tail to work with, weave the tail into the back of the piece. Cut the yarn from the ball and either use that tail to work more duplicate stitch or weave in that tail as well.

Mattress Stitch

Mattress stitch creates an invisible seam along two edges of a project. Place the pieces to be sewn together on a flat surface with the public sides (RS) facing you. The edges should be side by side and lined up where they need to be stitched together.

Thread a blunt tapestry needle with a strong yarn. The yarn does not have to be what was used to knit the project, but it should be close in color and very strong. It should be very difficult to break if pulled tight. Cut the yarn to approximately three times longer than the seam length to be sewn.

Beginning at the bottom edges of both pieces, insert the tapestry needle under one bar between the two edge stitches on the right piece and pull through to the front. Then insert the tapestry needle under the corresponding bar on the left piece and pull through to the front.

Going in where the yarn last came out on the right piece, insert the tapestry needle under two more bars on the right piece and pull through to the front, but don't pull tight. Going in where the yarn last came out of on the left piece, insert the tapestry needle under two more bars on the left piece and pull through to the front, but don't pull tight.

Repeat between * * working back and forth from your right piece to your left piece until the seam is complete. Carefully pull the yarn tight to cinch up the seam. Be sure to pull the fabric so that the seam isn't puckered before weaving in the tails on the wrong side of the piece.

Blocking

SPRAY / DRY BLOCKING

The most important thing to remember about blocking is that a piece can always be blocked more, but it can never be blocked less. Do not overstretch your finished garment. Be gentle in the blocking process and take your time.

I prefer to use the spray / dry blocking method whenever I block a piece; this is the default method used in the book unless noted otherwise. To do this, take the finished piece and lay it on blocking mats and pin to the desired shape or measurements. Take time to be sure that the entire piece is exactly how you want it to be. Using a spray bottle filled with filtered water, spray the finished piece to gently saturate the yarn. Pat down on the fabric carefully and spray again until the piece is wet, but not soaking. Leave it alone until the entire piece is completely dry.

If working with a thicker piece, such as a sweater, spray the inside of the sweater and the back of the sweater with water until it is saturated, but not soaking. Then pin the sweater down to the desired shape and measurements. Spray the front of the sweater and let dry.

WET BLOCKING

Unlike spray / dry blocking, where the entire piece is pinned out to shape while dry, wet blocking uses a soaking method before it is pinned out to shape. This method can drastically change your project gauge so be sure to treat your swatch in the same manner you plan to treat your project.

Fill a bowl or a sink with room temperature water. Add no-rinse wool wash or essential oils if desired. Without agitating the project too much (to avoid felting), submerge the project in the water, ensuring that the entire piece is under water. Do not let it sit in the water for too long.

Carefully drain the bowl or sink, supporting your piece as necessary to avoid the wet project from over-stretching. Carefully squeeze any excess water from your project. Be careful not to twist or wring the piece. Place the wet project on towels and roll up. Step on top of the towel roll to remove any excess moisture.

Unroll the towel and transfer the project to your desired blocking surface. Pin out the piece to the shape and/or dimensions as desired. Allow to dry entirely before unpinning. Do not block on top of towels as this can prolong the drying time.

ABBREVIATIONS

/ – used to separate inches from metric measurements
( ) – repeat between parentheses
* * – repeat between asterisks
Approx. – approximately
BO – bind off
bor – beginning of round/row
brk – (brioche knit stitch) knit the stitch together with its wrap
brkLdec – left-slanting brioche knit stitch decrease: slip 1 brioche stitch knitwise, brioche knit next 2 stitches together, pass slipped stitch over (2 stitches decreased)
brkRdec – right-slanting brioche decrease: slip 1 brioche stitch knitwise, knit next stitch, pass slipped stitch over. Slip remaining stitch to left-hand needle purlwise. Pass next brioche stitch over from left to right and off the needle. Move remaining stitch back to right hand needle purlwise (2 stitches decreased)
brkYObrk – (brk1, YO, brk1) into the same stitch (2 stitches increased)
brp – (brioche purl stitch) purl the stitch together with its wrap
C1/C2/C3, etc – color one/color two/color three, etc.
CC – contrasting color
cm – centimeter(s)
CO – cast on
dec – decrease(s/d)
DPN(s) – double pointed needle(s)
g – gram(s)
inc – increase(s/d)
K/k – knit
K1b – knit 1 in the stitch below
K2tog – knit two stitches together (1 stitch decreased)
K3tog – knit 3 stitches together (2 stitches decreased)
kf&b – knit into the front and the back of the next st (1 stitch increased)
ktbl – knit through back loop
ktfl – knit through front loop
LH – needle being held in left hand
m – meter(s)
M1L – make 1 left-slanting stitch (1 stitch increased)
M1LP – make 1 left-slanting stitch purlwise (1 stitch increased)
M1R – make 1 right-slanting stitch (1 stitch increased)
M1RP – make 1 right-slanting stitch purlwise (1 stitch increased)
MC – main color
P/p – purl
P2tog – purl 2 stitches together (1 stitch decreased)
P3tog – purl 3 stitches together (2 stitches decreased)
pf&b – purl into the front and the back of the next st (1 stitch increased)
pm – place stitch marker
psso – pass slipped stitch over (1 stitch decreased)
rem – remain(s/ing)
rep – repeat
RH – needle being held in right hand
rnd/rnds – round/rounds
RS – right side
sl – slip stitch(es) purlwise (unless otherwise noted)
sl1YO – slip 1 stitch purlwise while yarning over it
sl2K1p2sso – slip 2 stitches together purlwise, K1, pass 2 slipped stitches over the K1 (2 stitches decreased)
slm – slip stitch marker
sm – stitch marker
SSK – slip, slip, knit 2 slipped stitches together (1 stitch decreased)
SSSK – slip, slip, slip, knit all 3 slipped sts together (2 stitches decreased)
st. st – stockinette stitch (if working flat: knit one row, purl one row; if working in the round: knit every round)
st/sts – stitch/stitches
tbl(s) – through back loop(s)
turn – turn work so opposite side of work is facing you
w&t – wrap and turn (short row method)
WS – wrong side
wyib – with yarn held to the back (note: this will be the default for slipped stitches; if the yarn position is not noted in the pattern, it will be with the yarn held to the back)
wyif – with yarn held to the front
yd(s) – yard(s)
YO – yarn over (1 stitch increased)

YARN RESOURCE GUIDE

All of the yarns used in this book can be purchased from these wonderful retailers.

CASCADE YARNS
cascadeyarns.com

HANDMAIDEN
handmaiden.ca

KNIT PICKS
knitpicks.com

LA BIEN AIMÉE
labienaimee.com

MADELINETOSH
madelinetosh.com

MALABRIGO
malabrigoyarn.com

PLYMOUTH YARN
plymouthyarn.com

SPINCYCLE YARNS
spincycleyarns.com

THE FIBRE COMPANY
thefibreco.com

WONDERLAND YARNS
frabjousfibers.com

"IT IS GOOD TO LOVE
AS MUCH AS ONE CAN,
FOR THEREIN LIES TRUE
STRENGTH, AND HE WHO LOVES
MUCH DOES MUCH AND IS
CAPABLE OF MUCH, AND THAT
WHICH IS DONE WITH LOVE
IS WELL DONE."

—Vincent van Gogh to his brother Theo,
April 3, 1878

ABOUT THE ART

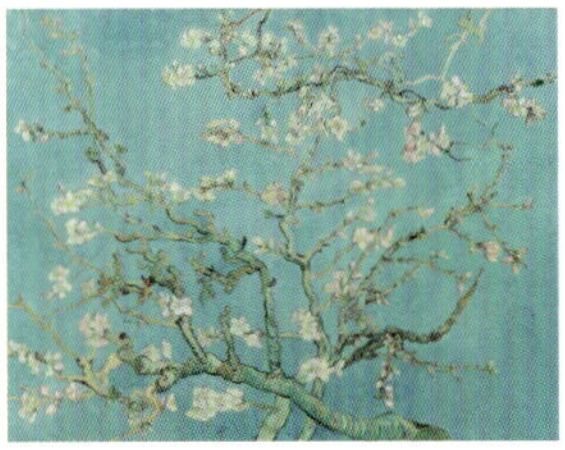

Vincent van Gogh (1853–1890)
Almond Blossom
Saint-Rémy-de-Provence, February 1890
Oil on canvas, 73.3 cm x 92.4 cm
Van Gogh Museum, Amsterdam
(Vincent van Gogh Foundation)

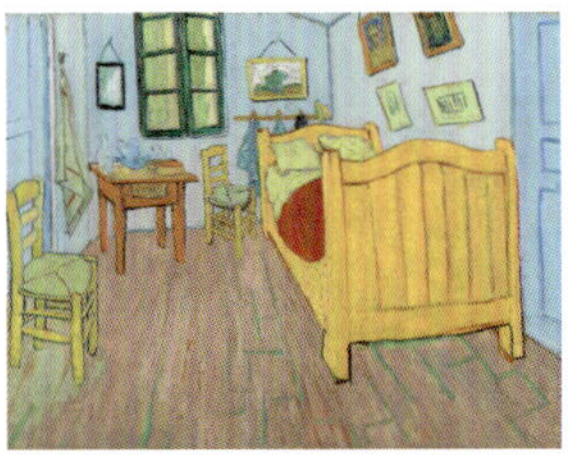

Vincent van Gogh (1853–1890)
The Bedroom
Arles, October 1888
Oil on canvas, 72.4 cm x 91.3 cm
Van Gogh Museum, Amsterdam
(Vincent van Gogh Foundation)

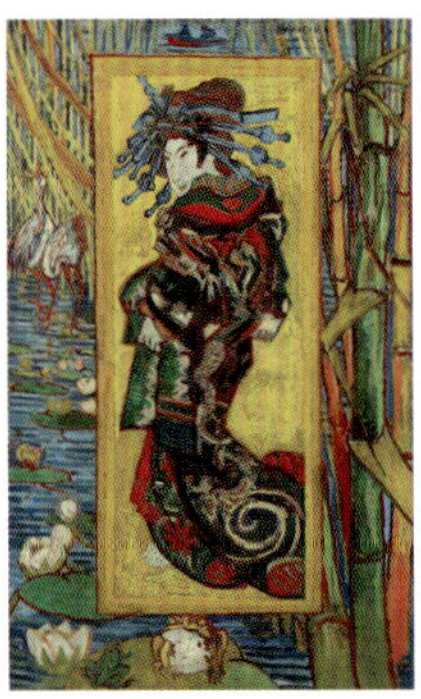

Vincent van Gogh (1853–1890)
Courtesan (after Eisen)
Paris, October–November 1887
Oil on cotton, 100.7 cm x 60.7 cm
Van Gogh Museum, Amsterdam
(Vincent van Gogh Foundation)

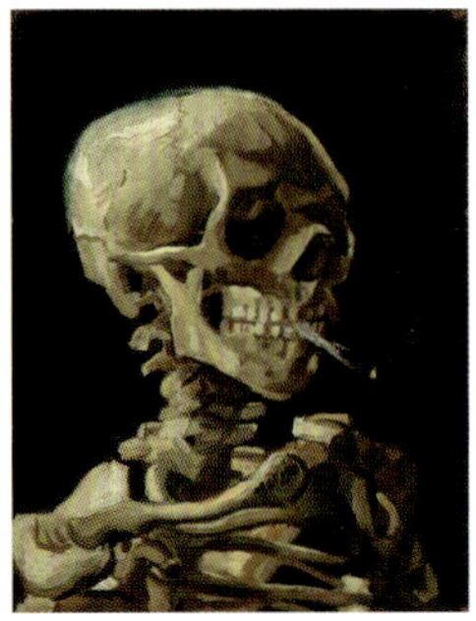

Vincent van Gogh (1853–1890)
Head of a Skeleton with Burning Cigarette
Antwerp, January–February 1886
Oil on canvas, 32.3 cm x 24.8 cm
Van Gogh Museum, Amsterdam
(Vincent van Gogh Foundation)

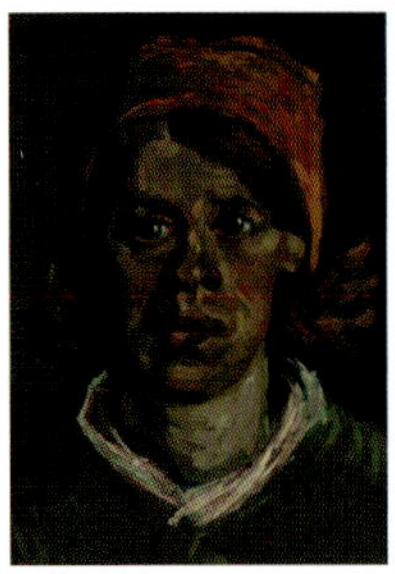

Vincent van Gogh (1853–1890)
Head of a Woman
Nuenen, April 1885
Oil on canvas, 43.2 cm x 30 cm x 2.2 cm
Van Gogh Museum, Amsterdam
(Vincent van Gogh Foundation)

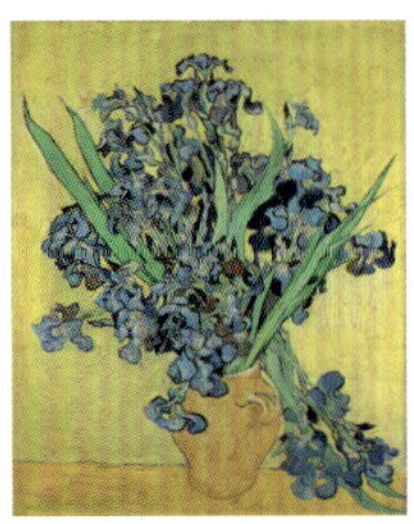

Vincent van Gogh (1853–1890)
Irises
Saint-Rémy-de-Provence, May 1890
Oil on canvas, 92.7 cm x 73.9 cm
Van Gogh Museum, Amsterdam
(Vincent van Gogh Foundation)

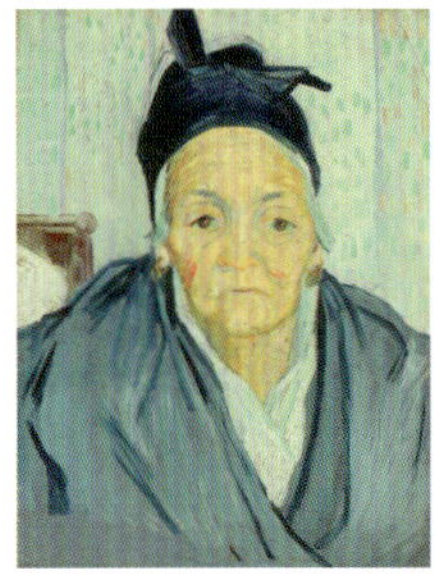

Vincent van Gogh (1853–1890)
An Old Woman of Arles
Arles, February 1888
Oil on canvas, 58 cm x 42 cm
Van Gogh Museum, Amsterdam
(Vincent van Gogh Foundation)

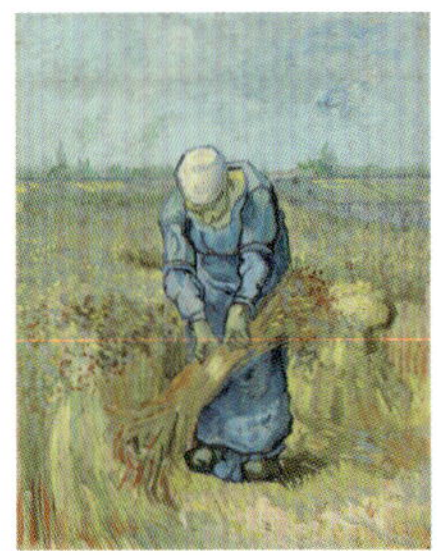

Vincent van Gogh (1853–1890)
Peasant Woman Binding Sheaves
(after Millet)
Saint-Rémy-de-Provence, September 1889
Oil on canvas on cardboard, 43.2 cm x 33.2 cm
Van Gogh Museum, Amsterdam
(Vincent van Gogh Foundation)

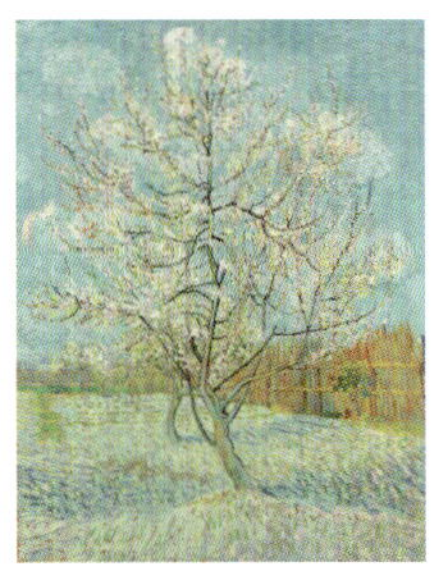

Vincent van Gogh (1853–1890)
The Pink Peach Tree
Arles, April–May 1888
Oil on canvas, 80.9 cm x 60.2 cm
Van Gogh Museum, Amsterdam
(Vincent van Gogh Foundation)

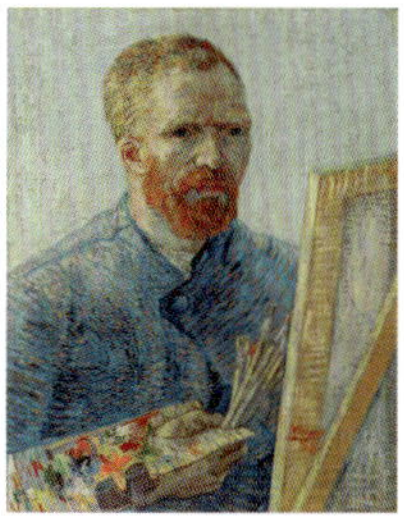

Vincent van Gogh (1853–1890)
Self-Portrait as a Painter
Paris, December 1887–February 1888
Oil on canvas, 65.1 cm x 50 cm
Van Gogh Museum, Amsterdam
(Vincent van Gogh Foundation)

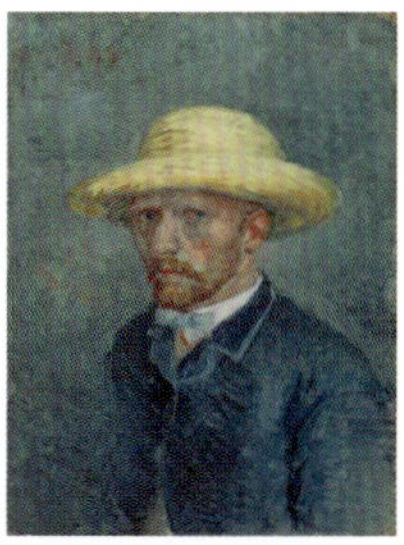

Vincent van Gogh (1853–1890)
Self-Portrait or Portrait of Theo van Gogh
Paris, Summer 1887
Oil on canvas, 19 cm x 14.1 cm
Van Gogh Museum, Amsterdam
(Vincent van Gogh Foundation)

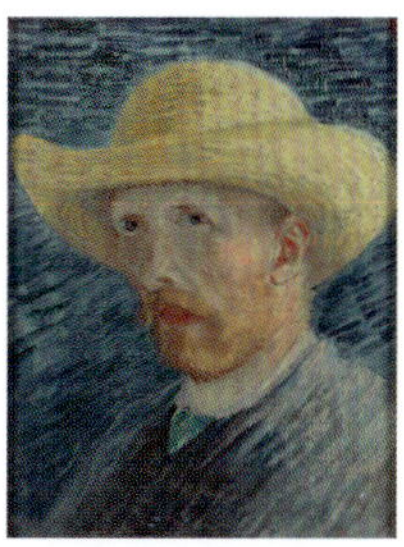

Vincent van Gogh (1853–1890)
Self-Portrait with Straw Hat
Paris, July–August 1887
Oil on canvas, 41.8 cm x 31.5 cm
Van Gogh Museum, Amsterdam
(Vincent van Gogh Foundation)

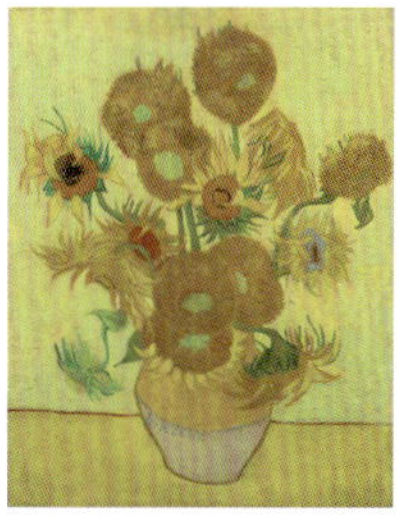

Vincent van Gogh (1853–1890)
Sunflowers
Arles, January 1889
Oil on canvas, 95 cm x 73 cm
Van Gogh Museum, Amsterdam
(Vincent van Gogh Foundation)

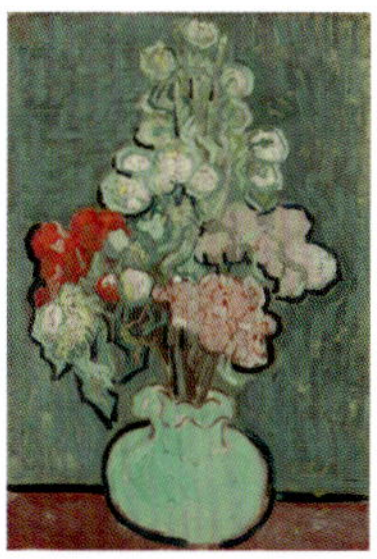

Vincent van Gogh (1853–1890)
Vase of Flowers
Oil on canvas, 42.2 cm x 29 cm
Auvers-sur-Oise, June 1890
Van Gogh Museum, Amsterdam
(Vincent van Gogh Foundation)

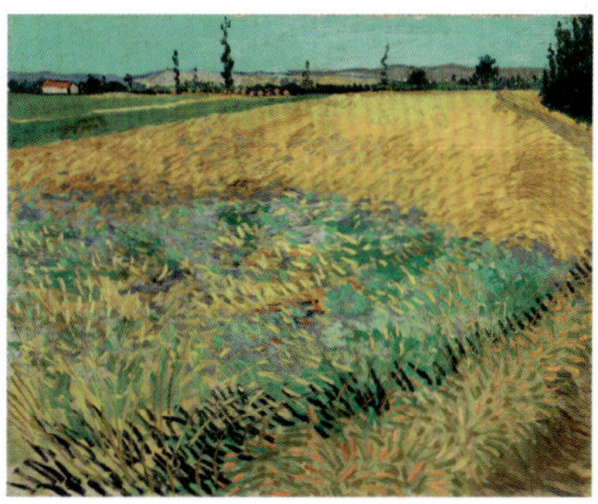

Vincent van Gogh (1853–1890)
Wheatfield
Arles, June 1888
Oil on canvas, 54 cm x 65 cm
Van Gogh Museum, Amsterdam
(Vincent van Gogh Foundation)

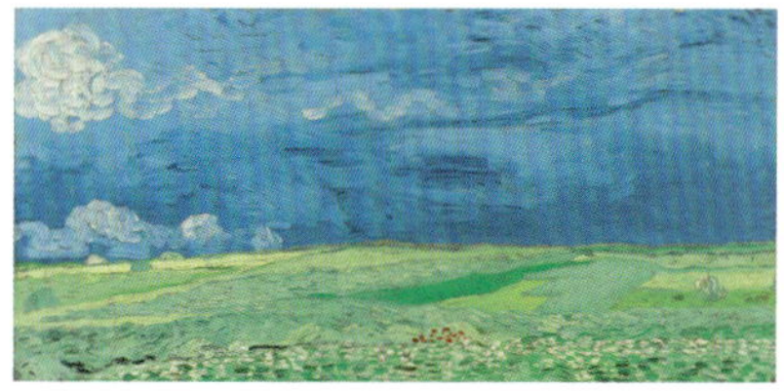

Vincent van Gogh (1853–1890)
Wheatfield under Thunderclouds
Auvers-sur-Oise, July 1890
Oil on canvas, 50.4 cm x 101.3 cm
Van Gogh Museum, Amsterdam
(Vincent van Gogh Foundation)

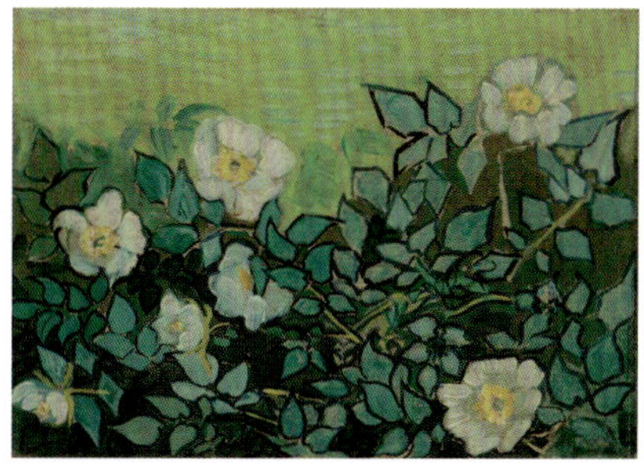

Vincent van Gogh (1853–1890)
Wild Roses
Saint-Rémy-de-Provence, May–June 1889
Oil on canvas, 24.5 cm x 33.5 cm
Van Gogh Museum, Amsterdam
(Vincent van Gogh Foundation)

ABOUT THE AUTHOR

Krista Ann is a nomadic knitter. In 2019, after twenty years in Southern California, she talked her husband into selling their house and almost all of their possessions to live life on the road. They moved with their fur baby, Phinny, into a twenty-six-foot RV travel trailer and began touring America.

When timing (and the pocketbook) allows for international travel, they leave Phinny with Grandma and Grandpa and hop on a plane to explore other countries. In 2022, Krista set foot (and knitted!) on all seven continents in a single year!

To pay for their adventures, Krista knits for costume and fashion designers. This job has allowed Krista to create some fun—and often unique—knit and crochet pieces for film, TV, commercials, and Paris Fashion Week runway shows. With filming happening all over the world, it doesn't matter where she is located as long as her knitting needles are within reach.

Some of the projects she has created pieces for include *Stranger Things* (Netflix), *The Mindy Project* (Hulu), *Tag, Annabelle Comes Home, Never Have I Ever* (Netflix), *iCarly* (Nickelodeon), *Hocus Pocus 2* (Disney+), and many other film, TV, and commercial projects.

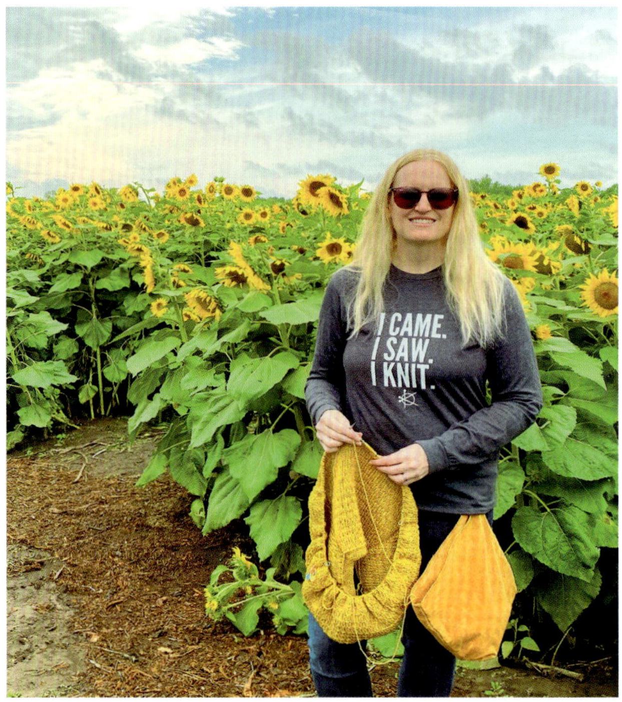

Krista loves designing knitwear and teaching knitting. With a multiple-subject teaching credential, becoming a knitting instructor was a natural transition. She loves teaching at local yarn shops during her travels as well as online via her own app, *The Knitting Rockstar Academy.*

Follow Krista's adventures and come join her for a class when she passes through your town. You can find her on Instagram at @explorewithknitsy or her website explorewithknitsy.com. And if you are looking to upgrade your knitting skills or enjoy endless fibery fun content, head over to knittingrockstar.com and become a member of *The Knitting Rockstar Academy!*

ACKNOWLEDGMENTS

No project—no matter how big or small—can be done alone and without the support of an awesome team of people. Thank you to Karyn Gerhard at Weldon Owen for your guidance and patience with a new author. Thank you to Sammy Holland at Insight Editions for putting the amazing Karyn and me in touch. Special shout-out to Meaghan Schmaltz, my rock star tech editor, and Ian Wickham from the Van Gogh Museum in Amsterdam for this wonderful collaboration opportunity.

Thank you to all of the yarn companies and indie dyers that continue to inspire designers like me with your amazing colors and fibers.

I wouldn't be where I am today without the love and support of my mom and dad as well as my mother-in-law and father-in-law. All four of you are an imperative part of my success and I'm grateful for all of your encouragement.

Endless thank-you hugs to my incredible husband, Garner, for everything you do to help make my life easier and keep me sane. And shout-out to our fur baby, Phinny, for making me take a break once in a while to give you snuggles (and chicken!).

This book is dedicated to my mom and dad for always allowing me to explore my own inner artistic creativity.

The countless trips to craft stores, endless dollars spent on art supplies, and multiple hours of late-night mess-making are finally paying off!

"I BELIEVE IN THE ABSOLUTE NECESSITY OF A NEW ART OF COLOUR, OF DRAWING AND— OF THE ARTISTIC LIFE. AND IF WE WORK IN THAT FAITH, IT SEEMS TO ME THAT THERE'S A CHANCE THAT OUR HOPES WON'T BE IN VAIN."

—Vincent van Gogh to his brother Theo,
March 16, 1888

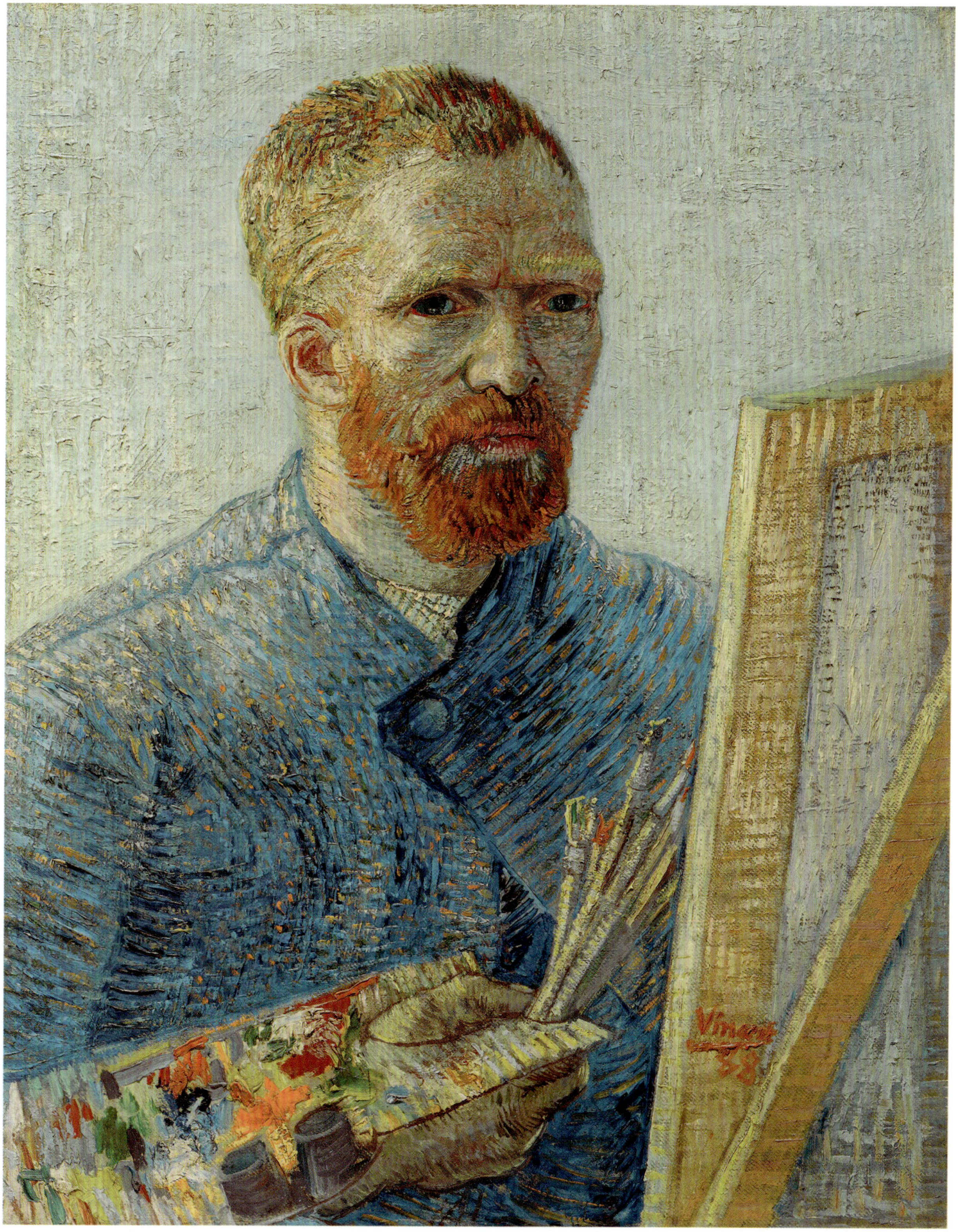

Self-portrait as Painter (p. 107)

weldon**owen**

an imprint of Insight Editions
P.O. Box 3088
San Rafael, CA 94912
www.weldonowen.com

CEO Raoul Goff
VP Publisher Roger Shaw
Editorial Director Katie Killebrew
Senior Editor Karyn Gerhard
Editorial Assistant Jon Ellis
VP Creative Chrissy Kwasnik
Art Director Allister Fein
VP Manufacturing Alix Nicholaeff
Sr. Production Manager Joshua Smith
Sr Production Manager, Subsidiary Rights Lina s Palma-Temena

Weldon Owen would also like to thank Jill Paice, B. J. Berti, and Karen Levy for their extraordinary work on this book.

Photography of finished pieces by Jill Paice

ISBN: 979-8-88674-175-9

Manufactured in China by Insight Editions
10 9 8 7 6 5 4 3 2

ROOTS of PEACE REPLANTED PAPER

Insight Editions, in association with Roots of Peace, will plant two trees for each tree used in the manufacturing of this book. Roots of Peace is an internationally renowned humanitarian organization dedicated to eradicating land mines worldwide and converting war-torn lands into productive farms and wildlife habitats. Roots of Peace will plant two million fruit and nut trees in Afghanistan and provide farmers there with the skills and support necessary for sustainable land use.

Van Gogh Museum Amsterdam

Your purchase supports the work of the Van Gogh Museum

vangoghmuseum.com